The Insiders

A STOCKHOLDER'S GUIDE TO WALL STREET

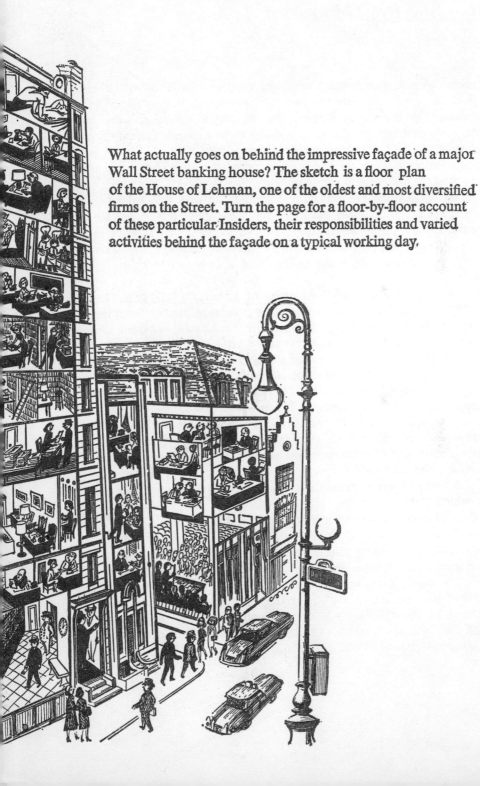

What actually goes on behind the impressive façade of a major
Wall Street banking house? The sketch is a floor plan
of the House of Lehman, one of the oldest and most diversified
firms on the Street. Turn the page for a floor-by-floor account
of these particular Insiders, their responsibilities and varied
activities behind the façade on a typical working day.

The Bustling House of Lehman

At eleven o'clock on a recent Wednesday morning, the House of Lehman, 1 William Street, Manhattan, was well launched in several different directions. On the eleventh floor, five telephone operators were busy placing the first of the 250 to 350 daily long-distance calls, while next door thirty clerks were mailing Lehman customers dividend checks from various corporations. In the firm's private gym, the masseur was kneading a late-working partner into condition.

On the tenth floor, tax experts and economists were exchanging views about a speech to be made by Jesse Siff, Lehman's chief economist, to a conference of presidents from R. H. Macy stores. In another room, Marcel Palmaro, the partner in charge of foreign operations, was decoding a cable from France about the financing of a monorail to be built out-side Paris.

On the floor below, several members of Lehman's Industrial Depart-ment were working on plans to arrange a private-placement financing for the Hertz Corp. On the eighth floor, Mathurin Allanos, once the chef at New York's elegant Le Pavillon restaurant, and his nine-man staff, were preparing a luncheon for ten partners and their four visitors. Two of the visitors, a magazine writer and a banker, would sit at the main table and share in the general conversation. (It ranged from the fiscal theories of Secretary of the Treasury Douglas Dillon to the possibilities of forming a publicly owned corporation to control professional football, basketball, hockey, and baseball teams.) Two executives of an electronics company contemplating a stock offering would lunch in one of the two private din-ing rooms with a Lehman partner.

On the seventh floor, Frank Morse, head of the municipal department, was winding up an offering of $25 million of 5½ per cent Montreal bonds. In Lehman's sixth floor library, one of the best in the Street, Miss Helen S. Johnston was assembling all available information on the toy industry. This was for a partner working to arrange the financing of a toy maker. Locked doors barred entry to the other room on that floor, where the portfolio committee of Lehman Corp. was holding its weekly review of investments. In the same room, Alan Hunter, the newly elected president of the One William Street Fund, was concluding a deal in which the fund acquired two smaller private investment companies with assests of $1,100,000 and issued 68,000 shares of its own stock in return.

Oil investments, one of Lehman's most successful fields of activity since World War II, are managed on the fifth floor. Here partner Ed Kennedy was discussing with insurance-company representatives the terms of a production-payment loan—a relatively complex type of oil-property financing that enables a small company to buy additional properties without paying out all of its profits.

On the fourth floor, organized confusion reigned. Bob Thayer, Lehman's syndicate manager, was coordinating the distribution of $6.5 million in first mortgage bonds and 140,000 shares of common stock of Northwest Natural Gas Co., while next door Donald Loomis, head of the registration department, was inserting some last-minute information in a prospectus to meet SEC requirements. In another room, Lehman's advertising director, Bertram S. Behrens, was checking an ad for the financial pages of the daily newspapers to be sure that "Lehman" appeared in the right size type and in the proper location.

On the third floor, partner Paul Manheim was busy in the partners' room reviewing with an assistant some of the portfolios in the Investment Advisory Service. The private offices of Robert Lehman and Monroe Gutman were empty; Lehman was in Paris, Gutman at the sixth-floor conference.

On the second floor, home of the retail sales department, salesmen were calling clients for indications of interest in a $27-million offering of 4½ per cent convertible debentures by Allied Stores.

On the main floor, clerks behind old-fashioned cages were taking in and handing out stock and bond certificates.

Meanwhile, in the narrow four-story annex added in 1940, the utility department was holding a meeting of a group of underwriters. Lehman made a bid on an offering of $25 million of bonds of Carolina Power & Light. It won the bid and now they were arranging a resale to the public. Across little Mill Lane, at 9 South William Street (right of picture), a "due diligence" meeting on an offering of Playskool Corp., a toy maker, was under way in the Lehman auditorium, the largest and most modern in Wall Street. (At a due-diligence meeting the underwriters are given an opportunity to assess the management at first hand and to ask searching questions of its officials and accountants.) On the upper floors of 9 South William, members of the Investment Advisory Service were reviewing portfolios.

Previous Books by the Editors of FORTUNE

A Stockholder's Guide to Wall Street

THE INSIDERS

by T. A. WISE
and the editors of FORTUNE

Drawing by Lucille Corcos

DOUBLEDAY & COMPANY, INC., *Garden City, New York,*

Contents

Acknowledgments

The following members of FORTUNE's Research Staff assisted in the preparation of this book: Nancy Bryan, Lorraine Carson, Patricia Hough, Carol Junge Loomis, Mary Melville, Betsy Stilwell Petersen, Malissa Redfield, Eleanor Nadler Schwartz.

Introduction

Almost everyone agrees about the vast influence of "Wall Street" on American business and on millions of American investors. And yet, oddly enough, hardly anyone off the Street knows much about the men who actually exercise this influence. They remain wraith-like figures, even to many sophisticated businessmen who invest heavily in the stock market. In part, their anonymity is traceable to a kind of "institutionalization" that has settled over the Street in the past couple of decades: where once it reverberated with chatter about boy wonders, lone wolves, and other interesting types, today the chatter is all about the big impersonal institutions—about whatever Merrill Lynch is recommending, say, or what the Prudential is putting its money into.

But a larger reason for the anonymity of Wall Street's powerful men is the fact that they live in a world of their own. The principal boundaries of the world, as many humorists have pointed out, are a river and a graveyard—i.e., the East River and the graveyard adjacent to Trinity Church; and Bowling Green to the south and, perhaps, Maiden Lane to the north. (If the insurance companies are thought of as part of the financial district, which they are, increasingly, then the northern boundary would be John Street; a case can also be made for taking in everything up to Chambers Street, where the Securities and Exchange Commission has its offices.) To thousands of the top executives clustered in midtown Manhattan, the Wall Street area might as well be in another city. Its occupants work different (somewhat earlier) hours from other businessmen in New York, and getting to their place of work is a maddening transportation problem. In short, other New Yorkers tend not to *see* the Wall Streeters, and to be foggy about their mode of operation. Of all the men portrayed in these pages, it seems likely, the two best known to the public are the two arch-swindlers, Lowell Birrell and Alexander Guterma.

One major purpose of this book is to penetrate the world of Wall Street, and especially to provide close-ups of the men who do most to direct its operations. The book is written from the investor's point of view, i.e., it examines the world of Wall Street with an eye to helping the investor understand his rights—and to understand his investments.

Many investors now tend to believe, optimistically, that their interests are watched over vigilantly. After all, corporations are required by state laws, by the laws of the various stock exchanges, and by the Securities and Exchange Commission, to disclose certain financial data to their stockholders, and, for that matter, to the public at large. The data is provided by the corporations, examined by their auditors, presented according to the generally accepted rules of accounting, perhaps discussed at the annual meeting, and often analyzed exhaustively in "market letters" written by close students of the securities markets. It is true that many stockholders have only the foggiest ideas about the companies they have invested their money in. They are unclear as to which of the company's products or stores are profitable, whether the company has enough working capital, whether a proposed merger makes any sense. But the uninformed stockholder nevertheless tends to think that, if he ever had the time to get around to it, he could answer all such questions readily enough. One minor purpose of this book is to disabuse him of that idea. The book points up the lacunae, the ambiguities, and the awful complexities in the reporting of financial information to the public today; and it considers some ideas for making the information easier to get at and understand.

*   *   *   *   *   *

The book is divided into four parts. The first part focuses on the auditors, the men who, more than any others, decide what information corporations shall report, and in what form they shall report it. Indeed, the auditors' professional society—the American Institute of Certified Public Accountants—is thought of as a kind of private financial legislature. The auditors themselves often seem remote and mysterious. The members of the Big Eight auditing firms, most of which are in the Wall Street area of New York, see a lot of each other, and are always apt to be *au courant* about each other's problems. The problems, however, often seem incomprehensible to those outside the auditors' universe; or, if comprehensible, they often seem technical and tedious. The two opening chapters of this book will try to make some of the current outstanding problems comprehensible, and also to suggest what is really at stake in their solution. In some cases, a lot is at stake, for auditors' decisions often get to the *substance* of business these days—not just to the form in which it is reported. (For an example of the way accounting can affect the actual conduct of a business, see page 29.) Along the way, these chapters will also have a hard look at the auditors themselves—at their mode of operation, the profitability of their own businesses, their solutions to a host of nagging ethical problems that envelop them, etc.

To an investor, perhaps the most interesting single fact about the auditors is that they often don't agree with one another. Two auditors in possession of the same data may construct two entirely different reports—a point illustrated in "The P.&L. of A&B," which appears on page 37. In this case, two companies with identical operations reported earnings of $.80 a share and $1.79 a share respectively, although both reports followed "generally accepted accounting procedure." A sophisticated investor reading the annual reports of two such companies (these two are imaginary) would probably have been able, after examining all the footnotes carefully, to ascertain what had actually happened at each. But there are some other situations in which, still following accepted accounting procedure, it is possible for a corporation to conceal from all outsiders just what it means when it says it earned such-and-such amount. The chapter on Atlas Plywood may suggest the extent to which even the biggest and most reputable auditing firms may disagree among themselves, and the implications that new auditing methods may have for stockholders in some situations.

Auditors don't disagree just about technical details; they also disagree, and violently, about the philosophical underpinnings of their profession. An outspoken minority of the auditors believes that, while the profession must retain some element of *judgment* in its work —or lose the right to be called a profession—it has altogether too many options facing it now, too much flexibility in its handling of financial reports. The majority does not acknowledge that things are that bad, and makes a case for maximum flexibility. These two views were articulated in a debate at the 1960 convention of the A.I.C.P.A. in Philadelphia. Since the debate, each of the two protagonists has written a letter to *Fortune* rebutting his opponent. Their original statements and the two letters (they have never been printed before) are reproduced in an appendix to this volume.

The second part of the book gets to close quarters with some very powerful operators on the Street: The brokerage business is examined in a portrait of Merrill Lynch, Pierce, Fenner & Smith, which is by far the biggest broker in the world (it would take a merger of the next four brokers to put together another Merrill Lynch), but which still has some serious competitive problems. The investment banking business is illuminated in a report on Lehman Brothers, the oldest, and probably the biggest, investment banker in the U.S. The offstage influence still exercised on public corporations by families of great and traditional wealth is shown in the chapter on the Milbanks, who "took over" at Commercial Solvents when they became dissatisfied with the company's management. Finally, this section includes portraits of nine individuals—and individual*ists*—who swing a lot of weight on Wall Street, although they are largely unknown outside the financial community.

The third part of the book consists of three fairly horrifying case histories. All of them serve to show, conclusively, that investors—and not just naive outsiders—can still be flimflammed and bamboozled by unscrupulous insiders who put their minds to it. The chapters on Birrell and Guterma may suggest how it is possible for companies listed on stock exchanges and regulated by the SEC to be robbed blind nevertheless. The chapter on H. L. Green, which was also a widely held corporation listed on the New York Stock Exchange, suggests that the stockholder is just about helpless when a corrupt insider works in collusion with an auditor. One incident in the chapter suggests the dimensions of the stockholders' problems: Even *after* the fraud at H. L. Green had been reported to the company's outside directors, they delayed almost a month before telling the public. They had good reasons for waiting—but meanwhile, hundreds of uninformed outsiders were buying into the company.

The final section of the book consists of two chapters discussing stockholders' legal rights and the realities underlying their present enforcement. The first of these chapters focuses on the corporate annual meeting, a ritual of long standing, deriving from a time when corporations ordinarily had only a few stockholders—few enough so that they could meet and realistically hope to set policy during the months ahead. The annual meeting in recent years has got to be much more elaborate and much less meaningful. As an exercise in democracy, it can hardly be taken seriously; and as a device for informing stockholders of the corporation's recent history and near-future prospects it is cumbersome and easy to improve on. Yet this curious institution is, oddly enough, being used to clarify some of the large ambiguities about the rights of stockholders and the obligations of corporations. A major portion of this chapter is devoted to an assessment of current legal thinking on both subjects.

The final chapter, on the SEC, offers a hard look at the present state of enforcement of the securities laws—ambiguous as they are. It is easy to criticize the commission itself, which always has the look of being harassed and behind in its work, and doubly afflicted by having so unclear a mandate. It is also easy to make a case that the commission devotes an inordinate amount of its time to fighting off a few outrageous swindlers, who are usually small potatoes, and not doing too well with them; while really sizable cases are either ignored or dealt with arbitrarily. Finally, it is easy to demonstrate that many rules of the SEC are simply ignored, and with impunity, by businessmen who find them a nuisance; in the Goldfine case, for example, it was revealed that for seven years his East Boston Co., which was listed on the Boston Stock Exchange, never got around to filing a proper report with the SEC—and nothing was done about it until the case became a national issue. All these problems are tackled in this last chapter.

There are, in sum, a lot of different powers being exercised in downtown Manhattan. And if the Wall Street community still looks like a closed little world, the investor who remains ignorant of its inhabitants does so at his peril.

*   *   *   *   *   *

Except for the exchange reproduced as the appendix to this volume, all of this material is based on articles that appeared in *Fortune,* mostly in 1959 and 1960. Some of the earlier material was brought up to date in 1962. In addition, the *Fortune* articles were cut in order to avoid repetition in the book.

The author of all the articles is T. A. Wise, who joined the *Fortune* staff in 1957, when he was already well known as an outstanding financial reporter. He wrote the articles on Birrell and Guterma in collaboration with Spencer Klaw, and the article on the powerful individualists with George J. W. Goodman.

PART ONE

The Men Who Make the Rules

I

The Auditors Have Arrived

It is a curious and noteworthy fact that the tremendous growth of the U.S. accounting profession in the postwar years has taken place almost unnoticed by most Americans. In the same years, other proliferating white-collar types—advertising and public-relations men, union and corporation lawyers, stockbrokers, research scientists—have impinged heavily on the national consciousness; news stories about such men are often in the papers, and their prototypes appear regularly in novels and television dramas. But the rise of the accountants has occurred quietly. To most businessmen, the names of the big accounting firms are familiar, principally because of the way the names recur at the end of published annual reports; but not many businessmen know, or have even heard of, the men discussed on the following pages, who are the senior partners of the nation's largest accounting firms. They are among the most powerful men anywhere in business today.

In a way, their anonymity is in keeping with the traditions of the profession, which have always called for a rather aloof public posture. Elbert Hubbard's description of "the typical auditor" many years ago had him "cold, passive, noncommittal, with eyes like codfish . . . minus bowels, passion or a sense of humor." The modern auditor is likely to have all three, but he is still unlikely to step out of the shadows very often. One reason for this reticent posture is that an auditor is privy to the secrets of many businessmen, and they naturally feel easier about this relationship if the auditor seems to be a man of reserve and discretion. Moreover, an auditor must preserve his independence in dealing with present or prospective clients. The chiefs of the profession—the leading lights of the Big Eight firms— live very much in a world of their own. Six of the eight have their main offices within a few blocks of one another in New York's Wall Street area; they see a lot of and know a lot about one another. Their firms audit about 80 per cent of all the corporations listed with the Securities and Exchange Commission. But not many line executives know how these eight men operate: how much money they make, and how much their firms make, how they have been steadily taking on new functions, how they get new business, and how they have been coping with an extraordinary range of ethical and intellectual problems.

These operations do not constitute all the news about the auditors these days. The profession today is fighting a number of quiet but intense battles to clarify and make consistent the accounting principles used in the U.S. It is a truism in the profession, though it still seems a bit shocking to many businessmen, that two different accountants in possession of the same figures may construct two considerably dissimilar balance sheets. The principal issues in the battle between accountants, and the profession's prospects for resolving them, will be described in the next chapter.

A few figures and definitions are in order at the outset. When some of the more prestigious members of the profession are asked whether they consider themselves auditors or accountants, they may take a deep breath and reply that they are "independent certified public accountants." On the other hand, the Census Bureau just lumps "accountants and auditors" together. The difference between an accountant and an auditor is a chronic source of confusion, but the operational distinction is a simple one. All accountants assist in the preparation of financial statements according to the principles they believe to be generally accepted by the profession. An audit is an *examination* of such a statement, and an auditor is simply an accountant checking the work of someone else—often another accountant. The great majority of those listed by the Census Bureau are not recognized as accountants by the profession, and most of them are, realistically, plain bookkeepers, untrained in the many rigorous disciplines, the concepts, and the case lore of modern accountancy, and unrecognized by any state authorities. Just about 121,000 have acquired this recognition: these include the 76,000 certified public accountants in the U.S. (about 12,000 work for the Big Eight) and 45,000 who have "licenses" issued in thirty-three states to do public accounting.

Not all the C.P.A.s have the same qualifications—these vary from state to state—but all of them have, at least, passed a rigorous examination that is given twice each year and is prepared by the American Institute of Certified Public Accountants. The examination covers accounting practice and theory, auditing, and commercial law; it is given in several installments, each of which begins at the same moment in every state, and all together it usually consumes about nineteen hours, spread over a Wednesday-to-Friday period. Before the examination, the questions are kept under close security; they are delivered in armored trucks to the examination centers and opened in the examination rooms before witnesses.

The C.P.A.'s competition is not limited to other C.P.A.s. The 45,000 "licensed public accountants" can legally do everything the C.P.A.s can do, even though many have not passed an examination (they got into business before the enactment of the present laws regulating accounting). In seventeen states (including Massachusetts and Pennsylvania) *anyone* can call himself a public accountant —i.e., no license is issued. There are perhaps 10,000 such unlicensed, uncertified public accountants in these states, and they too are entitled to do anything a C.P.A. can do.

The growth of the profession has taken place in less than a century. As recently as 1900, there were eactly 243 C.P.A.s in the U.S., and no more than 1000 persons employed in all the nation's accounting firms. And the rate of growth is still accelerating: the profession expects to pick up an additional 40,000-odd C.P.A.s by 1970. Accountants' numbers and influence are increasing in other countries as well as in the U.S.; but the scope and diversity of U.S. capitalism have made this country the modern center of the profession, and the American Institute of Certified Public Accountants is always playing host to droves of visitors from Italy, Japan, Israel, and many other nations, who are eager to learn how auditing, and accounting in general, are practiced here.

A beginning in breweries

The steadily expanding influence of the auditors derives, in general, from two sources: (1) the increasing complexity of the modern industrial world, and (2) its greater emphasis on *accountability*, meaning the need of one man to refer his actions to judgment by standards he shares with other men. The classical nineteenth-century entrepreneur had little need for an accountant in the modern sense; he was accountable to the law of the land and his own conscience, but beyond that he was the sole judge of whether his performance was meritorious. A very different situation is that of professional managers controlling the property of unknown stockholders, dealing with institutionalized creditors, and entrusted with a host of social tasks from the generation of taxable revenues to the production of essential weapons. Under these circumstances, it becomes a matter of the utmost public importance to know how the management of a public corporation is performing. Accountancy has created several concepts that are useful in evaluating these performances. "Depreciation" is one such concept, "earned surplus" is another, and "net working capital" is a third. Aside from the help such measurements give the public, it is important *within* any top management group to be able to evaluate objectively the performance of subordinates, and accountancy contributes many techniques to the discharge of this responsibility.

The accounting profession in this country can be traced back to about 1880, when some English and Scottish investors began to put their money into U.S. securities. The securities they picked were mostly brewery stocks, which were then regarded in Great Britain as the worthiest of blue chips. The investors who bought heavily into American breweries sent their own auditing firms over here to check on the health of these investments. Two members of the Big Eight, Price Waterhouse and Peat, Marwick & Mitchell, were originally British firms that got their start in the U.S. this way. Today, of course, they are entirely American-owned but have working relationships with the British partnerships.

By the time of World War I, the ownership of public securities had become fairly widespread, and there was a growing awareness of the need for more uniformity in financial reporting. The nation's first Secretary of Commerce (in the Wilson Administration), William C. Redfield, was a businessman who had been engaged shortly before taking office in an effort to merge several companies. The merger collapsed when he realized that some of the companies involved were substantially overvalued. He discussed the generally chaotic state of financial reporting with officials of the Federal Reserve Board, and persuaded several of them to take the lead in setting down some guidelines for businessmen. In 1917, with the help of the accounting profession, the board produced a memorandum, subsequently published in booklet form, called "Approved Methods for the Preparation of Balance Sheet Statements." This booklet did a lot to systematize financial reporting, and also to make businessmen aware of the need to employ accountants who understood what was required in making reports.

The moral of McKesson & Robbins

During the 1920s the New York Stock Exchange also boosted the accountants' business by waging a continuous campaign to get corporations to provide more financial information. In 1933, after the crash, the Exchange, with advice from the American Institute of Certified Public Accountants, initiated a whole new series of standards for the treatment of unrealized profit, capital surplus, earned surplus, and other corporate financial items. The standards were incorporated into the accounting principles approved by the institute. That same year the Exchange also began requiring of all listed corporations an audit certificate by an independent C.P.A. Both of these developments did a lot to enhance the prestige and acceptance of the independent accountant.

The sensational revelations of the McKesson & Robbins case in 1939 temporarily impaired the profession's new prestige, but in the end, by showing the need for much more careful auditing practices, the case brought the profession a great deal of new business. When it was first revealed that the head of the drug company had swindled it of millions, principally by carrying fictitious inventories on the books, it was obvious that the profession had to revise completely many of its accepted methods of verification. The SEC investigation showed that the audit of McKesson & Robbins by Price Waterhouse had "conformed . . . to what was generally considered mandatory."

While the case was still warm, the A.I.C.P.A. set up a review committee, which proposed that future audits include direct verification of inventory, by personal inspection of warehouses where that seems necessary; direct communication between auditor and debtor on a corporation's receivables; and the selection of auditors by directors, with the approval of the stockholders, who, in addition, should be entitled to a description of the scope of the auditor's work, and to read his opinion in a separate section of the annual report.

E.P.T. gets the business

The profusion of taxes, and tax complications, have also accelerated the growth of the profession. Many Americans had their first contacts with accountants in the period just after 1913, the year when the first income-tax law was passed. Four years later, in 1917, the government passed its first excess-profits tax. Manufacturers now found that they had to calculate their profits in relation to the capital invested in their firms—a new and burdensome chore for many firms that had never systematically distinguished between, say, maintenance costs and new investment, and now found themselves obliged to reconstruct their books from the ground up. The first E.P.T., like those during World War II and the Korean War, generated a lot of business for the accountants.

Their tax practice is still growing. All of the Big Eight firms have tax departments staffed by anywhere between 100 and 250 specialists. Their clients today include not only corporations and wealthy individuals, but an increasing number of upper-middle-income citizens who find it necessary or convenient to pay $100 or $200 to have their accountancy chores handled by a national firm. No one knows just how many such people there are, but some accountants figure the total market for individuals at about 1,500,000—this being roughly the number of individuals whose taxable income is over $20,000, and who can expect that the Internal Revenue Service will probably audit their returns.

In building their tax business, the accountants have got into a battle with the legal profession. Back in 1913, lawyers generally shied away from tax work because it was highly technical and involved accounting concepts with which many of them were unfamiliar. But in the 1930s, as the tax rates mounted and tax problems entered increasingly into business and personal decisions, lawyers began to feel that they had let the accountants get too firm a hold on something good. The dispute came to a boil in 1943, when a client in New York balked at paying his accountant a $500 bill on the grounds that, in preparing his tax return, the accountant had given *legal* advice, which he was not professionally qualified to do. The accountant sued. The legal profession sensed an opportunity and the New York County Lawyers Association entered the case on behalf of the defendant. In alarm, the New York Society of C.P.A.s rushed to support the plaintiff. Later, a similar case cropped up in California. In both cases the courts ruled that the accountants were illegally engaging in the practice of law.

Both professional groups felt that the dispute was unseemly. In 1957 they agreed not to engage in any more court contests on such disputes, but instead to refer any cases that came up to a special mediating committee made up of representatives of both professions. However, neither profession has yielded an inch on its own asserted right to practice in the field of taxes.

Accounting to Royal Little

In the postwar years the rise of the accountants has been accelerated by three rather special phenomena: a vast wave of corporate mergers; the need for better accounting in the financial affairs of labor unions, pension and welfare funds, foundations, and other institutions; and the push of the big auditing firms into a vast, sprawling area they call "general management services."

The first two of these new phenomena are well known. During the 1950s the number of mergers involving manufacturing companies, for example, rose from about 300 to about 500 a year. Furthermore, mergers that do not come off—that bog down over some disagreement—also represent a substantial volume of accounting business. Royal Little of Textron, Inc., had his auditor, Arthur Young & Co., do preliminary investigations of over 100 companies during one recent five-year period alone; only twenty-five of the companies were eventually merged into Textron.

It seems likely that the market for noncorporate accounting services will continue to be expanded. The 1959 disclosure law requires labor unions to file financial statements with the Department of Labor but does not require these to be audited unless the Secretary requests an audit. Over 50,000 unions are affected, and most of them have by now filed their statements—mostly unaudited. The value of such statements is questioned in many quarters, and eventually, it seems likely, auditing of these statements will become widespread. Auditing of the nation's 15,000 welfare and pension funds has improved considerably since the passage, in 1958, of a law which requires that the funds' administrators account to the Secretary of Labor for all contributions, salaries, and fees, the rates given insurance carriers, and a variety of other data on investments and loans. Finally, there is a mounting pressure to get better audits of charitable and philanthropic funds. It was intensified by the scandal early in 1960 over the finances of the Sister Elizabeth Kenny Foundation. When this foundation's finances were first audited back in 1951, Arthur Andersen & Co. refused to certify the financial statement attached to the report because the executives did not want to disclose that it had cost $975,000 to collect $1,240,000. It later turned out that these executives had prevented the Andersen audit from reaching the foundation's board of directors. And eight more years passed before the public learned what was happening to the money it had contributed to the foundation.

Bread and toll booths

The "management service" business has burgeoned in the accounting profession during the past few years. Many accountants find it confusing and hard to justify, but others consider it a logical and lucrative extension of what they have been doing in the financial field all along.

In effect, the auditors are going into competition with the management consultants. The independent auditor called upon to examine a corporation's financial records often becomes aware of the full range of problems facing the company—sometimes more acutely aware than management itself. Moreover, many auditors are real experts in some fields—e.g., a man who has spent twenty years auditing department stores often knows more about merchandising than some of his clients—and it was probably inevitable that such auditors, observing the surge of business to professional management-consultant firms, would feel a desire to sell their own expertise too. Moreover, many clients of auditors were requesting their help in developing systems to keep track of affairs and of records that were growing increasingly complex.

Some of the big auditing firms have committed themselves wholeheartedly to the management-services field. Ernst & Ernst, Peat, Marwick, and Price Waterhouse have staffs of 250 in their management-service divisions, and offer clients literally any management services they want. Ernst & Ernst, for example, will tackle any assignment in labor negotiations, personnel selection (it has its own staff psychologists available for consulting), new-product planning, and factory design and layout. A while back, E.&E. took on the job of working out a control system for the New York State Thruway: it determined the number of men needed to man the toll booths at the heavy traffic periods, and it set up a record system to check the number of tickets sold. Arthur Young helped Becton, Dickinson & Co., the medical-supply firm, to determine the market for a disposable surgical needle it had developed, the price the needle should sell for, and the way it should be promoted. But many big auditing firms will handle only a few kinds of management chores. For example, a bakery firm asked

Lybrand, Ross to help it solve the problem of determining the optimum number of loaves to bake—i.e., so that it would not always have large amounts unsold and wasted on rainy days, and not run short on sunny days. Lybrand, Ross considered the job to be primarily mathematical, and since the firm has its own research department, which is well able to apply mathematical techniques to inventory sampling and other accounting problems, it felt that it could take on the job.

An accounting firm's revenues are derived, of course, from renting out the services of its staff. Junior accountants in the big firms earn perhaps $6000 a year, and senior accountants perhaps $8000 to $13,000. These are the firm's "production workers" and, at the same time, its physical assets, and an idle junior or senior accountant is viewed with the same dismay with which a manufacturing company might view an idle plant. In general, a big firm feels it can be profitable if its juniors and seniors are working for customers 75 per cent of the time. At this rate they would ordinarily generate revenues about two times their salaries, which would comfortably cover their own costs to the firm, and also the salaries of their superiors: the "managers" ($13,000 to $21,000), who run the offices, and the senior partners ($25,000 and up), who handle any large questions that arise with clients and in general devote most of their time to what might be called "diplomacy"—e.g., persuading clients that furniture cannot be written off in two years, or making recommendations on some other phase of the client's business, or pitching for new business.

This pitch is hampered by several kinds of restrictions. Not only is advertising unethical, but any competitive bidding is frowned on, and so is contacting a prospect without the knowledge of its incumbent auditing firm. Free-for-all competition is permissible only when a new company, which has never had an auditing firm, comes into the daylight. Then a direct approach can be made.

The elaborate procedures that surround the getting of new business can be seen in a switch in auditing firms made in 1960 by Allied Stores, one of the nation's largest department-store chains. First, Allied broke the bad news to the firm of Touche, Ross, Bailey & Smart that it was going to look for a new auditor. It then invited Ernst & Ernst and Arthur Andersen to visit its executive offices and make "presentations" for the account. Both auditing firms had meetings with several Allied executives in order to learn some of the particular requirements of the corporation. (As a matter of professional courtesy, Touche, Ross was kept notified of all these meetings.) Then the two firms sent delegations to Allied's offices on Fifth Avenue in New York and recited their own experience, made some promises about the time that their top men could personally give the account, and volunteered to discuss fees. The Ernst & Ernst delegation consisted of Hassel Tippit, the firm's senior partner, William Stowe, the head of the New York office, who would be in direct charge of the account, and several staff men; the Arthur Andersen delegation was headed by senior partner Leonard Spacek. The results of these meetings were communicated to a committee of Allied's directors, which had been appointed by the whole board to make a recommendation.

Ernst & Ernst had several advantages in this competition. It had been Allied's auditor back in the 1940s, and was familiar with the company. It had pioneered the development of the last-in-first-out (LIFO) method of inventory valuation in the retail field. A substantial number of its ninety-five branch offices were near Allied's eighty-five stores, and E.&E. prepared a map that brought home the point forcefully at the presentations. The next day Ernst & Ernst was told it had the job—subject, of course, to the approval of the Allied directors.

Price cutting by auditors

As it happened, there was no detailed discussion of fees in these negotiations; Allied simply made it clear that it expected the fees to be in the normal range. But ordinarily such presentations do include some fairly explicit talk about costs and fees. Price competition between auditors can be intense—though price cutting in order to get an account is officially deplored in the profession. Auditing firms generally calculate their fees in relation to the time they expect their personnel to be occupied on an account; but a firm with a high proportion of its junior and senior accountants idle may submit a bid well under "the normal range" just to get them working again. Al Jennings, the senior partner of Lybrand, Ross Bros. & Montgomery, recalled recently that his firm had lost a big account to another of the Big Eight, which put in a "loss-leader" bid—after it had managed to wangle an invitation to make a presentation. Firms often submit such bids in the hope that after they get a foot in the door, they can gradually expand the volume of their work and their fees.

Another large influence on the bids that auditors submit, and on their costs in handling an account, is the extent of the client's own internal controls. A sizable number of large corporations have recently been building up their internal auditing staffs, in order to maintain consistent surveillance and control over their systems and procedures, to guard against fraud, etc. This internal auditing cuts down the independent auditor's case load considerably, and huge companies like General Motors and A.T.&T., which have such internal systems, are able to hold down the fees they pay their independent accountants.

In setting his fees, the independent auditor has to make a calculation about the length of time it will take him to familiarize himself with a company. Its sales volume is only a rough guide, but its "complexity"—the number of operations it performs, the number of branches or divisions—matters considerably. Merrill Lynch, Pierce, Fenner & Smith, possibly the most complex "service company" in the world, paid Haskins & Sells $164,000 in 1959.

In general, the auditing firm's work load is heaviest in the first year, when it is just getting to know the corporation, and some auditors expect to lose money on a big account in this year—even with normal fees. The loss should be recovered in the second year, when the work load drops by perhaps 25 per cent. In the third year the account pulls into the black. An auditor cannot very well submit a loss-leader bid if there is any danger of his losing the account within a few years, and many auditors are chary of bidding for business where there is a tendency to rotate auditors. For many years E. I. du Pont de Nemours & Co. has been the outstanding exponent of the rotation philosophy. The company used to change its auditors every three years; recently the time has been lengthened somewhat.

A question of rotation

The rotation problem is a delicate subject in the auditing profession. Some corporations have formal policies calling for the rotation of auditors. They believe that their stockholders are entitled to receive fresh and objective views of their financial operations, and that an old, established auditor may begin simply to take the company's practices for granted. Some companies want to be sure that the auditor's loyalty is to his own organization and not to the officials he is supposed to be reporting on, who get to be his friends after a while. Finally, there is the problem that an auditor who has worked a long time on one account may develop a kind of vested interest in not uncovering any frauds or financial irregularities—i.e., any such discovery would reflect on his own handling of the account in the past.

Auditing firms do not have, to any great extent, the problem, usually associated with the advertising business, of the partner who "controls an account" and is able to walk off with it. The rotation of auditors on an account is one obvious deterrent. Even when some partners in auditing firms develop close and friendly relationships with the executives in client firms, it is hard for the client to justify giving them the account, because stability and manpower, rather than any special creative talent, are what auditing firms must primarily offer. One exception: in 1947, George Bailey, the partner in charge of the Detroit office of Ernst & Ernst, fell out with A. C. Ernst, and managed to take the Chrysler Corp. and many other clients away from the firm. Chrysler agreed to go with Bailey, but stipulated that he must have a large enough organization to service the account nationwide. Bailey then pulled together the firm of Touche, Niven, Bailey & Smart (now Touche, Ross, Bailey & Smart), today a member of the Big Eight, and still handling Chrysler's business.

How profitable are the big firms? For many big firms, in an average year, about 20 per cent of total revenues can be considered net income—i.e., it is available for distribution to the partners and for working capital. Auditing firms have one substantial expense that most other companies in "service" industries do not have. This is the cost of liability insurance—to protect the firm from any stockholder suit charging negligence in the event that a client suffers a substantial loss traceable to professional incompetence. (If such a charge were proved, the partnership would, of course, be fully liable for the entire amount.) Any of the Big Eight firms is likely to carry as much as $15 million of this insurance. (Coverage in such large amounts is offered only by Lloyds of London.) The auditing firms all prefer not to publicize the existence of this insurance on the ground that anyone contemplating a fraud is likely to be encouraged by the thought that everyone involved is insured.

The problem of "bigness"

What sets the Big Eight apart from most other auditing firms is not only their size and influence, but also the fact that they are national —and international—in the scope of their operations. The bulk of public accounting in the U.S. is done by 25,000-odd small, local firms. In between these and the giants are a number of well-known semi-national firms, whose senior partners are also influential in the profession. These include Seidman & Seidman, Scovell Wellington,

S. D. Leidesdorf, Main & Co., Horwath & Horwath, and Alexander Grant. Like the Big Eight, many of these firms are headquartered in New York; however, they characteristically have only a few branch offices and their gross revenues run below $10 million.

The problem of "bigness" agitates the accounting profession as much as it does many manufacturing industries. Virtually any member of the Big Eight or of the semi-national firms will say that the backbone of the profession is the small, local, independent accounting firm. Such firms still are the training grounds for the great majority of independent accountants. These firms have the great bulk of the personal tax business, and most of whatever auditing is done for the more than four million "small business" enterprises in the U.S. But these local firms have never been able to compete effectively with the national and semi-national firms for the business of big clients—i.e., those that generate over $10,000 a year in fees. The local firms face a continuing succession of tragedies as the small and medium-sized companies they have grown up with locally grow too big for them. It often happens that a local company separates from a local auditor when the company makes its first public offering of stock; at such times the underwriters are likely to insist that the prospectus bear the name of a national auditing firm—to ensure that a competent job will be done, and perhaps for reasons of prestige too.

Some small auditing firms have tried to cope with this problem by merging with other small firms. La France, Walker, Jackley & Saville, with eighty-five professional accountants, sixteen partners, and branch offices in eleven cities, was formed in 1959 in a merger of nine small firms—none of which had more than seven professional employees before the merger. But more often the small firms are absorbed into the medium firms and the Big Eight. Alexander Grant, for example, merged four local firms into its organization.

Within the American Institute of Certified Public Accountants, the smaller firms have been pushing for a series of reforms that would help them to maintain their own identities and remain competitive. Many of them would like the institute's ethical code to include a ban on the vast "publishing activities" of big firms. The latter do, in fact, turn out a steady stream of booklets and magazines explaining and analyzing the operations of state tax codes, the functions of management service divisions, the problems arising out of new SEC regulations, etc. There is a vast amount of real scholarship in these publications, but the small firms feel that there is also a vast amount of promotion for their sponsors. The small firms would like the ethical code to ban the continued use of a deceased partner's name in a firm's name—i.e., they want to prevent the Big Eight from continuing to cash in on the immense prestige of some of their founders.*

To help the small firms the institute is now sponsoring a professional training program designed for accountants in two-to-five-partner firms. The program includes, for example, training in the application of management services to small business. It also includes, oddly enough, a study of the special economic problems of small accounting firms—which are often considerable, principally because the partners are apt to be young and inexperienced, and trained in handling other companies' accounting problems, not their own.

The widespread introduction of electronic data-processing equipment in the accounting profession recently has left some auditors with a feeling that the profession's economics are about to be transformed. E.D.P. equipment has vastly increased the efficiency of many routine operations of the big clients, especially the so-called "posting and footing" operations. (This is what the profession calls routine bookkeeping work, e.g., checking classifications.) The new equipment will increasingly cut down the proportion of junior accountants required by the big firms. Haskins & Sells, for example, used twenty juniors back in 1950 to make a headquarters audit for one of the big farm-equipment firms. In 1960 it used only seven. Seidman & Seidman reports that the ratio of junior accountants to seniors in its firm has declined by 25 per cent in the past two years. One interesting application of the use of E.D.P. by a *small* firm is provided by Young, Skutt & Breitenwischer of Jackson, Michigan. The firm was approached in 1959 by a local manufacturer who had bought a computer and then found he could not really keep it busy. He suggested that the accountants take it off his hands, use it in their own operations, and rent it out to their clients when they were not using it. This scheme has worked out nicely so far.

The auditing boom in Washington

The increasing influence of accountants and auditors has not

---

* The appearance of this chapter as an article in *Fortune* was the occasion of still another fight between the big and small firms about "advertising." One small firm contended that, in allowing themselves to be interviewed by *Fortune,* the Big Eight partners had violated the A.I.C.P.A.'s ethical code. However, the institute's Committee on Professional Ethics disagreed.

been confined to private business. Accountants are proliferating furiously in the great public bureaucracies as well, and at all levels, from the municipalities to the federal government. Auditors and accountants are the fastest growing of all occupations in the federal government; there were 16,845 in 1960. Of the FBI's some 6000 special agents, over 700 were trained accountants. In the General Accounting Office there were 1800 professional accountants—over 400 of these were C.P.A.s, among them the Controller General himself.

The rise of accountants in government, as in private industry, is essentially a reflection of the endless complexity of the modern world. At many levels of government today, accountants are inextricably involved in the formation of policy—often because they are the only officials able to make sense of a modern government budget. When he was budget director of the City of New York, Abraham Beame completely dominated many policy-making sessions of the city's Board of Estimate, principally because he was apt to be the only official present who knew what was possible within the scope of the city budget. Professor Wallace Sayre of Columbia University, who made a detailed study of the workings of the city government, said that Beame was "the single most powerful official in the city." At the national level, President Eisenhower's Budget Director Maurice

STANDINGS OF THE TEAMS

The Big Eight partnerships dominate the auditing world, and their senior partners provide that world with most of its leadership and direction. These firms operate in a stately and dignified environment, mostly in the Wall Street area, and the competition among them often seems to be muffled by rules about "ethics." Nevertheless, the competition is real.

Unlike advertising agencies and law firms, auditing firms do not consider it unethical to serve clients competing against one another, and several of the Big Eight firms have important specialties in certain industries. Arthur Young & Co. has been strongest in the oil and gas fields. Touche, Ross, Bailey & Smart does auditing for both Macy's and Gimbels, and for scores of other retail corporations. Arthur Andersen & Co. originally made its reputation unraveling the snarled affairs of the Insull utility empire, and still maintains a strong position in utilities: today Andersen audits perhaps a third of all U.S. utility companies. (However, it does not have the business of the world's largest utility, the American Telephone & Telegraph Co., which is audited by Lybrand, Ross Bros. & Montgomery.)

One firm that has expanded in almost all possible directions is Peat, Marwick, Mitchell & Co., which has got to be the largest in the profession

Stans, who is a C.P.A., played an important role in several major policy decisions, including a very controversial decision to cut back the B-70 program to the development of a single prototype.

The whole federal system of accounting was overhauled more than a decade ago with the passage of the Budget and Accounting Procedures Act of 1950. This called for much more complete disclosure of the government's financial operations, and authorized the establishment of new accounting and reporting systems for each executive agency of the government. It directed the Bureau of the Budget, the Secretary of the Treasury, and the Controller General to conduct a joint program for the improvement of cost accounting in the government. Before 1950, federal accounting systems were dominated completely by the General Accounting Office and the Treasury Department, with the emphasis on "allotment accounting," which was designed to keep agencies' expenses and obligations under control. Few attempts were then made to use cost accounting so that agencies could present budgets that systematically related their costs to their proposed operations. The 1950 act required the Executive Department to project its requirements through the Bureau of the Budget. With the Eisenhower Administration's greater emphasis on balancing the budget, the bureau's power and prestige were steadily expanded. The budget director now receives an earlier and more de-

through an aggressive program of mergers. Its biggest single lift came in 1950, when it absorbed the established old firm of Barrow, Wade, Guthrie & Co. Price Waterhouse has always had a broad client base, and although smaller today than several other firms, it still audits more listed corporations than anyone else. It also retains a substantial foreign business through its contacts with affiliated firms, working in an international P.W. partnership. Haskins & Sells, which was the first major auditing firm founded by American accountants—most of the early firms were British in origin—also has a broadly based clientele, which includes the largest U.S. industrial corporation, General Motors, and hundreds of very small clients too. (In the world of the Big Eight, a small client is ordinarily thought of as one whose fees do not get above $10,000 a year.) Ernst & Ernst has built up its business substantially by moving very heavily into the "management services" field, in which it pioneered.

Because they are private partnerships, none of the Big Eight firms are required to disclose any information about their size or revenues. The last time any such data were spread on the record was in 1939, when the Securities and Exchange Commission was investigating the McKesson & Robbins scandal, and auditing practices generally. At that time the SEC report indicated that Price Waterhouse was the largest firm in the U.S.

tailed picture of the operations of the Executive Department than any other individual; and this fact makes a policy role for him inevitable. He has maintained this role in the Kennedy Administration.

Why auditors are uneasy

Many accountants and auditors, although delighted with the volume of new business and new responsibilities they acquired during the 1950s, will confess to a kind of uneasiness about their situation. Their uneasiness stems from a feeling that the profession has not yet done a satisfactory job of resolving all the uncertainties and ambiguities as to the proper ethical conduct of auditors in situations where their private interests seem to clash with their clients'. But there is an even larger ambiguity as to what constitutes "generally accepted accounting principles." And many auditors believe that it is an urgent matter to resolve these before the profession is inundated by the load of new business it expects by 1970. The ambiguities are more than mere details; they are numerous and fundamental, and many auditors believe that unless they are resolved, the interpretation of many financial statements will come down to an elaborate guessing game. The nature of these ambiguities, and the prospects for resolving them, will be discussed in the next chapter.

~~~~~~

Peat, Marwick then had twenty-five partners and Arthur Andersen fifteen. The figures on partners shown below are not strictly comparable, since some firms have several classes of partnerships and others do not; however, these and other figures do at least make it clear that the relative sizes of the firms have changed a lot since 1939. The figures are *Fortune*'s estimates as of the end of 1960, and are based on information from a wide variety of sources. None of the firms named have confirmed these figures, but several have acknowledged that they are in the right range.

Firm	*Partners*	*Offices*	*Est. gross* (in millions)
Peat, Marwick, Mitchell & Co.	190	60	$45
Arthur Andersen & Co.	171	28	40
Ernst & Ernst	132	95	36
Price Waterhouse & Co.	101	40	35
Haskins & Sells	176	36	33
Lybrand, Ross Bros. & Montgomery	131	23	28
Arthur Young & Co.	104	28	26
Touche, Ross, Bailey & Smart ..	71	27	17

2

Some Large Questions for the Auditors

"The beginning of wisdom," say the Chinese, "is to call things by their right names." The 76,000 certified public accountants in the U.S. are every year becoming more aware that finding the "right" names for business operations may be the most arduous part of the unending search for a more understandable, more rational,

THE FATHER OF THE BALANCE SHEET

The father of the accounting profession is an unsung, largely unremembered Franciscan monk, Fra Luca Pacioli, who gave the world double-entry bookkeeping, and was the greatest mathematician of his day (*c.* 1445–1523). He was also a teacher, a professor of sacred theology, and a friend and associate of some of the great statesmen, painters, musicians, and churchmen of his period, including Leonardo da Vinci, Pope Leo X, and Pope Julius II. Pacioli's exposition of double-entry bookkeeping was acclaimed at the time by Leonardo, and Goethe later described it as "one of the finest discoveries of the human intellect." Oswald Spengler asserted in *The Decline of the West* that Pacioli's work ranked in importance with the discovery of the New World and the theory of the rotation of the earth around the sun.

It was sometime in the thirteenth century that merchants in Italy began to keep track of their business affairs by making two entries, one of debit and one of credit. Essential to this innovation was a growing awareness of companies as *continuing* enterprises. Before the innovation, each transaction had simply been viewed separately—some merchants kept journals bound in different colors to record different kinds of transactions—and the concept of "balance" on a single ledger had been unknown. The income statement was also unknown, except as it applied to single transactions; no attempt was made to determine whether a business was operated profitably over a specific period, such as a year or two.

It was Pacioli's contribution to sense the revolutionary implications of

more honest, and more efficient business society. When the terms that measure business performance are used inflexibly, business practice may be unduly constricted. But when these terms are used too loosely, business practice may degenerate into confusion and mistrust.

At their convention in Philadelphia in 1960, the C.P.A.s labored mightily to find a set of principles that would minimize both dangers. They need such principles as underpinnings for their professional code of ethics and to gain more respect for their professional independence.

One afternoon during the convention, about a thousand of the most distinguished C.P.A.s in the U.S. gathered in the Rose Garden Room of the Bellevue-Stratford Hotel to hear what was billed as a debate on the principles of their profession. An uninitiated visitor wandering into the room might have thought at first that they were arguing over some minor, tedious technicalities, and so might have

~~~~~~

these changes. He recorded and classified them, and set forth the necessary elements of a balance sheet in a special supplement to his *Summa Arithmetica*. His outline of the proper use of the journal and general ledger could be used, with only minor alterations, by a bookkeeper working today.

He was forty-nine in 1494, when this work was published. Born in Borgo San Sepolcro, a small town in central Italy, he was early apprenticed to a wealthy merchant family. When he was twenty, he went to Venice to tutor the sons of a rich merchant. Later he studied at the great universities of the day. In 1470 he joined the Franciscan order and began to teach mathematics and also theology. After the *Summa de Aritmetica* appeared, he and Leonardo collaborated on a book about science and mathematics, *De Divina Proportione*, with Leonardo doing the illustrations and Pacioli supplying the text. He died around 1523—the exact date is uncertain.

For centuries afterward, his text on accounting was translated and often plagiarized. A version reached England and Scotland in the Elizabethan era, and there found its most hospitable soil, flourishing as England embarked on its great era of exploration, with joint stock companies financing the ventures. Double-entry bookkeeping became much more important in England in the eighteenth century, when the laws on the limited liability of corporations were passed. These laws enabled corporations to acquire sizable assets, and so to plan ahead for periods of years. Balance sheets got to be infinitely more complex—and accountants came into their own.

been puzzled by the passions that were manifestly stirred up. The C.P.A.s themselves knew that the debate concerned a lot more than technicalities. They knew that they—the members of the American Institute of Certified Public Accountants—were in a position to influence considerably both the financial reports of companies and the business practices to which the reports refer. In recent years the A.I.C.P.A. has, in fact, become a kind of private financial legislature; working within the limits imposed by tax and securities laws, its members advise businessmen as to correct and permissible procedures to be followed in reporting their financial affairs. What now bothers many members of the profession, and what occasioned the debate, is the fact that the limits of permissibility stretch pretty far these days.

The case against flexibility was argued by Leonard Spacek, the senior partner of Arthur Andersen & Co. Spacek is regarded within the profession as something of a rebel. He knew that he was speaking to a predominantly hostile audience, and he made no attempt to conciliate it; peering sternly from the lectern through thick glasses, never smiling, never raising or lowering his voice, he set forth the case for greater uniformity in accounting procedures. His opponent and opening speaker in the debate was Maurice Peloubet, the white-haired senior partner of Pcgson, Peloubet & Co., whose benign and avuncular manner contrasted sharply with Spacek's. Peloubet argued forcefully that businessmen *should* have maximum flexibility in handling their financial affairs. (The text of their statements, together with rebuttals that were written afterward, appear in the Appendix, beginning on page 203.)

Spacek's firm has been crusading aggressively for more uniformity. It has circulated a booklet citing twenty different issues on which the institute's own position differs from the practice of many of its members, or on which the institute's position is unclear, or on which new financial developments have raised new questions about the institute's position.

"The truth as it actually is"

The problems the profession is concerned about may be suggested, briefly at this point, by citing some figures:

• In one recent ten-year period, Texaco reported earnings some $213 million below what it might have if it had adopted different (but also acceptable) methods of accounting for intangible costs involved in drilling operations.

• The Great Atlantic & Pacific Tea Co.'s balance sheet shows about $700 million less of debt than it would if the company had followed a policy of owning its stores rather than one of sale and lease-back. Although the company is under a long-term obligation on the stores, these lease commitments do not have to appear on the balance sheet as debt.

• The American Electric Power Co. has been able to increase its stockholders' equity by some $127 million by crediting deferred federal income taxes to a restricted earned surplus.

• In 1958 the Transamerica Corp. increased its assets figure almost fourfold, to $149 million, by reporting its subsidiaries at book value instead of original cost.

The institute has been aware for several years that it will have to take a position either for continued flexibility in handling financial statements or for uniformity. C.P.A.s have been zealous in their insistence that their work calls for a high degree of judgment; yet at the same time they have been apprehensive that their judgments, unless tied to some systematic set of principles, will come to seem arbitrary. Some members of the profession talk ambitiously of the "principles" on which accounting practices rest, and of the "postulates" on which the principles rest—as though the whole edifice had been constructed logically, like theorems in geometry. Yet there is no definitive list of principles or postulates, and many of the practices have simply evolved *ad hoc*.

In the debate in Philadelphia, Spacek made it clear that his quest for uniformity was related to a desire to help investors "find the truth as it actually is." Peloubet, by contrast, ridiculed the notion that there is "some sort of absolute truth . . . This exists nowhere else and will not be found in the practice of accounting"—which merely requires "that the conventions and assumptions on which the accounts are prepared should be clearly stated." Peloubet's view on this matter has generally prevailed within the profession over the years. The late George O. May, who was often identified as the dean of the modern U.S. accounting profession, once remarked that the "world of business . . . is subject to constant and sometimes violent change and full of uncertainties." He added that the works of accountants "cannot rise higher in the scale of certainty than the events which they reflect."

The effort to cut through all the ambiguities in modern accounting gained momentum at the 1957 convention of the A.I.C.P.A., with a speech by Alvin R. Jennings, the senior partner of Lybrand, Ross Bros. & Montgomery. Jennings proposed that the profession buttress its theoretical underpinnings, in part by organizing a sizable new research effort. Specifically, he persuaded the members to support a new research division, staffed by both academicians and practitioners, that would codify, analyze, and recommend changes in prevailing accounting practice. Also the organization of an Accounting Principles Board, which would work out an agreed-upon body of doctrine, was an indirect result of his proposals. The board was organized in 1959 and has been addressing itself to the issues raised by Spacek—himself a member of the board.

The ethics of auditors

The accountants' intensified concern about their principles is related to their consciousness that the importance and status of their profession have been rising rapidly; but that even so it lacks the independence and authority that come from having at its back a systematic body of solid and settled principles. The lawyer serves his client, but he takes his guidance from a body of law and knowledge on which the client's beliefs and wishes have no influence. The accountant occupies a much lower place on the scale of independency. His code will not, of course, allow him to put his name to an outright untruth. But he is sometimes caught in a position where there is no agreement in his profession about the way "the truth" shall be stated—and this makes it harder for him to be independent of his client's demands.

In 1959, for example, the Alaska Juneau Gold Mining Co. pressed its auditor, Arthur Andersen, to permit a revaluation (upward) of certain of the company's properties to offset partially a substantial net reduction in the over-all assets. The Andersen firm did not agree that any properties should be written up, although it conceded that the case was not clear-cut. Alaska Juneau thereupon switched to Arthur Young & Co., whose partners, after careful study, felt there was merit in the management's position. This sequence of events suggests the pressures that auditors are often under, and the range of ethical problems they face in the absence of agreed-upon accounting principles. At the Philadelphia convention the institute's efforts to clarify its rules about members' independence, and about their ethical obligations in general, consumed more time than, and created as much of a fuss as, the debate over accounting principles.

Some of the ethical prohibitions confronting C.P.A.s are clear-cut. It is plainly a violation of the code to advertise or solicit new business, or to tell outsiders about clients' business transactions. But other situations are not easy to resolve. Consider two very sticky problems recently faced by auditors:

Not long ago a partner in one of the Big Eight national firms made the arresting discovery that some employees of one corporation he was auditing received payments from a supplier company that he was also auditing. The partner was ethically bound not to reveal this information to the executives of the first corporation (i.e., because it involved confidential information obtained in the course of auditing the supplier company). At the same time, he was bound to protect the first corporation from repetition of the practice. He finally resolved the matter by asking the chief executive officer of this corporation to state the company policy on such payments. When he was told that they were forbidden, he disclosed that the policy was being violated—but left it up to the management to detect and halt these practices.

A partner in another Big Eight firm found, in checking the books of one client, that a high proportion of its assets consisted of receivables from another client—which, the auditor knew, was close to bankruptcy. He could not reveal this fact to the first company; yet he had to insist that larger reserves than usual be set up against possible losses on the receivables. The management of the first company made it clear that they thought his demand unreasonable. This left the auditor in a painful and precarious position, but he stuck to his guns, and eventually management accepted his recommendation.

Independence—but how much?

The ethical problem that commanded most attention at Philadelphia concerned the "independence issue." This issue involves a lot more than the problem of the client exerting pressure on an auditor who wants to keep an account. The issue also embraces some questions about auditors' impartiality in handling secure accounts.

It is clear that an auditor must not have, or even seem to have, any motive for failing to disclose misleading information in his client's accounts. The SEC has ruled that no auditor can be considered independent if he has a financial interest in a client; and auditors practicing before the commission cannot own shares or serve as directors or officers of corporations whose financial statements they audit in connection with public offerings. The Big Eight firms generally have adopted this principle, and as a matter of policy bar their partners and managers from owning stock in or serving as directors of any client corporation. A partner in Price Waterhouse, for example, is barred from investing in about 400 listed companies.

Several leaders of the A.I.C.P.A. have been prodding the institute to require *all* C.P.A. firms to follow the Big Eight in barring such investments. The Illinois state society has already passed rules forbidding an auditor to express an opinion on the financial statement of a concern in which he has any financial interest or with which he is associated as a director, officer, or promoter. But at the Philadelphia convention the institute leaders ran into trouble when they tried to get the membership to bar such holdings formally.

Spokesmen for some of the small firms argued that the concept of independence could not be linked mechanically to the absence of such holdings. In some cases, they said, they had been asked to help out young enterprises, often when these were close to bankruptcy. In many such cases, these auditors argued, they had been willing to help the companies conserve cash by taking payment in stock; now it would be unfair to make them dispose of this stock in order to keep the accounts. Furthermore, they contended, only a small proportion of the nation's C.P.A.s practice before the SEC, and it would be unfair to saddle a majority of the profession with standards that are relevant only for a minority.

The whole debate was intensely embarrassing to the leaders of the institute. Part of their embarrassment arose from the strong feeling of many members that the Big Eight, and the semi-national firms, too, already have too much influence in the institute—and the more rigorous standards were plainly modeled on Big Eight practice. The dispute accentuated the divided interest of the big and small firms and highlighted the fact that they have different standards of ethics. Supporters of the proposed standards, not anticipating a proxy contest, had done no campaigning or proxy soliciting. The small firms —the one-to-five-man outfits—did solicit proxies against the proposed rule, and apparently they got enough to make its adoption doubtful. As soon as it was doubtful, its proponents grew leery of bringing it to a vote at all; the one thing they did *not* want was a vote showing the institute membership against stricter standards. After a great deal of parliamentary maneuvering and a certain amount of unparliamentary chaos—at one point five overlapping and contradictory motions were being entertained by the chair—there was a vote to defer the issue until 1961. (At the 1961 Convention, the stricter standards were adopted overwhelmingly; however, they will not go into effect until 1964.)

How to try a C.P.A.

The conduct of certified public accountants is subject to several different kinds of discipline. Some of it is imposed by state licensing authorities, which, however, have widely varying standards. Some of the discipline is exerted by state C.P.A. societies, whose standards are in principle—but not always in practice—as high as the national organization's. In addition, a C.P.A. who certifies financial statements concerning securities of any listed company must agree to observe the regulations of the SEC. Finally, he may join the American Institute of C.P.A.s and agree to abide by its code of ethics. (The institute has about 44,000 of the 76,000 licensed C.P.A.s in the U.S.) Of all these organizations, the American Institute exerts the tightest discipline.

Some of the state licensing authorities and associations have, in fact, been powerless to require accountants to adhere to their presumed standards. C.P.A.s who have been expelled from the A.I.C.P.A. often continue to practice undisturbed by the state authorities. One C.P.A. was expelled by the institute after he pleaded *nolo contendere* in a federal tax-fraud case; he had been charged with allowing his client, a hardware retailer, to manipulate profit figures in such a way that he evaded $125,000 in income taxes over a four-year period. The auditor is still practicing in Pennsylvania.

The institute has three penalties it may invoke against transgressors. It may admonish, suspend, or expel them. Many of the admonitions are for borderline offenses—e.g., for seeming to violate the rule against self-advertisement by allowing a local bank to tell its depositors that a C.P.A. who is a "tax expert" will be available for consultation at certain hours. Suspensions and expulsions are for more serious offenses, are relatively rare, and cannot be invoked without a trial. In the period from May, 1956, to December, 1961, twenty-nine members of the institute were brought to trial. Sixteen were expelled, eleven were suspended, and two were acquitted.

The trial procedure is quite formal. First, a fifteen-member Com-

mittee on Professional Ethics establishes a prima-facie case that the
rules of conduct have been violated. Then the case is handed over
to a twenty-one-man trial board. The accused C.P.A. may be, and
usually is, represented by counsel. The case is presented by the chairman of the Committee on Professional Ethics, and the whole trial
rarely takes longer than a day—usually only two or three hours. It
requires a simple majority of the trial board to suspend a member
from the institute, and a two-thirds vote to expel him.

Despite all the parliamentary uproar over "independence," most of
the men at Philadelphia were aware that the larger problem facing
their profession was the fuzziness about the basic principles of accounting. The institute's current attempt to clarify these principles
is not its first. Indeed, it had a Committee on Accounting Procedure
before its new Accounting Principles Board was set up, and the
former issued basic opinions for twenty years, beginning in 1939.
There are now fifty-one bulletins outlining accepted accounting
principles, and some regard them as a sort of catechism of the profession. They do, in fact, constitute the most authoritative written
guides to good accounting practice. But accountants have had
varying degrees of loyalty to these bulletins, at least one of them having been virtually ignored by the profession. (This stated the preferred
method of writing off plant and equipment under the wartime rapid-
depreciation laws.) A more recent bulletin, dealing with the procedure to be followed in treating welfare and pension plans, was two
years in preparation, went through fifteen drafts, was finally exposed
to the profession, then was revised, re-exposed, and then formally issued. It still has not gained complete acceptance.

Can the Accounting Principles Board gain a more widespread acceptance of *its* recommendations? The new board has at least one
large advantage over the old committee: its members are aware that
the confusions about acceptable practices cannot be ended merely
by issuing a lot of specific recommendations—and they are resolved
that the board shall clarify first principles first. With the principles
clarified, it may be easier to get agreement on practices.

On the other hand, the new board has some new problems. One
problem is simply that tax laws and securities regulations are much
more complex than they used to be. In the complexity there is at least
some room for businessmen to maneuver—to make decisions more
freely—and any attempt to codify the handling of related financial
data reduces the area of freedom, and will surely meet some resist-

ance. A related difficulty has arisen from the steady shift in emphasis and interest away from the balance sheet and toward the income statement. Investors, security analysts, bankers, and even some creditors have grown more interested in the earnings capacities of companies than in their assets and liabilities. (It is almost forgotten today that until the passage of the Securities Act in 1933 many public corporations did not even issue income statements; the curious investor could deduce the income only from changes in net worth shown on successive balance sheets.) The tremendous premium placed by the stock market today on high earning capacities suggests that reforms tending to lower some companies' reported earnings will meet with considerable resistance.

Oily financial statements

Perhaps the most spectacular example of the flexibility of modern accounting is provided by the disparate handling of the oil industry. At present there are several alternative procedures, all "generally accepted," that may be followed in accounting for the intangible costs of drilling productive wells—at least, in accounting to stockholders. In tax reports to the U. S. Government, almost all oil companies charge off their intangible drilling costs against income in the year the cost is incurred. But in their published reports, oil companies generally follow one of three procedures. The first, which seems to be the most conservative (because it results in lower reported earnings), is used by Amerada Petroleum Corp. in reporting its domestic results. In the U.S., Amerada charges all intangible drilling costs against income immediately. ("Tangible" costs, i.e., of equipment, are of course depreciated at varying rates.) Under the Amerada procedure, a company with, say, $200,000 of income and $100,000 of intangible drilling costs would report the balance of $100,000 as taxable income. After paying the 52 per cent corporate income tax, the company would show a net profit of $48,000—exactly in line with its tax return.

The second procedure, perhaps the most liberal, is followed by Standard Oil of New Jersey and many other companies. Jersey does not charge any intangible drilling costs on producing wells against income, at least not at the time the well is drilled. Instead, the intangible costs of productive wells are capitalized; and so they show up on the balance sheet as new assets, and not on the income statement as expenses. Under the Jersey method, therefore, the company with $200,-000 of income would report all of this amount. However, companies using this method report to their stockholders only the actual taxes paid to the government—$52,000 in this case—which means that they can report a net profit of $148,000, roughly three times as much as a company using the Amerada method.

Midway between these two extremes, and increasingly popular with accountants, is a reporting procedure followed by Texaco and Shell Oil and others. Like Jersey, these companies immediately put the intangible costs of productive wells on their books as assets; and if they have the same $200,000 of income, they do not deduct these costs from it. But unlike Jersey, these companies reduce their reported income by an amortization charge equal to the taxes saved, in addition to the charge for taxes actually paid—i.e., they show a total charge of $104,000 and so report a net of $96,000. They take the $52,000 amortization charge as a reduction of the $100,000 cost of developing the well; and so the net asset that appears on the balance sheet is the $48,000 difference. This asset is charged against income over the useful life of the well—perhaps at the rate of $4800 a year if the well is presumed to be good for ten years.

In sum, then, three different oil companies, each with revenues of $200,000, each with intangible development costs of $100,000, and each actually paying the U. S. Government $52,000 in taxes, might report three considerably different net-income figures to the public: $48,000, $96,000, or $148,000—and all three would be following "generally accepted accounting procedure." Furthermore, *none of the companies would be under any obligation to tell the public which procedure they were following;* they would only be obliged to indicate if and when and how they changed their procedures. Texaco, Shell, and Jersey Standard do not indicate in their annual reports how they account for intangible development costs. (Amerada does make its accounting practice clear.)

The businessman aghast at all this flexibility can be reassured on one point at least: Amerada's procedure results in lower earnings reports, and Jersey's in higher, only in the short run. In the long run, and *ceteris paribus,* the accounting procedure adopted will have little effect on earnings. Eventually, Amerada's reported earnings will be bolstered by revenues from wells it has already written off. And eventually, Jersey's reported income will be depressed by the amortization costs of its wells.

Hot water in pools

Investors also have a problem in evaluating the financial data relating to mergers; and the New York Stock Exchange has asked the American Institute of Certified Public Accountants to straighten out a large, continuing confusion about two different kinds of mergers: purchases and pools. In principle, a merger may take place (*a*) when one company purchases another, or (*b*) when two companies pool their interests. In either case, there is likely to be an exchange of stock. The difference is that in a purchase the smaller company becomes a part of the parent; in a "pooling of interests" the companies are simply blended into one, whose assets, liabilities, and net worth are the sum of these pairs of items on the two original balance sheets. Perhaps a half of all big mergers these days are pools.

Why should the distinction be of any interest to investors? Consider some recent examples:

Not long ago, C. I. T. Financial Corp. merged with the privately owned Home Finance Service. To swing the merger, C.I.T. had to give stock with a market value of $5,600,000 in exchange for Home Finance stock with a book value of $3,600,000. If the merger had been construed as a purchase, C.I.T.'s assets would have had to reflect an additional $2-million cost, and amortizing this amount might have created a steady drain on reported profits in the years following. Instead, C.I.T. reported a pooling of interests with Home Finance—and so it had no problem.

The Automatic Canteen Co. of America was recently involved in two mergers. In one of them it exchanged 82,500 shares of its own stock for Nationwide Food Service, Inc. In the second merger, six weeks later, Automatic Canteen exchanged 40,970 shares for the stock of the A. B. T. Manufacturing Corp. In this second merger the stock exchanged was about equal in value, and the deal was called an acquisition. But in the first case the Automatic Canteen stock was worth some $2 million more than the book value of the company it merged with; and calling this deal an acquisition might have required a write-off of the differential. The deal was called a pooling.

Here again, the basic problem is that public corporations have considerable latitude in reporting on their earnings and financial position. The A.I.C.P.A. has, to be sure, outlined a number of standards that accountants are supposed to follow in determining whether a merger can be considered a pooling: the institute says, for example, that the relative sizes of two companies should not be wildly out of line, and specifically suggests that the smaller company's assets should not be less than 5 per cent of the larger company's. Actually, Automatic Canteen acquired Nationwide Food Service in exchange for only 1.6 per cent of its own stock. Yet it would be unfair to suggest that the deal violated accepted accounting procedure. For different C.P.A.s assign different weights to the several standards, and no one of them is considered controlling.

Pension rights and wrongs

Another large accounting problem, also unresolved by the profession, concerns the proper method of reporting on pension funds. Ever since the first great wave of corporate pension plans broke over the profession a decade ago, accountants have been trying to grapple with the two kinds of costs involved in pension planning. One cost, which has created few problems, reflects the pension credits built up by the employees in the current year. The other cost, which *has* created problems, is incurred in amortizing the employees' "past service liability." The main accounting questions were, and still are, how this liability should appear on the balance sheet, and how much of it should be charged against income every year.

Corporate responses to both questions have varied widely. When U. S. Steel inaugurated its pension plan in 1950, the corporation's unamortized past-service liability was estimated at $574 million—an amount equal to half the market value of all the common and preferred stock at the time! In most subsequent years U. S. Steel has made payments for past-service charges. But in 1958 the corporation contended that past-service charges were amortized adequately and that it did not have to make a payment that year. Price Waterhouse had no real grounds for rejecting the company's contention, but insisted on inserting in the annual report a long paragraph spelling out the change that had taken place. The effect of the change, in any case, was to increase the reported net profit that year from $200 million to $300 million (i.e., the pension cost was reduced by about $100 million). In 1959, U. S. Steel resumed its payments for past-service costs, but in 1960 discontinued them again.

The institute has done little to clarify pension reporting practices. In 1956 it issued a bulletin to the effect that financial statements should at least indicate the present liability, actuarially calculated, of future pension commitments. But the institute has never got any agreement on the best way to charge for past-service costs, and some sizable corporations do not even make charges for *current*-service costs. Until 1960, for example, American Tobacco had an unfunded pension plan, and the only pension charges shown in its financial statements were actual payments to retired employees. At the other extreme, the Gillette Co. is one of the few large corporations that have funded substantially all their past-service liability. And in between are a fair number of corporations that contribute to pension funds each year only the additional obligation incurred that year—with no contributions for past-service liability.

Accounting and inflation

In general, many auditors believe, most of the big disagreements in their profession concern proper methods of allocating costs over periods of time. And some auditors believe that the biggest disagreement of all during the next decade will concern what they call "price-level depreciation"—a method of allocating costs over periods of time when prices are fluctuating.

The debate begins with the concept of depreciation itself. Originally, accountants thought of depreciation simply as an amortization of costs incurred in the past. But since World War II a second concept has become more widespread—the "shoebox" concept of depreciation charges as a *reserve* put aside for replacement of worn-out plant and equipment. This new concept brought a new problem with it. In a period when the purchasing power of the dollar has been declining, it obviously requires more dollars to replace worn-out plant and equipment. Some accountants, including Spacek of Arthur Andersen, contend that present depreciation charges are not realistic. They believe that annual depreciation charges, whether calculated on a straight-line or accelerated basis, should be increased (or, conceivably, decreased) as the cost of living changes. Thomas Higgins, the senior partner of Arthur Young & Co., suggests that the profession might get into price-level depreciation by encouraging its corporate clients to publish two sets of figures—one adjusted for prices, the other unadjusted. A body of opinion in the A.I.C.P.A. is still against any such change, however. Carman Blough, for many years the institute's very influential research head (he retired recently), does not believe that inflation has yet been severe enough to distort the meaning of present depreciation figures. Anyway, he argues, why should price-level accounting be limited to depreciation? Blough points out, for example, that no auditor has proposed charging against income any figure for insurance costs higher than the actual costs, even though insurance premiums are sure to rise in an inflationary era. (Higgins is for using price-level reporting on any item that is "material"—which presumably excludes corporate insurance charges.)

While price-level depreciation is not an accepted accounting method in the U.S., it is accepted in Europe, and more U.S. investors are likely to begin encountering the practice as the securities of more foreign corporations are traded in U.S. markets. In 1956, for example, Simca, the French auto company, sold some capital shares in the U.S. In its prospectus, which was passed by the SEC, Simca noted that under French tax law it was permitted to account for the loss in purchasing power of the franc by putting a higher figure on its fixed assets. Simca has continued to depreciate its assets on the basis of the adjusted figures. Philips' Gloeilampenfabrieken, a Dutch electrical manufacturer with many U.S. shareholders, uses price-level depreciation regularly.

One large difficulty about price-level depreciation is that, in a time of rising prices, the additional charges against income might depress earnings. Several years back, Professor Ralph C. Jones of Yale made a study of this problem for the American Accounting Association (an organization composed primarily of teachers of accounting). One of the companies Jones studied was the New York Telephone Co., a member of the Bell family. His figures show that in 1946–52, New York Telephone reported 50 per cent more income than it would have reported if depreciation charges had been inflated along with the dollar.

The power to decide

It is clear that the profession's principal unresolved problems will have to be solved, ultimately, by the A.I.C.P.A. and its new Accounting Principles Board. It is also clear that the actual powers of the institute and the board are still undefined. The scope of these powers was tested early in 1960, in a case raised by three subsidiaries of the American Electric Power Co., which sought a court injunction to prevent the institute from issuing an "interpretation" of one of its prior opinions. Much of the ammunition against the institute was supplied by Donald C. Cook, president of A.E.P., who happens to be a member of the institute. Cook and his company argued that the influence of the institute had already led the SEC to propose a change in its approved procedure on the recording of deferred tax payments; the proposal was, in fact, eventually adopted. (Cook also happens to be a former chairman of the SEC.) Until the institute and the SEC acted, A.E.P. had been allowed to carry deferred tax payments on its books in a "restricted earned surplus," which technically forms part of the stockholders' equity. The change would have had the immediate effect of reducing this equity by $67 million; and Cook contended that the reduction would make it harder for the company to borrow money, and oblige it to sell stock instead—which, he also contended, was more expensive.

The institute's powers are especially ambiguous as they relate to regulated companies—e.g., railroads, airlines, public utilities, whose rates are regulated, and also banks, savings-and-loan companies, insurance companies, and stockbrokers, where regulation is concerned mainly with protecting consumers against fraud. Perhaps because these companies are regulated in so many other ways—to protect passengers, depositors, policyholders, etc.—not much concern has been given to the problems of their *stockholders,* and many such companies are not required to have audited financial statements. It is often hard for investors to make any meaningful evaluation of these companies as business enterprises. Accounting in the banking and insurance fields, for example, shows a preoccupation with the companies' solvency but is weak on their earning power. Fewer than 20 per cent of the nation's 14,000 banks are audited by independent certified public accountants. Robert A. Eden, a savings-and-loan executive who has extensively studied the varying accounting methods in use, said recently, "Two otherwise identical savings banks might report net income differing by thousands and even hundreds of thousands of dollars . . . might differ in total assets over the years by possibly millions of dollars."

Where the power ends

If accountants need some clarification of their powers, they also need a greater public awareness of where that power and responsibility end. Many businessmen are surprised to learn that a corporate financial statement is the responsibility of management, not of the auditing firm. The chief executive of a corporation must give his auditors a letter of representation in which he states that, to the best of his knowledge and belief, all the information in the report is true and fairly presented. Technically, and legally, the auditor is responsible only for the honesty of his own opinion certificate, in which he ordinarily says that his investigations have led him to believe that the company's assets, liabilities, and earnings reports are fairly presented.

Not, of course, that the certificate is an unimportant matter. Any qualifications that may be expressed in it are attentively noted by investors these days. Stockholders are questioning auditors more frequently and more intensively at annual meetings, and often demanding to know why corporations changed their auditors. Questions about conflict-of-interest situations, as at Chrysler Corp., are increasingly directed at the auditors, as well as at management. The selection of independent auditors is more often being submitted for stockholder approval. Some auditors believe that the time may soon come when U.S. stockholders will have the same legal rights as British stockholders, who are entitled, at annual meetings, to have both the old and new auditing firms present when there is any change in auditors. One way or another, it seems likely that auditors in the U.S. will be answering a lot of questions in the next few years.

THE P. & L. OF A. & B.

	COMPANY A	COMPANY B
Sales	$10,000,000	$10,000,000
Costs and expenses		
Cost of goods	$ 6,000,000	$ 6,000,000
Selling costs	1,500,000	1,500,000
LIFO inventory reserve	400,000	—
Depreciation	400,000	300,000
Research costs	100,000	20,000
Pension costs	200,000	50,000
Officers' compensation		
Base salaries	200,000	200,000
Bonuses	200,000	—
Total costs and expenses	$ 9,000,000	$ 8,070,000
Profit before income taxes	$ 1,000,000	$ 1,930,000
Income taxes	520,000	1,004,000
	$ 480,000	$ 926,000
Capital gain (after taxes)	—	150,000
Net profit reported	$ 480,000	$ 1,076,000
Per share (600,000 shares)	$ .80	$ 1.79

In a famous 1960 debate before the nation's distinguished auditors (see appendix, page 204), Leonard Spacek of Arthur Andersen & Co. and Mau-

GAS AND TAXES AND THE FPC

One example of the new role of accounting is provided by a case recently before the Federal Power Commission. The case is a prime example of the manner in which accountants today affect the substance of business (and not just the way business transactions are reported).

The case concerns the Northern Natural Gas Co., a utility with customers spread over the Midwest. Northern has a number of subsidiaries, one of which is a gas-producing company. The producing subsidiary had losses aggregating about $5,500,000 in 1957 and 1958; if applied against future profits, they would reduce its tax liability by some $2,800,000. However, the producing company could not generate enough profits to get the full benefit of the tax credits unless it did one of two things: cut back its costs, by reducing exploration activities, or increase its revenues, by selling off rights to some future production. The effect of either course would be to hold down the company's gas reserves.

This problem was attentively noted by the parent company's financial officials, who decided that it could best be solved by consolidating the

rice Peloubet of Pogson, Peloubet & Co. argued about accounting principles in general, and about two profit-and-loss statements in particular. These were for two imaginary companies, A and B, which are presumed to have had the same volume and kind of business. Despite this similarity, B reported higher earnings than A. Both of them used acceptable accounting methods. Spacek deplored such flexibility in accounting and Peloubet defended it.

In general, company B has increased its reported income by deferring costs:

• B uses a first-in-first-out (FIFO) method of inventory valuation, and so has no need for the $400,000 inventory reserve set up by company A.

• B avoids a $100,000 charge against income by using straight-line depreciation; A uses accelerated depreciation.

• B amortizes its research costs over a five-year period, while A takes its costs immediately.

• A funds all current pension costs—i.e., it puts into a reserve an amount equal to the cost of the employee's current service and amortization of his past service. B funds only an amount equal to the discounted value of an employee's present interest in a pension plan, with this amount not to exceed the company's current legal liability.

• A paid its officers a cash bonus, while B granted them stock options, which are not charged to income—though eventually they may act as a drag on per-share income.

• Both companies had capital gains. A credited the gain to earned surplus, B to income.

parent and subsidiary tax returns. This would give the tax credits to Northern, which never has any trouble showing a good profit. In return, Northern would reimburse the producing subsidiary by paying it about $2,800,000. Northern's auditor, Arthur Andersen & Co., advised it that the maneuver conformed to acceptable accounting practice.

The FPC accountants were alarmed about one aspect of the deal, however. They conceded that Northern and its subsidiaries had every legal right to consolidate their tax returns, but they challenged the propriety of the $2,800,000 payment to the producing company; they argued that Northern should keep this amount, or rather, since utilities' profits are always reflected in their rates, that Northern should give its customers a refund.

The question at issue—can a parent corporation reimburse a subsidiary for tax credits when a consolidated return is filed—looks technical and supremely uninteresting. But if the FPC staff is upheld, then the utility customers will get a $2,800,000 windfall and the producing company's reserves will be diminished. Which would seem to be fairly substantive matters

3

Atlas Plywood: When the Auditors Disagreed

The Atlas Plywood Corp. of Boston, for many years a major U.S. producer of plywood, is no longer in business. Many of the stockholders who invested in it during the mid-1950s undoubtedly wish that it had *never* been in business; they lost heavily, especially in 1956–57, when Atlas common fell from around $15 a share to around $4. What made the case especially exasperating was the near-impossibility of finding out exactly what had happened at Atlas and who was at fault. How could a company that had enjoyed twenty-three years of uninterrupted profits suddenly suffer a $10-million loss? The two prestigious auditing firms involved in the case could not agree on an answer to that question—or to several others. Here are the principal characters and organizations involved:

• *Peat, Marwick, Mitchell & Co*—Now the biggest auditing firm in the U.S., it had been the auditor for Atlas for over twenty years. The Atlas account was supervised by Boston partner Howard Hansen.

• *Willard Heinrich*—Appointed treasurer of Atlas in 1957. In 1947 Heinrich, as treasurer-controller for Georgia-Pacific Corp., had a disagreement with his firm's auditors, Peat, Marwick, after which the Georgia-Pacific account was taken away from Peat, Marwick.

• *Arthur Andersen & Co.*—Another of the Big Eight auditing firms, often regarded as an irritating maverick by the other seven, mainly because its managing partner, Leonard Spacek, sounds off critically in public about some of the traditional and generally accepted practices of the profession. (See appendix, page 204.) Arthur Andersen & Co. had been the successor firm to Peat, Marwick after the clash with Heinrich at Georgia-Pacific. In 1956 it had also replaced Peat, Marwick as auditor for the Chicago & North Western Railway just as Spacek was inaugurating a series of blistering, widely publicized, and controversial speeches criticizing a number of the railroad industry's accounting policies, established by the ICC and accepted by most other auditors—including Peat, Marwick.

• *Maurice Marcel Clairmont*—A former Romanian textile manufacturer who came to the U.S. in 1941 and became a "specialist in mismanaged companies." Clairmont was the central figure in a long struggle over control of Rice-Stix, Inc., of St. Louis; he lost, but came away with a profit in seven figures. He was involved in a similar battle for Russell Manufacturing Co. of Middletown, Connecticut, lost again, and again profitably. He became chairman of the Atlas Plywood executive committee in September, 1956.

• *Dorchester Industries Inc.*—The investment company through which Clairmont gained control of Atlas Plywood. Its key stockholders, who later became directors of the Boston corporation, included Simon Jaglom, a Russian-born importer of Polish hams, reportedly worth over $10 million; Jack I. Poses, a wholesaler of cosmetics and perfumes; and Dewey D. Stone, president of a New England textile-finishing company.

The changing of the auditors

In April, 1957, partner Howard E. Hansen, of Peat, Marwick's Boston office, went to the Statler Office Building to call on Willard Heinrich, newly appointed treasurer of Atlas Plywood Corp. In view of Peat, Marwick's past experience with Heinrich, Hansen was quite prepared to hear from him that Atlas was changing auditors. As a matter of fact, Hansen knew that Heinrich had already asked three other accounting firms to submit proposals on the Atlas audit.

After Hansen was ushered into Heinrich's office there was a brief exchange of pleasantries. And then Heinrich did tell him, precisely as anticipated, that Peat, Marwick was losing the Atlas account. But Hansen had had no premonition of what came next. Heinrich said the recently reshuffled Atlas management was planning to *sue* Peat, Marwick on the grounds that it had certified faulty and misleading financial statements in the Atlas annual reports.

Minutes later the shocking news was communicated to Peat, Marwick partners in Boston and New York. It prompted the partners to make a decision without precedent: they would withhold from anyone in Atlas or in any successor auditing firm the Peat, Marwick working papers on the Atlas Plywood audit. An auditor's working papers consist of the preliminary notes, records of calculations, instructions, and explanations used in the preparation of an audit. Normally an auditing firm would make these available to a successor auditing firm as a matter of professional courtesy, but courts have ruled that these working papers are the auditor's property and the Peat, Marwick partners thought it prudent to safeguard the papers against the day they might have to defend in court their long service for Atlas.

A short time later Peat, Marwick was officially notified that its successor at Atlas was Arthur Andersen & Co. A partner of Arthur Andersen called and asked to see the Atlas working papers. The answer was a polite but firm "no."

A request for restitution

In July, the Peat, Marwick partners discovered they had not yet drained the bitter cup. Clairmont invited them to confer with him in New York. It turned out that he had but one thing on his mind: he wanted Peat, Marwick to make a cash settlement as restitution to Atlas for failure to make a proper audit of its books. If a settlement was made, Clairmont said, Atlas would not sue. He did not say how much money would be necessary.

The Peat, Marwick men were as puzzled as they were angered. Arthur Andersen had not yet completed its audit. Even if Clairmont had some preliminary notions of what it would show, how could he state with certainty that the former auditors had made an improper audit?

A clue to Clairmont's thinking was provided at the end of August, when the Atlas annual report, for the year ending June 30, 1957, audited by Arthur Andersen, was made public. It was a bombshell.

To hell in one year

In the year between the last Peat, Marwick audit and Andersen's audit, Atlas Plywood had apparently gone to hell. Sales had skidded from $58,400,000 to $51,600,000. In place of a $404,198 profit, there was an operating loss, the first since 1933; it was a whopper: $4,518,645. And to add to the anguish, a series of special charges against income totaling $6,300,000 brought the over-all 1957 loss to $10 million (after a tax credit of $588,000). Atlas' assets had dwindled from $36 million to $26 million. Inventories had shrunk from more than $13 million to $8 million, and a husky reserve of $700,-

000 was set up for doubtful accounts, instead of $150,000, as in the previous year. Another $450,000 was charged off as uncollectible.

Moreover, a letter to the stockholders, signed by Treasurer Heinrich, forecast a grim future for the company and its stockholders. He described Atlas as a company so badly managed that only heroic sacrifice and accomplishment by the new management could put it back on its feet.

Soon afterward, the dismayed stockholders learned that the company was undergoing radical changes. Only eleven of the thirty-three plants it had at the beginning of 1956 were operating two years later. During that interval, the number of employees dropped from 4000 to 1600. The board of directors and the executive staff were largely replaced.

Another such abrupt and complete reversal of fortunes as the one that smote Atlas would be difficult, if not impossible, to find in recent corporation history. Equally extraordinary was the auditors' certificate attached to the report.

It was a "qualified" certificate. In auditing terminology this meant that Andersen had some reservations about the accuracy of the information provided in the profit-and-loss statement. Parts of the special charges of more than $6 million, Andersen explained in the certificate, might conceivably have been charged off in 1956, 1955, or earlier years—i.e., when Peat, Marwick was auditing Atlas.

A puzzled stockholder might wonder whether the 1957 report would have been just as gloomy if Peat, Marwick had done the audit. Or was the catastrophe attributable to the change in management that took place during the year? In approaching these questions, warily, we can begin by reviewing Atlas' earlier history.

The boss who sorted the mail

The company was formed in 1925 by a merger of five small New England plywood producers. From 1936 on it was run by a tight-fisted, stiff-necked Bostonian named Elmore I. MacPhie, who carried one-man rule to an eccentric extreme. (He sometimes supervised distribution of the mail.) MacPhie rarely told his directors or his executives any of his plans beforehand. Atlas executives couldn't even learn from their own mistakes, since MacPhie didn't give them a chance to atone for any.

MacPhie's production and merchandising policies were simple: he played it by ear. In good years he went all out on production, sold to marginal customers to gain a higher markup and fatter profit. In bad years MacPhie squeezed out a profit, no matter how small, by stringent economy. After World War II, when Atlas bumped into competition in the container market from the paperboard manufacturers, MacPhie moved into the paperboard field too, but slowly and on a small scale. To diversify the company's plywood line, MacPhie went into production of hardwood panels—unluckily, just before cheaper Japanese imports began flooding the U.S. market. Under MacPhie, Atlas expanded by purchasing stock control of Plywood, Inc., which operated warehouses and mills in the Middle and Far West—but Plywood, Inc., had little timberland and so was vulnerable to price squeezes when the demand for wood and wood-pulp products was soaring. And yet, MacPhie was remarkably successful. Atlas never operated in the red during his presidency.

But in 1954, as sales fell 14 per cent and profits 64 per cent, it was apparent that increased competition was becoming a serious operating problem. Some Atlas directors and officers clamored for a change in policy. MacPhie was still resisting the pressure to make him change his ad hoc method of running the company when in March, 1955, at sixty-six, he died.

No provision had been made for an orderly succession; there were no large stockholders to give direction to the management. MacPhie, abnormally sensitive to any threat to his authority, had seen to that. His death now released some long-nurtured, long-repressed resentments and ambitions. MacPhie's family was shocked when some of his former associates came to pay their last respects—reeling from a cocktail party. And at least three of MacPhie's executives thought they could step into his shoes as president. They staged a prolonged tussle for the post before Robert A. Muller, a senior vice president with an engineering background, won out and became the successor of the deceased Elmore MacPhie as president of Atlas Plywood Corp.

Robert Muller is a suave, handsome man of impressive bearing and convincing speech. Some of his former associates at Atlas say that he is a terrific plywood man. His critics—they include MacPhie's family—say he wasn't up to the job of president and invoke the ghost of MacPhie to prove their point: shortly before he died, they recall, MacPhie renewed his previous warnings not to let Muller succeed him. (Muller's friends acknowledge MacPhie's hostility, but ascribe it to a clash of mutually abrasive personalities.)

At any rate, Muller set out confidently in June, 1955, to shore up Atlas' weakening profit position. He budgeted for a $10-million an-

nual sales increase in fiscal 1957 and 1958. To tighten Atlas' control
of its profit-making subsidiary, Plywood, Inc., the minority-stock-
holder interest in that company was to be bought out. The subsidiary's
timber hunger was to be assuaged by the purchase, for $9 million, of
cutting rights to a section of northern California timberland owned
by the Hearst interests.

To help finance this program, Muller and fellow director David
Van Alstyne Jr., head of the Wall Street banking house of Van Alstyne, Noel & Co., arranged an offering of $3 million in sinking-fund
debentures and $3 million in convertible debentures. This offering
was the door through which Maurice Marcel Clairmont stepped into
the affairs of Atlas. He already owned several thousand shares of Atlas
common, bought at the time he was getting out of a fight for control
of one company, Rice-Stix, Inc., of St. Louis, and about to step into
a tussle for another, Russell Manufacturing of Middletown, Connecticut.

Losing with a profit

Clairmont is a slender man with twin patches of black hair cling-
ing to a balding head, and a constantly worried look on his sallow
face. He had gained temporary control of Rice-Stix, one of the nation's biggest soft-goods manufacturers and wholesalers, earlier in
1955. He relinquished control of the company when his partners became, as he puts it, "too greedy" and wanted to sell out to an opposition group at a handsome profit. Clairmont reluctantly went along.
Though he himself realized a profit of over $1 million, he says the
profit could have been greater if his partners had stuck with him.

As part of his share in the Rice-Stix settlement, Clairmont got options on 40,000 shares of Russell Manufacturing common, exercis-
able at $11.50 per share. (Russell common was then selling around
$10 a share.)

Clairmont assumed the chairmanship of the Russell board at a time
when the company, a producer of automotive and belting products,
was losing money. He concluded immediately that the situation
would get worse unless he moved in on it. He brought in new executives, changed auditors, suggested liquidating some of the assets, and
announced that Russell needed a loan of perhaps as much as $500,-
000.

Businessmen in Middletown, alarmed by the prospects of liquidation at Russell, thereupon bought Clairmont's option position for

$50,000 and in June, 1956, took over the company. By this time the company had begun to make money. Clairmont says he willingly let himself be bought out, because with total assets of only $5 million Russell was "too small a situation" to interest him.

Under the new management (headed by a president brought in by Clairmont) Russell rapidly improved. All debt and tax delinquencies were wiped out without borrowing, and Russell reported earnings of around $541,000 in 1957. Two-thirds of its profits, incidentally, came from automotive parts, the end of the business that Clairmont had particularly wanted to liquidate.

After two frustrations

Clairmont now turned to a new—and much bigger—"situation" in Atlas. At the time the company had a good financial record. Market price of its stock was substantially below its book value.*

Toward the end of 1955, when the proposed new financing for Atlas was announced, Clairmont had asked Van Alstyne to sell him a substantial block of the convertible debentures. Van Alstyne sold him a large number of the convertibles, but could not supply as much as Clairmont wanted. Clairmont then worked through other underwriters handling the issue to pick up more of the securities. When Van Alstyne completed the underwriting Atlas had 220,000 shares of convertible preferred and over 800,000 shares of common outstanding, and three separate bond issues, including one made in 1953 under MacPhie. Clairmont and friends of his held more than half of the convertible debentures—a fact that the Atlas management, which had never had any large block of its securities held by one individual or group, found somewhat disturbing.

Invitation to a proxy fight

One month after the financing was completed Muller learned that one of his earlier rivals for the presidency was planning a proxy fight with the aid of a customer's man at Harris, Upham & Co., one of the largest Wall Street brokerage houses. Muller, aware of Clair-

---

* Atlas common was traded but "unlisted" on the American Stock Exchange, meaning it was not subject to the same SEC disclosure requirements as fully listed stocks. Its executives and large stockholders, for example, did not have to make public their trading in Atlas shares.

mont's position as a holder of Atlas securities, invited him to join the board, hoping thus to armor himself for the proxy fight.

Now Clairmont set up Dorchester Industries, Inc., as an investment company to buy Atlas common. By July, 1956, when Clairmont accepted Muller's invitation and joined the board, Dorchester's holdings of the common represented the largest individual block. The proxy-fight threat evaporated, but Muller soon realized he had invited a camel to stick its nose under the corporate tent flap. At the September, 1956, annual meeting, four of Clairmont's associates joined the Atlas board.

Almost from the day he joined the board, and, according to members of the old management, before he could have completely familiarized himself with Atlas affairs, Clairmont had displayed nervous concern over the condition of the company, its plants and management. When his Dorchester associates joined the board his jitters increased noticeably. He began to talk of selling plants and cutting back Atlas' activities in the plywood business.

Clairmont says he was upset by what he learned of Atlas once he was on the inside. It is true that the competition from Japanese imports and paperboard was hurting Atlas more and more. And though at first, says Clairmont, his Dorchester group supported Muller's expansion program, "every time we turned around we found a new skeleton in the closet."

The first clear indication of how differently Muller and Clairmont viewed the future of Atlas came when the new board cut the 1957 sales budget. Muller had set his sights on a $70-million volume for the year, and, in addition to the Hearst purchase, he had made commitments for the purchase of lumber in the open market to reach that goal. The board discarded Muller's sales target, terming it unrealistic. Reviewing what happened, Muller says, "When you have a situation in which the president and board don't agree, you are not going to make any progress. So I got out."

A chuckle from a ghost

Muller's reign ended in January, 1957, after a turbulent eighteen months, and the shade of Elmore MacPhie must have enjoyed a ghostly chuckle. Wholesale resignations and firings followed Muller's departure. The atmosphere in the traditionally restrained Atlas offices became dramatically charged.

Changes in Atlas' structure then came fast. "Unprofitable" plants and warehouses were closed and sold as fast as possible. Some were bought by local people, some by other plywood companies like U. S. Plywood and E. L. Bruce Co. Six plants were sold for a total of about $1,100,000, with most of the payment deferred for three years to five years. The Hearst timber contract and others were terminated.

Along the line Clairmont brought Willard Heinrich into the company as treasurer. Heinrich took over his duties on April 1, 1957. He examined the Atlas books, raised his hands in horror, and said the only thing to do was to make an unusually thorough audit of the company's accounts, inventories, and assets.

Why was it necessary to change auditors at Atlas? Heinrich says that Arthur Andersen & Co. had more experience in the plywood field than Peat, Marwick, and that it was desirable to get as much experienced judgment on Atlas as possible. It is a fact that Andersen audits for the largest plywood companies, but it is also true that Peat, Marwick works for more than forty lumber and plywood companies.

"Unfounded and unmitigated"

As we have noted above, the next annual report of Atlas Plywood, which included the financial statements audited by Andersen, together with Heinrich's letter to the stockholders, was a sizzling indictment of the old management. Here are some of the detailed charges made by Heinrich together with comments by Muller or Frank Harney, former senior vice president and last of the old management to leave:

► Heinrich said that the cost system under the old management did not reflect actual production costs.

Frank Harney says that this statement is "an unfounded and unmitigated lie."

► Heinrich said that purchasing was inadequately centralized.

Harney says that except for advantageous local buying, Atlas purchasing was centralized and strongly supervised in the home office.

► Heinrich said that the Hearst contract was a "burdensome commitment," since the timber could be used by only one marginal plant, which was shut down a few months after the contract was signed.

Muller and Harney retort that the mill had to be shut down because the plywood market had dropped sharply, a fact they could not have foreseen.

Expanding on the statements made in Heinrich's letter, Clairmont says that his management began selling plants only after studying all of them carefully and determining which could be kept and operated profitably. But, he adds, it did not take much study to spot some plants not worth keeping. He cites a plant built at Camden, Ohio, to supply Frigidaire and a few other appliance-industry customers with cleated corrugated cartons. Later, more advantageous contracts caused the appliance companies to withdraw much of their business from the Atlas plant, leaving it a heavy loser.

Atlas had two plants in North Carolina, a small, profitable one at Williamston, and a big, unprofitable one at Plymouth, twenty miles away. Clairmont contends that the two plants were making the same products, and neither was running at full capacity. So he sold the Williamston plant, kept the bigger one at Plymouth. Local interests bought the Williamston plant and soon had it operating in the black.

A modern plant that Atlas built in Center, Texas, four years earlier Clairmont sold to E. L. Bruce Co. for 25 per cent of its replacement cost, or slightly over $400,000.

Some things left undone

Several sections in the 1957 Atlas report seemed directed as much at Peat, Marwick as at the old management.

One is a tabulation, prepared by Heinrich, explaining how $8,500,-000 of write-downs and reserves had been made. Accompanying the table are statements about correcting "timber depletion treatment in prior years" and "a large quantity of obsolete and unusable supplies . . . never charged off or written down." These remarks could be interpreted as an indication that the previous auditors had left undone some things they should have done.

Moreover, the paragraph immediately following the treasurer's tabulation refers to Andersen in such a way that the casual reader might assume that this particular tabulation was approved by the new auditor.

Walter Oliphant, the Andersen partner who supervised the Atlas audit, suggests that he does not wish to be associated with Heinrich's jab at the previous auditors. He requested that a statement be inserted at this point in the report to remind the reader that Andersen's opinions on the write-downs could be found in its own certificate.

And yet the Andersen certificate is no kinder to Peat, Marwick.

It says Andersen was not present to observe and examine the "realizable value" or "economic usefulness" of inventories and assets at the end of fiscal 1956, or to set up any necessary provision for losses on commitments and lawsuits, and consequently could not certify "what portion of the net loss including special charges" should have been attributed to the era of the Peat, Marwick audits. The meaning is clear: some portion of the loss should have been taken earlier.

Oliphant admits that the wording of Andersen's certificate, when read in conjunction with Heinrich's letter, could be interpreted as criticism of one auditing firm by another but denies it was his intention to criticize Peat, Marwick's 1956 work.

While avoiding any expression of outrage at the Andersen certificate, Arthur Tolman, head of Peat, Marwick's Boston office, who was responsible with partner Hansen for the earlier Atlas audits, says the rest of the annual report is "calculated to slam." He goes on: "Frankly, there's quite a bit there that borders on the libelous."

As to the Andersen certificate, both Tolman and senior partner William M. Black say they consider it "unusual." Tolman adds that the qualifying paragraph, in his opinion, makes "irrelevant" comments and raises issues that are "beyond the duty of the accountant to determine." Tolman's "irrelevant" refers to Andersen's statement that it could not determine the "economic usefulness" of some of the Atlas assets.

What of the threatened suit against Peat, Marwick? Clairmont now vehemently denies he ever threatened a suit against Peat, Marwick for improper auditing. He says he threatened to sue only for the working papers and—according to Clairmont's newly hired public-relations counsel—never had any real intent of translating even that threat into action.

The old cry of "liquidation"

But to stockholders a debate over the proprieties of the auditing profession does not answer the question: would Atlas have shown a loss if there had been no change in auditors or management?

The Clairmont group, of course, does not doubt it for a second. Some members of the old management, Muller included, grudgingly admit Atlas would have shown an operating loss in 1957. There were too many problems facing the company and the plywood market had one of its worst years in history. The drop in plywood prices that year hurt U. S. Plywood earnings and those of other companies in the field—though none were hit as hard as Atlas was.

The severity of the loss shown in the Atlas report, coupled with the speed with which Clairmont moved in diminishing the company's operations, immediately raised the familiar cry of "liquidation" among some stockholders and old employees.

At the 1957 annual meeting Clairmont stated that his group had no intention of disposing of all the plants and would keep those company plants that could be profitably operated. But all but one of the plants in operation were losing money. Meanwhile the company's cash assets, resulting from inventory liquidation and plant sales, were mounting rapidly. On June 30, 1957, Atlas had over $5 million in cash and government bonds. By the end of September the amount had jumped to $8 million and by December was close to $10 million. Perhaps the best clue to Clairmont's intention at the time was provided by a "blind" ad he inserted in the business section of the New York *Times* on Sunday, December 8. Here's how it read:

. . . .

Acquisition Wanted
Listed corporation with substantial liquid funds and tax-loss carry-forward will buy a profitable company on the following basis.

(1) Prefer manufacturer of paper board, paper packaging or other paper products, mechanical rubber or plastics manufacturer, building material products, but will also consider other fields.

(2) Must have stable record of earnings averaging at least $500,-000 annually before taxes.

(3) Company must be owned to extent of at least 60% by individual, family, or small group.

(4) *Will purchase for cash.* Mechanism of acquisition will be such as *to avoid capital gains taxes for sellers.* [Italics supplied.]

(5) Must have capable management willing to remain. Brokers and finders protected. Please reply in confidence to Chairman of the Board.

. . . .

This ad produced no tangible results for Atlas. But in the spring of 1959 Financial General Corp., a New York holding company, began buying Atlas Plywood shares. After much dickering and negotiating, Clairmont agreed to join forces with the new group. In September 1960, with Clairmont serving as chairman, the company's name was changed to Atlas General Industries. Two months later Clairmont was out. It was the third time he had made a profit while losing a company.

A hangover for the auditors

This transaction by no means ended the case for the auditors concerned. The SEC had made an effort to clarify at least the facts of the case when, in October, 1958 Atlas Plywood was forced to file another annual report for the year ending June 30, 1957. This demand forced Clairmont and Heinrich to resume their discussions with Peat, Marwick about the availability of the firm's working papers for that year.

William Black, senior partner of the firm, responded by demanding a letter stating whether or not the Atlas Plywood management had found anything in the books or records of the company that indicated any improper auditing by his firm. Heinrich wrote that there was no such evidence on the record, although his remarks excluded the period covered by the disputed working papers. Black insisted that Clairmont sign the letter. Clairmont instead signed a statement saying that the letter had been issued with the approval of the Atlas board of directors. Peat, Marwick then turned its working papers over to Arthur Andersen, which examined them and reported that the company's statements for both 1957 and 1958 had been fairly represented. Thus in the end, Andersen agreed that Peat, Marwick had been following accepted principles even if they were not the principles Andersen itself would have followed.

But this agreement only seemed to magnify some other large questions. Why, first of all, had there been that big discrepancy between the figures for 1956 and 1957? Part of the answer may be that Atlas had different objectives in each year. One management, under MacPhie and Robert Muller, had been operating Atlas as a going plywood company and so its auditors had valued the assets for their earning power. But Clairmont and Heinrich had brought in a new set of auditors and, very possibly, suggested that they look at the company with liquidation in mind.

This change in corporate "philosophy" does not, however, explain the huge write-down for "special charges." A careful scrutiny of subsequent annual reports suggests that the write-down was overly pessimistic; in 1959, as it turned out, Atlas sold its written-down timberland properties for a $5.1-million *profit*.

By the time the accountants finally straightened out their working papers and the dispute had become academic, the stock was back up to $15 per share. But by that time the damage had been done, so far as hundreds of stockholders were concerned. It was probably not much comfort to them to reflect that the wild gyrations on the company's financial statements had all conformed to "generally accepted principles of accounting."

PART TWO

The Powerhouses in Operation

4

Merrill Lynch: The Biggest Broker in the World

"Like Gaul, our opinion of Merrill Lynch is divided into three parts: part admiration, part envy, and one hell of a lot of determination not to let it run away with the industry." Thus a partner in a competing brokerage house recently summed up Wall Street's mixed reaction to the biggest firm with the longest name in the U.S. securities business. Admiration and envy are surely deserved. In the two decades since its founding, Merrill Lynch, Pierce, Fenner & Smith has set a scorching pace for the rest of the financial community. It has broken more taboos, opened more offices, employed more salesmen, and attracted more customers than any other Wall Street brokerage house. And to a remarkable degree it deserves credit for reviving Wall Street's confidence in itself and for bringing back a once cynical public to the securities markets en masse.

In the process Merrill Lynch has become a giant, and a starkly lonely giant at that, in the securities business. In 1961 it handled more than $20 billion worth of stocks, bonds, and commodities, and boasted no less than 540,000 active clients, or close to 4 per cent of all U.S. individual stockholders. In 1961 the firm collected $19 million in interest on amounts it lent those customers who trade on margin. For serving these customers, Merrill Lynch's rewards at first glance appear small. Gross revenues last year ran to only $181 million, and earnings after taxes (and after a $16-million contribution to employee benefit funds) to $22 million on invested capital of $91 million. These are, indeed, piddling figures compared to the sales and earnings of the great industrial enterprises whose shares it handles.

But it should be remembered that the securities business, while essential to the entire U.S. economy, operates on paper-thin profits, and the fact is that, comparatively, Merrill Lynch has always stood and now stands head and body above all its competitors. Its revenues *are approximately* three and a half times those of Bache & Co., its nearest competitor in the brokerage field, and it would take a merger of the country's four next-largest brokerage firms to create an organization doing as much business as M.L.P.F.&S. Moreover, Merrill Lynch has not contented itself with brokerage, but has struck out boldly into the field of investment banking and now ranks sixth among all U.S. corporate underwriters.

Nor is there any indication that Merrill Lynch will slow down. Even while the Dow-Jones industrial average was dropping eighty-five points in 1960, M.L.P.F.&S. went ahead calmly and confidently with its plans for expansion. In 1962 its advertising space budget was increased to $2,700,000, a $500,000 jump over last year. Its training program, which was the first of its kind in Wall Street, now "processes" some 300 graduates annually, almost double the 1958 rate. To its 150 offices, M.L.P.F.&S. plans to add thirty more in the next three to five years, each office representing an investment of $250,000, for a total outlay of $7,500,000. In addition, it has remodeled or relocated 52 offices in the past two years, at a minimum cost of $2 million. All told, Merrill Lynch is spending in its expansion program more than eleven of the Street's top twenty-five brokerage firms currently possess in the way of capital. And this expansion has been world-wide. Merrill Lynch has 14 offices overseas, ranging from Beirut to Tokyo, and including two on the edge of the Iron Curtain, in West Berlin and Hong Kong. The firm is setting up special securities-research divisions to cover foreign investments for Americans and U.S. securities for foreigners.

Such optimistic expansion has a variety of effects on the whole financial community. For one thing, Merrill Lynch's increasing investment in new electronic equipment to handle its own business will undoubtedly speed up the technological revolution now going forward in Wall Street. For another, the gap between M.L.P.F.&S. and the rest of the brokerage pack is tremendous and will grow even wider in the next few years unless the competition makes up its mind not to be outdistanced any further. Francis I. du Pont, Walston, Shearson, Hammill, and others are pulling up their socks. More important, the pace that Merrill Lynch is setting may accelerate mergers and expansions among both brokerage and underwriting firms. Traditionally, many of the better-known brokerage firms have kept clear of underwriting, and most underwriters have kept their brokerage business to a minimum. Now established brokerage houses like E. F. Hutton are paying increasing attention to underwriting, while key underwriting firms have come to lean heavily on brokerage firms to distribute the securities they handle. The next and logical step in some cases may well be expansions and mergers.

Merrill Lynch's expansion plans clearly envisage a further spread of security ownership. At the present time there are about 17 million security owners in the U.S. or 11.5 per cent of the adult population. If the recent rate of growth is maintained, the number of security owners should increase to at least 26 million by 1970. Merrill Lynch has launched a new selling program to boost the New York Stock Exchange's dawdling Monthly Investment Plan, which permits an investor to buy as little as $40 per quarter in Big Board securities. Even more important, there has been a noticeable softening in Merrill Lynch's hostility to mutual funds. Should Merrill Lynch decide to associate itself actively with a mutual fund, its managerial and sales fees would almost certainly be cut and this would cause a further hubbub in the Street. In any case, Merrill Lynch is confident that "People's Capitalism" is still in its adolescence.

The breakeven point

Merrill Lynch's confidence reflects a faith that U.S. industry still has a huge profit-making potential. It could be, of course, that Merrill Lynch is overestimating the market and overlooking some factors that are bound to affect the economy in the Sixties—the threat of overcapacity; the tapering off of the inflation that made equities so attractive in the postwar years; the increase of foreign competition, to mention a few. Yet even if Merrill Lynch's outside expectations prove overly optimistic, it figures that it can break even on less than a 1,700,000-share day on the Big Board. In 1961 the average daily turnover was 4,085,000. Actually Merrill Lynch expects that by the middle of the decade six to eight-million share days may be routine and that when they come M.L.P.F.&S. will be ready.

The man charged with keeping M.L.P.F.&S. in its dominant position isn't a Merrill, or a Lynch, or a Pierce, or a Fenner, or even a Smith, but a fellow named Michael McCarthy. He is a deliberate, determined, but soft-spoken man who was not well known at all in Wall Street until recently. A native of Minnesota and a graduate of Safeway Stores, McCarthy went to work for Charles Merrill back in

1940, at about the time that Merrill was beginning to knit the firm together out of four separate brokerage firms—Merrill Lynch, E. A. Pierce, Cassatt & Co., and Fenner & Beane. In those days it seemed it would take decades to overcome public distrust of the securities markets and keep ninety-four offices and 322 salesmen really busy. But Charlie Merrill was a brilliant and impatient bantam, who set out to revamp the methods of security selling completely. He introduced informative but informal advertising; eliminated service charges for customers' monthly statements and for holding securities; and supplied research free of charge. One of his most controversial edicts was that salesmen be paid on a straight salary basis to assure customers that the advice they received was not given simply to "churn" an account and earn a commission.

Charlie Merrill's new techniques worked, but in the mid-Forties he suffered a coronary, and for the next decade the active management of the firm was in the hands of his old Amherst classmate, Winthrop Smith. In 1956 Merrill died and in 1957 Smith's health also began to fail. (He died in 1961.) In December of that year McCarthy was named managing partner. His first and not his least important decision was that Merrill Lynch had outgrown the partnership form of organization. With the exception of the ailing Smith and E. A. Pierce, all the partners whose names are on the firm masthead were gone from the scene, although some of their sons were still active and many were substantial stockholders. In January, 1959, the firm was turned from a partnership into a private corporation, with a Merrill trust holding some 10 per cent of its shares and the rest scattered, at last count, among 329 owners. The move meant financial sacrifice for some partners who had to pay extra taxes when the change-over was made. But incorporation ensured continuity of the firm's capital and also made it easier to move up new talent into active ownership and top managerial jobs.

Today, with the title of chairman, McCarthy bosses a closely knit team of men including president George J. Leness, who has been responsible for developing the firm's underwriting business; Donald T. Regan, vice president for administration; and James E. Thomson, vice president in charge of operations. Merrill Lynch has been called "conference happy," and in fact its internal communications and liaison system has been developed into a humming machine. Every two to three months a group of the firm's 150 branch-office managers is brought into headquarters at 70 Pine Street in New York for two weeks, to chew over their respective problems and be briefed on changes in policy. In the past few years sixty-five office managers have been replaced, and McCarthy has intimated that another sixty or more office managerships may be available in the next two to five years. Meanwhile the home office plays host almost daily to salesmen, dubbed "account executives," who come in to refresh their education. Wall Street is famous for its standoffish and cliquey attitudes. Merrill Lynch practices a kind of open-door policy with its employees as well as with the public, and it is a matter of note that any branch-office manager, from San Francisco or Zanesville, Ohio, can reach McCarthy personally by picking up a phone.

Charlie thought it up

Through all its ramified activities, however, Merrill Lynch practices a pretty clearly defined strategy—a strategy first laid down by Charlie Merrill himself. In drumming up new clients and holding them, the firm uses a three-pronged attack. Its opening onslaught is crisp, freshly written advertising that serves to draw customers into its offices. There the individual salesman takes over and seeks to determine the customer's peculiar needs. The salesman in his turn is backed up by a huge research department that has the responsibility for providing a good selection of stocks and bonds.

The whole approach is meant to impress on the public's mind the image of a broker who is completely reliable and ready at any time to discuss the client's problems fully and frankly. M.L.P.F.&S. runs ads regularly in over 200 newspapers and national magazines, intriguingly explaining how to open an account—but never failing to cite both the rewards and risks of becoming an investor. Frequently an M.L.P.F.&S. branch will insert a modest announcement in the local paper that a series of lectures will be given free of charge in the evening at its local office. Invariably the office will be swamped and the lectures will have to be stretched out to accommodate all the people who want to attend. M.L.P.F.&S. gives some 650 of these investment talks annually and also takes part in a number of the 3000 investor-information programs sponsored by the New York Stock Exchange with member firms. M.L.P.F.&S. sometimes even moves into county fairs, where agents in tents, alongside prize-winning apple pies, bark out the attractions of investing.

Not the least of Merrill Lynch's sales pitch is the fact that it has tried to hold brokerage charges to a minimum. Three times in the past ten years it has opposed the raising of brokerage commission rates, which are set by the New York Stock Exchange and now average about 1 per cent, though, of course, varying with the size of the transaction. Merrill Lynch has continued its policy of providing free research and other service facilities such as holding shares, a general practice now, although some brokers believe that the Stock Exchange should require charges for these services. Because Merrill Lynch has fought hard against this idea, it has been criticized for being a price cutter. The criticism causes scarcely a shrug at 70 Pine Street. Merrill Lynch believes in competition.

As a result of its efforts, Merrill Lynch's clientele has risen from 145,000 to 540,000 in the past decade. Moreover, its clients appear to have prospered. In 1957, according to a Merrill Lynch survey of its active customers, a typical investor was between thirty-one and forty, was a salaried employee earning about $10,000 annually, had been buying securities for six to ten years, and had a portfolio of securities valued at under $5000. A 1959 survey showed that the typical M.L.P.F.&S. investor, now slightly older, had an income ranging from $7,000 to $20,000 and his security portfolio had been built up to over $10,000.

According to the New York Stock Exchange, which is leading a campaign for broader share ownership, over 850,000 novices across the country are now becoming new stockholders every year. Some hardened Wall Streeters believe, of course, that these novices will vanish into thin air if market prices begin a long-term drop, and that the whole drive for new investors will boomerang. Merrill Lynch just doesn't think so. True, a little tremor of apprehension runs through M.L.P.F.&S. when the market turns sharply down, as it did early in 1960. But the comforting fact is that, even during the drop, new accounts were being opened at a rate equal to, and in some cases greater than, the 1959 rate. New accounts held up well again during the market drop in early 1962. Since this trend is also reported by the mutual-fund companies, it may indeed be a sign that the new breed of investors is made of sterner stuff or has greater confidence in its own judgment than previous generations.

Merrill Lynch isn't just counting on investor confidence and heavy advertising to get and hold its clients. From the beginning the firm has turned out well-trained salesmen, and today 1375 of its 2054 salesmen are graduates of the company's own schools. At those schools they are not only indoctrinated in the technicalities of stocks and bonds but are also imbued with a sense of responsibility. On the latter score the record of Merrill Lynch is remarkably good, considering all the temptations confronting any huge sales organization. In the past fifteen years the firm has been wrapped on the knuckles only once by the SEC for pushing its wares too hard. That occurred when an overzealous salesman jumped the gun in giving out information on an underwriting of Royal Dutch/Shell. The SEC cracked down and M.L.P.F.&S. was forced to withdraw from the underwriting.

Right now, indeed, Merrill Lynch is more concerned about pepping up its salesmen than restraining them. Most of the graduates of its schools grew up in the great bull market of the early Fifties, when selling was easy, and many of them have come to rely too much on the firm's big advertising efforts. When stocks turned down in 1958 and again in 1960, some salesmen became virtually mute when faced by a customer who had a loss in a security that Merrill Lynch had recommended. Victor Cook, head of the firm's huge downtown Manhattan office, recently warned his fellow-managers they would have to re-alert their men to the fact that they are expected to be investment advisers, not just order takers. "Don't let them sit there with their tails between their legs because the account has a loss. That's when the investor needs the advice the most. Turn to your research department to help upgrade the investment. Put his money to work."

Crack in the cement

Over the years Merrill Lynch has gradually been forced to change its methods of salesman compensation in order to hold its top men. Charles Merrill's idea of paying salesmen a flat salary instead of putting them on a commission basis worked fine at first and did much to overcome the public's fear that brokers were out simply to turn shares over. But the Merrill policy began to lose some of its appeal to salesmen as trading increased in volume and salesmen in competing firms began raking in larger and larger compensation. To meet this problem Merrill Lynch modified its original approach: to salary it has added an adjusted compensation plan (1942), calculated twice a year on the basis of a salesman's intake; a profit-sharing plan (1945); a pension plan (1959); and finally the opportunity to become a stockholder (1960). The net of these changes is that in good years, such as 1961, relatively young salesmen may earn as much as $15,000 to $20,000 from salaries and other benefits, and more experienced men may earn $50,000 or more.

Despite this, several top-flight account executives left Merrill Lynch in 1958 and 1959, drawn by the lure of earning a higher annual income than Merrill Lynch pays even under its adjusted plan. Moreover, smaller firms can often offer partnerships and top executive positions, which are already filled at Merrill Lynch. Until recently salesmen were slow to switch jobs, because they found that their customers were loyal to Merrill Lynch and would not follow them if they took a new job. Over the last several years, however, this cement has shown signs of cracking. There has been a tremendous increase of interest in speculative shares of the kind that Merrill Lynch has not cared to push officially. In a number of cases salesmen have nevertheless counseled their clients to get into these equities and have made money for them. In this case the client is apt to follow the salesman to a new firm if he makes a change.

A question of "selection"

This has caused long thoughts among McCarthy and his lieutenants as to some basic policies, and in particular has directed their attention to Merrill Lynch's research department. The department, which bears the heavy responsibility of analyzing and evaluating securities, has a budget of almost $3 million a year, and employs some 175 researchers. About half of them are security analysts, who keep salesmen up to date on changes going on in particular stock groups. The other half are portfolio analysts and correspondents who review the security holdings of Merrill Lynch clients or non-clients (free of charge, of course) and last year handled about 125,000 requests for such service. Four times a year the research department puts out a comprehensive "Security and Industry Survey," commenting on the general business situation, and listing certain stocks as "selected issues" for certain purposes—i.e., growth, stability, speculative appeal, etc. This selected list is then constantly updated on almost a day-by-day basis.

Inevitably, as Merrill Lynch has grown in size, its advice about stocks has tended to become more conservative. The surest way to disappoint a neophyte capitalist is to steer him into a speculative issue that fails to fulfill expectations. In addition Merrill Lynch has discovered that what it says about stocks can powerfully affect the market. In 1958, for instance, Merrill Lynch listed Raytheon common among its selected issues. It was then selling for $17 per share and in subsequent months zoomed to $73 per share. Then, in 1959, Merrill Lynch learned that Raytheon's executive vice president, Harold Geneen, was resigning, and removed Raytheon from its selected list. Promptly Raytheon shares fell nine points.

Experiences like this make the research department extremely careful about making even the mildest kind of recommendation, and particularly on thinly held issues. On the other hand, if it pushes conservatism too far the firm will lose not only salesmen but customers. McCarthy is well aware of this problem, and lately, under its chief, John H. Moller, research has been recommending more securities in the speculative groups such as electronics and airlines. In addition, Merrill Lynch encourages trading in the commodity markets for those who wish and can afford to take a real flyer. It believes that such markets afford overlooked opportunities to confirmed dice throwers. Even here, however, M.L.P.F.&S. enforces some restrictions. It will not, for instance, open a commodity account for women except in very special circumstances. And commodity traders are expected to have a net worth of at least $20,000 before they can begin to operate. Merrill Lynch is hopeful that commodity trading, in which it now has about 7500 customers, may expand. It expects great expansion in its over-the-counter trading of unlisted securities, of which it already handles about $3 billion a year.

$1,800,000 worth of errors

With its immense and continually growing operations on the Big Board and other exchanges, the company faces an ever growing traffic problem. By its very nature the brokerage business involves an enormous amount of paper work and computations, as customers' orders move from the salesmen and brokerage office to the trading floor of an exchange, and as the executed orders in turn move back to the customers via the accounting department. As the market grows, so does the job of record keeping. At the present time Merrill Lynch handles from 20,000 to 28,000 trades daily and has over 2,200,000 positions on its books. Last year losses due mostly to simple clerical errors ran to some $1,800,000. And five years from now the sheer mechanical load of doing business will be at least double.

The answer, Merrill Lynch believes, lies in improved technology, and here it has pioneered all along the line, not just to keep abreast of the traffic but also to cut costs. In 1958 it converted its accounting system to the use of I.B.M. 705 electronic computers. This equipment does in seven or eight minutes work that used to take one hour, and this saving more than offsets the monthly rental charges on the computers, which run to about $160,000. Since 1958, of course, the accounting load has increased and Merrill Lynch has now installed the greatly improved I.B.M. 7074 computer.

Electronic technology is also being used to conserve the salesman's time and to make it more productive. Salesmen normally handle about 200 accounts, though some have been known to handle as many as 1200. Merrill Lynch has been using the Kilberg Dialaphone—a new instrument that, attached to a regular phone, in effect gives a salesman 850 timesaving private lines to his clients. It is using a special Western Union facsimile transmission system that permits an order to flow from a salesman's desk to the trading floor and back with less handling and greater speed than was possible before. Along with some other brokerage houses, M.L.P.F. &S. has installed the Scantlin Electronics Quotron, a compact memory machine. This device is being used to record on tape the sales on the Big Board, and later will include the American Exchange and the bid and ask quotations of over-the-counter stocks and commodities. With the press of a button, a salesman will be able to obtain the latest price or a run of prices on a wide range of items in any one of those markets. The over-the-counter market would appear to be the chief beneficiary of the Quotron, since it will provide more prompt and complete information, hence create greater investor confidence.

Some enthusiasts foresee a day not too far distant when the whole process of buying and selling securities will be just about completely automated. An order would then move directly from brokerage office to the trading floor, where instead of hundreds of shouting, milling members there would be batteries of purring computers, whispering to one another. The completed order would move back to the brokerage office and pass through all billing, margin, and mailing procedures in a matter of minutes, or seconds. While this is an overdrawn picture so far as elimination of the floor activity goes, it is not pure dream by any means. By 1963 or 1964 Merrill Lynch expects that most of the steps in executing an order will in fact be part of an automatic electronic sequence.

At the same time M.L.P.F.&S. emphasizes that the brokerage business will always depend on human brains and human judgment, based on expanding knowledge. To further such knowledge it has given a $50,000 grant to establish a Center for Research on Security Prices at the University of Chicago. As its first project the center plans to process through computers financial data about every stock on the Big Board for the past thirty-five years. The end result, it is hoped, will be a thorough analysis of security price changes, and the key factors causing them.

Underwriting upheaval

While these developments will help improve Merrill Lynch's brokerage service, the firm is also strengthening its less-publicized but increasingly important role as an underwriter. Back in 1947, when the U. S. Department of Justice filed antitrust charges against seventeen major investment-banking firms, M.L.P.F.&S. didn't even warrant a mention. It was on the outside of an almost closed club of financial firms. These firms in turn have been dominated by strong personalities whose prestige and contacts are crucial in landing an underwriting deal. They include such men as Perry Hall at Morgan Stanley, Sidney Weinberg at Goldman, Sachs, Joseph Ripley at Harriman Ripley, and Harold Stuart at Halsey, Stuart.

Today the picture has drastically changed. The old top-drawer firms are still very much in business though their leading personalities are now in their sixties and seventies. But Merrill Lynch has moved up in the underwriting world and now occupies sixth place in terms of the value of public corporate issues managed or co-managed. A principal reason is that as a chain broker, possessed of a big selling organization, Merrill Lynch can do an excellent job of rapidly distributing the issues it handles in relatively small packages across a nation. In 1959, when it offered a million shares of Transitron Electronic, its average sale per customer was forty-five shares. Transitron happened to be a hot issue, but even with sticky ones M.L.P.F.&S. has shown what a vast selling organization can do. In 1960, on an offering of 1,400,000 shares of Columbia Gas System, dozens of members of the underwriting syndicate withdrew at the last minute because they thought the offering price was too high. Merrill Lynch stepped up its own selling efforts to 628,000 shares, four or five times as many as originally expected, and sold out in one afternoon.

Just as the individual investor has grown more savvy about the stocks he's willing to buy, so has the corporate issuer become more sophisticated about how its shares should be placed. A utility company in South Carolina, for example, may want a certain percentage of its shares to be sold in its home state to provide sympathetic local support when it files for rate increases. Some issuers now want to know how each member of an underwriting syndicate performs, and if one or two don't live up to their promises, they may be eliminated from the next syndicate.

Another development strengthening M.L.P.F.&S.'s position as an underwriter is the growth of "secondary" sales of large blocks of stock. These have grown in importance in Wall Street since the outbreak of World War II, when large amounts of British- and French-held shares had to be sold in the U.S. without breaking the markets. After the war the growth of institutional investors and the impact of taxes on estate liquidations added to the secondary distribution pattern. In 1958 *Investment Dealers' Digest* reported 311 secondary offerings of various types valued at over $402 million, and by 1961 the total had dropped to 209 though the value rose to $536 million.

In 1961, Merrill Lynch participated in handling approximately one out of every four of those secondary offerings, principally because it can often handle the distribution within its own organization, and tell the seller how the offering has worked out within an hour. Confident of its ability in the underwriting arena, the management increased the amount of capital allocated to this division to permit aggregate corporate commitments at any one time to go from $15 million up to $20 million. And additional capital has been allocated to the municipal business, allowing commitments of up to $9 million.

Whither now, M.L.P.F.&S.?

What other fields are there for M.L.P.F.&S. to conquer? Two areas suggest themselves—mutual funds and foreign operations. From its inception, M.L.P.F.&S. has stubbornly refused to sell mutual funds, which have turned out to be one of the fastest-growing segments of the investment business. The firm's coolness toward mutual funds dates back to Charles Merrill's belief that an investor should make his own decisions and that the sales charges of open-end trusts, averaging 8 per cent, plus a management fee, ate up too much of the investor's money. Probably, too, Merrill did not expect the funds to be as successful as they've been to date.

Mike McCarthy and his associates are not intimating that they are considering breaking with their past policy. They firmly believe the small investor can be well served by the New York Stock Exchange's Monthly Investment Plan. Of the 105,000 plans in operation, Merrill Lynch opened 65,000 and now, in cooperation with the exchange and with other firms, it has developed a new, simplified contract to be used in a heavy, direct-mail sales campaign. But the subject of mutual funds, once virtually banned, is now coming up more frequently in discussions both inside and outside the firm. Indeed, there has been considerable speculation to the effect that Merrill Lynch may one day hitch up with or help organize a mutual fund that would omit any management fee and reduce the sales load to, say, 3 per cent. If this ever happened, it would cause a real revolution in mutual funds.

A Yankee abroad

With respect to developing foreign business, Merrill Lynch is enthusiastic but is something of a Johnny-come-lately. Other brokerage firms such as Fahnestock & Co., H. Hentz & Co., and Bache went abroad earlier and are more experienced in the ways of sophisticated foreign investors. At first Merrill Lynch naturally concentrated primarily on the vast domestic U.S. market, to which its selling methods were peculiarly adapted. Now it has turned its attention overseas and characteristically it is resolved to make up for lost time.

In venturing abroad, Merrill Lynch has had to trim its exuberant selling methods to local customs. In Switzerland, for example, citizens traditionally buy and sell both foreign and domestic securities through Swiss banks. The Swiss bankers, who are also members of the various Swiss exchanges, feared that Merrill Lynch's policies would induce Swiss nationals to bypass the banks in buying foreign securities. Merrill Lynch and the Swiss bankers then reached a "gentleman's agreement" by which Americans in Switzerland could purchase U.S. securities directly through M.L.P.F.&S., but Swiss citizens would be referred to their banks even though it meant a higher cost to the individual Swiss. Since then Merrill Lynch, instead of trying to appeal to the public, has concentrated on demonstrating the quality of its services to the banking fraternity.

Merrill Lynch also, of course, faces all the normal risks of operating under foreign governments. It went to Cuba when everything looked propitious, but has had to close down its operations there in the face of Castro's Communism. On the other side of the world, in Hong Kong, it has carved out a niche for itself and proudly advertises that it is promoting capitalism "just thirty-five miles from the bamboo curtain." Despite occasional unrest in Japan, Merrill Lynch also has high hopes for that country. It is particularly attracted to Japan because that country's security regulations were adapted largely from those obtaining in the U.S. Indeed, when Michael McCarthy visited Tokyo in 1959, he found that some of the Japanese brokers had adopted almost every Merrill Lynch procedure, including the pamphlets and brochures. McCarthy also found that the Japanese security business was booming, with share ownership up from under 500,000 in 1945 to some 13.5 million today.

"I asked the head of one of the principal Japanese brokerage firms if he would permit me to estimate the annual gross profit of his firm," says McCarthy. "He agreed. I estimated $6 million and he said I was pretty darn close. Right then I was convinced we should have an office in Tokyo."

The impact of Merrill Lynch has now been felt in the conservative financial community of London. An office was opened there late in 1960 and almost immediately debate began on the wisdom of permitting the firm's advertising-promotional tactics to be introduced. Now there are signs that the Merrill Lynch approach is gaining favor. The London Exchange, adopting some of the innovations pioneered by the New York Stock Exchange, now encourages visitors, conducts advertising programs, and even produces films explaining its function and operation to the public. The London press has been throwing out some hints that the City could use a spot of Merrill Lynch's approach to spreading security ownership. In this new climate the firm of Merrill Lynch, Pierce, Fenner & Smith should touch a responsive cord among the British who so dearly cherish long names. In any case, London should provide the firm with an ideal European showcase for demonstrating the social and economic effectiveness of Charles Merrill's investment philosophy.

1959 BROKERAGE AND UNDERWRITING STANDINGS

Fifteen biggest brokers— gross income		Fifteen leading underwriters—corporate underwritings managed or co-managed	
(in millions)		(in millions)	
1. Merrill Lynch	$136	First Boston	$1,042
2. Bache	38	Morgan Stanley	965
3. Francis I. du Pont	31.2	Lehman	880
4. E. F. Hutton	30	Blyth	868
5. Paine, Webber, Jackson & Curtis	29.1	White, Weld	833
6. Dean Witter	*	Merrill Lynch	815
7. Walston	27.2	Kuhn, Loeb	696
8. Goodbody	24.8	Halsey, Stuart	650
9. Shearson, Hammill	24	Eastman Dillon	456
10. Loeb, Rhoades	23	Stone & Webster	388
11. Harris, Upham	22	Goldman, Sachs	366
12. Reynolds	21.6	Dillon, Read	363
13. Hayden, Stone	21.5	Smith, Barney	350
14. Eastman Dillon, Union Securities	*	Kidder, Peabody	275
15. Thomson & McKinnon	18	Harriman Ripley	245

* Gross income figure not available.

Though brokers and investment bankers continually pry into the business of other companies, they are traditionally tight-lipped about their own affairs. With the notable exception of First Boston, most Wall Street firms are either partnerships or private corporations and hence are required to make public only their balance sheets. Merrill Lynch alone, among the privately owned firms, issues an annual report giving a full account of its income and profits.

Nevertheless, *Fortune* has undertaken above to rank the major brokerage houses and to indicate the comparative size of their incomes. This has been done on the basis of data, filed with various regulatory agencies, that give the number of offices and employees, size of capital, and customers' debit balances. *Fortune* has also secured for all but two of the houses unofficial but authoritative gross income figures.

Income is, of course, not the measure of efficiency or profitability and there is considerable variation in the kinds of business that the firms do.

Some, like Harris, Upham and Thomson & McKinnon, are purely brokers. Many combine brokerage with underwriting and other investment-banking activities. Several—notably Loeb, Rhoades, Hayden, Stone, and Reynolds—have an additional network of "correspondent" firms, for which they execute orders, take care of stock clearance, and perform other services in return for an average 40 per cent share of commissions. They handle substantially more business than their income figures indicate, and the lower overhead on such business means a higher net profit.

Firms that specialize in underwriting are as fond of privacy as the brokers and are ranked above according to public corporate offerings that they managed or co-managed, as reported by *Investment Dealers' Digest*. The leading underwriter, First Boston Corp., a publicly owned company, reports income and profits, which ran last year to $15 million and $2,800,000 respectively. Only Merrill Lynch and Eastman Dillon qualify both as top brokers and leading underwriters, but there will almost certainly be an increasing overlap between these types of business in the future.

5

The Bustling House of Lehman

A baroquely ornamented building at 1 William Street, a discreet distance from a formal Wall Street address, houses the distinguished investment-banking partnership, Lehman Brothers. To anybody with a feel for the artistry of finance, the building is an atelier where imagination, craftsmanship, and an all-important sense of timing are combined to bring forth a few financial works of art and numerous fashionable securities to satisfy the demands of coldly calculating professional investors as well as the less exacting but more hopeful requirements of the general investor.

In the intensively competitive investment-banking business, the Lehman name today carries with it a solid ring of prestige and authority. And for good reason:

• The House of Lehman, its American beginnings going back one hundred and eleven years, is the oldest continuing partnership in investment banking today.

• Lehman partners and their associates sit on the boards of over thirty-five major U.S. corporations, scores of smaller ones, and serve as trustees of many philanthropic organizations.

• The partnership annually guides, by direct management or advice, some $2 billion to $3 billion of investment funds.

• Lehman Brothers has achieved the greatest postwar growth of any Wall Street house, and has been one of the biggest profit makers—many believe the biggest—in the business.

• To many ordinary investors, not likely to deal directly with investment bankers, Lehman Brothers is favorably known for its management of Lehman Corp. With over $350 million of assets, Lehman Corp. is, after Tri-Continental Corp., the largest closed-end diversified investment-trust company in the U.S. It is also the only trust linked to a major investment bank that emerged from the 1929 crash with its prestige not only intact but enhanced.

And many other investors are interested in Lehman Brothers chiefly as the sponsor of the One William Street Fund, an open-end investment company. This venture was started at a propitious time—in February, 1958, at the bottom of a bear market—with some $235 million of capital paid in. Despite the good timing, the fund did poorly for a few years, principally because Lehman had no real experience in the kind of hard selling a mutual fund needs for growth. But since 1960 the fund has done better. At the end of 1961, its net assets were up to $311 million, its asset value per share was up to $15.41 (vs. $11.56 when the fund was started).

Today the Lehman firm sedulously cultivates an air of dignified reserve, even secrecy, but individual Lehman family members and their banking associates have been much in the national eye. In polo there was partner Tommy Hitchcock Jr., who was killed in World War II, one of the few ten-goal players in the U.S. In the art world there is the famed collection of the late Philip Lehman and his son, Robert, the only Lehman now a partner in the firm. In atomic energy there was Alex Sachs, a Lehman associate, who helped Albert Einstein arouse Franklin Roosevelt's interest in nuclear fission in 1939; the late John Hancock, who with Bernard Baruch drafted the first U.N. plan to control the atom. In politics there is Herbert Lehman, ex-Governor of New York, ex-Senator; in jurisprudence Herbert's late brother, Irving, who served as Chief Justice of the New York State Court of Appeals.

Specialties of the house

Today no other top Wall Street firm is so active in so many money-making fields. The twenty-three partners of Lehman Brothers and their associates perform all the traditional functions of investment banking. Syndication of a large stock issue, the management of an underwriting or a selling group, the arduous work that accompanies a competitive bidding effort, all these workaday tasks are carried out with an aplomb based on long experience. Yet Lehman's skill in these matters can be matched by many other houses of issue in Wall Street. And in many specialized banking fields, in fact, other firms are better known and more proficient than Lehman Brothers.

In the handling of commercial paper, for example, Lehman's one-time partner, Goldman, Sachs, has no peer. In brokerage commission business, no firm is in the same class as Merrill Lynch. No house can hope to stand with Halsey, Stuart in the utility bond market, at least not so long as "loner" Stuart is willing to buy a whole issue whether or not he is assured of a market or a profit for the securities. No house can boast a string of blue-blood corporations comparable to those Morgan Stanley underwrites. First Boston's position in government bonds, and Kidder, Peabody's in mutual funds—these also would be conceded by Lehman.

But no firm can match Lehman for sheer virtuosity. During the 1950–53 antitrust suit against the investment-banking industry, Lehman's lawyers argued that the firm's "special attitudes form a continuity of character that it is impossible to confuse with the modes of business of the other sixteen defendant firms. The investment-banking activity of the firm is but a part of its completely independently conceived relation to industry."

The firm, naturally, takes the underwriting "part" of its business very seriously, and preens itself when it manages (or co-manages with Lazard Frères) an underwriting for a major corporation such as Burroughs Corp. or R.C.A. And the underwriting business has continued growing steadily at Lehman. But the excitement and infectious enthusiasm of Lehmanites really spill over when the less publicized but more profitable aspects of investment banking are mentioned. Lehman partners are active arbitragers, oil wildcatters, serve as professional directors, economic forecasters, management consultants, and jacks-of-all-financial-trades. Lehman partners regard the firm's chief specialties as private placements, the raising of venture capital, the creation of new business, and putting old corporate assets to work in new form. In the process of accomplishing these various objectives, Lehman Brothers brings into play a wide assortment of services and talents, and has created a distinctive role as a counselor to U.S. industry.

The lunch menu

Lehman's "special attitudes" begin to foam and bubble at 9 A.M. every Monday morning in one of the small meeting rooms adjoining the partners' huge room on the third floor. There the firm's executive committee, composed of seven partners—they take turns acting as committee chairman—meets to review all the current and proposed business for the firm. This executive committee was formed in 1960 to formalize a tradition that had been carried on for years. The tradition called for a majority of the partners to discuss and decide business problems while lunching around the walnut dining table.

The seven-man executive committee now screens all the important subjects to weed out the projects that are impractical or too small for Lehman; it postpones discussion of those that require more information; any deals that survive this screening are put on the agenda for the luncheon.

There is a minimum of protocol. Only three seats are sacrosanct. Robert Lehman presides at the head of the table flanked by the two senior partners in point of service and prestige, Paul Mazur and Monroe Gutman. The other partners sit according to comfort and convenience. Mazur, who keeps alert to most of the projects under way, sets the session in motion, announcing the most urgent topic on the agenda or calling on a partner to bring everybody up to date on a particular situation. Once the topic is thrown on the table it's open for discussion or comment by any of the twenty-three partners. If it becomes a policy matter, e.g., whether Lehman should or should not underwrite a new issue, a vote will be called.

At these Monday lunches the partners are also likely to discuss a variety of problems confronting the corporations on whose boards they serve. The main question might be, for example, whether certain security issues should be postponed in view of tumbling stock prices. There might be discussion, too, of whether a manufacturing company whose profits were declining should cut its dividend. At one meeting, a partner on the board of a corporation that wanted to merge with a paper company raised the following question: Since the paper company was allied with a rival banking house, should Lehman approach the company directly or consult the other banking house first? Another partner talked about a Canadian mining company that was seeking new capital; was Lehman interested in underwriting for this industry or this company? At least ten other topics might be discussed before the luncheon broke up.

At the Monday meetings leads for new business are often discussed to see if any partner has background information that may be helpful. In many cases the question boils down to the approach that Lehman should make to win a new underwriting position. It doesn't hurt, for example, for executives of an issuing firm to know that Lehman partners use their product. (Partners of virtually every investment house, Lehman included, were driving a Ford Motor Co. model—usually high-priced—when that famous issue was negotiated.)

"New business" is a portentous phrase, of course, around 1 William Street. To the newer members of the firm, new business is an important element in winning personal recognition; to older members it opens a vista of fresh relationships, novel problems, and the hope that some new deal may be as smashing a success as was Lehman's underwriting of Hertz Corp. and, more recently, Litton Industries, one of the hottest electronic firms set up in the postwar.

The all-important dealers

When touring the country scouting for new business, Lehman partners try constantly to improve the distribution organization that is so important to Lehman's underwriting activities. Lehman has some 600 independent broker-dealers that it can normally count on to move securities. Seldom are more than 100 of these firms required to make commitments on any individual underwriting or selling group, however. Some of the dealers handle only bonds, other firms specialize in the more speculative issues. Some have strong ties with regional institutional investors, others sell only to individuals. The hunt for dealer talent becomes more important when money is tight, for in underwriting, even as in the auto industry, salesmen will meet stiff customer resistance if the price looks high.

The prime responsibility for deciding whether a specific security dealer is doing a good merchandising job belongs to the syndicate manager. At Lehman, Robert Thayer, an associate, holds that title, and he is responsible for Lehman's relationships with other investment bankers and dealers. This relationship differs considerably from the wholesaler-retailer ties in other industries, for in underwriting and selling securities there is a written contract specifying the exact underwriting terms for each issue, and if a dealer-member of a selling group fails to stick by the contract, he can be penalized. A dealer may, for example, sell a newly issued security below the agreed-upon public offering price before the selling group is officially disbanded. If during an underwriting a syndicate manager finds newly issued stock bouncing back into the market, he usually can track down its source rapidly (all stock certificates are numbered). As a penalty, the offending dealer may lose his selling-group commission.

Profitable periphery

Syndicate selling is the fundamental business of investment banking and the Lehman partners are still, in large measure, merchants of money, intermediaries between those who want to produce goods and men seeking outlets for surplus funds. But over the years Lehman has erected a network of additional services and functions around this original one of moving money from investor to industry. For as the economy has grown more complex, the factors that bankers must take into consideration when making a decision about financing have also become more complex. To keep the partnership alert to the action and interaction of money, business, and the forces that play upon both, Lehman has set up a number of service departments. The three principal ones are the Industrial Department, the Economics Department, and the Investment Advisory Service.

The Industrial Department is, in effect, a comprehensive research organization that analyzes and makes recommendations on most projects brought before Lehman. It also acts as a management-engineering firm; in the 1950–53 banker conspiracy suit, for example, the Industrial Department was described by Lehman as "a sounding board against which management can project its ideas." The twenty-man department includes lawyers, accountants, engineers, men who have run their own businesses as well as eager graduates of the Harvard Business School and the Wharton School of Finance and Commerce.

Each week the Industrial Department processes reports on some 200 going or contemplated projects. It will send men out to examine the physical properties of a company whose stock Lehman may underwrite, recruit executive talent for a client firm, make efficiency studies, and appraise properties (Albert List had a complete evaluation of his properties made by Lehman before he merged them into the old RKO Pictures Corp.). It will also seek out merger possibilities.

The Economics Department provides Lehman clients and subscribers with broad analyses of national economic trends. In 1959, for example, the department prepared a special report on the long-term trend of business in the U.S. through 1975. (Using 1953 as a base year the study projects an increase of more than 100 per cent in industrial production by 1975, a 15 per cent decline in the average hourly work week, an increase of over 75 per cent in out put per man hour.)

The third department, the Investment Advisory Service, was organized by partner Paul Manheim in 1951. It is the largest investment advisory service operated by any investment house and in the past five years has bulked larger at Lehman every year. Lehman doesn't publicize its advisory service or solicit accounts. In fact, it won't take an account with less than $500,000 of capital. Until recently, moreover, it would not sell the service to show people, remembering the needling given Goldman, Sachs by ex-client Eddie Cantor in the early Thirties. Cantor had made a sizable investment in the Goldman Sachs Trading Corp., the multi-million-dollar investment company that withered away in the 1929 crash. He later made this investment debacle part of his act: an actor would run out while Cantor was on stage, and Cantor would indentify him as "the man who wants more margin for my Goldman Sachs Trading stock."

Since there is approximately $1 billion under the direct guidance of the advisory service—and even larger sums are indirectly influenced by it—the service's advice can easily affect security prices. Great care is taken to ensure that no Lehman employee can profit from advance knowledge of the service's recommendations. Nobody connected with Lehman is permitted to trade a stock recommended by the I.A.S. until after clients have been advised. And I.A.S. maintains a research staff completely independent of Lehman Corp.'s or One William Street's research staff.

From stores to oil

Lehman has long been the principal investment banker to the U.S. retailing industry and the firm has done most of the underwriting for ten of the nation's largest retail companies, including Gimbels, May, and Federated Department Stores. But after Lehman Brothers split with Goldman, Sachs in 1925 (see box, page 88), Robert Lehman sought out new fields for financing. Lehman Brothers channeled money and talent into investment trusts and into aviation, office equipment, and textiles. It helped raise money for several airlines, including Pan American, Continental, and National Airlines. It also helped finance tobacco companies.

But since World War II, Lehman Brothers has made its greatest strides in the oil industry. It has financed Kerr-McGee Oil and Murphy Corp., arranged Sinclair Oil's purchase of Southern Production and American Republic Oil. All told, Lehman has probably done more than $1 billion of financing for the oil industry since 1946, and handled the purchase of oil properties for some companies to the tune of $400 million to $500 million.

Misses and bites

Lehman Brothers makes no claim, of course, to any infallible formula for spotting or developing profitable situations. Though Lehman helped build the early financial strength of Burlington Mills and Schenley Industries, for example, it could not cope with the demands of those rugged individualists J. Spencer Love and Lewis Rosenstiel, who subsequently took their business elsewhere. And Lehman is still struggling with Fruehauf Trailer; although Lehman since 1948 has raised over $315 million in new money for a Fruehauf sales-finance company, the trailer maker has not been able to show a sustained earnings record. Underwood Corp., one of Lehman's earliest underwriting clients, has nose-dived in Wall Street esteem as a result of losing more than $50 million between January, 1956 and January 1962. (It was bought by Italian interests in 1960.)

Lehman has also been chastised by critics for pushing "popular stocks"; e.g., since World War II, Lehman has promoted the securities of electronics companies and Canadian oil firms. Then, there's the contention that Lehman always gets a "bite" of any situation it sponsors—unless the issuing firm is very big or very smart.

Lehman, in reply to this charge, contends that in any underwriting arrangement both issuer and underwriter should benefit. Often a small company enlists Lehman's aid as banker because Lehman's sponsorship is more important to investors than the unknown company's past business record. For that kind of sponsorship there's a price and it usually is paid in the form of stock or stock options. Lehman thinks such an arrangement binds the underwriter to the company and ensures that Lehman will work hard to strengthen the firm's finances.

Money in Monterey

Lehman's adeptness at making money on special situations was well demonstrated in its creation of Monterey Oil in California. In 1950, Ed Kennedy, then a Lehman associate, learned at a petroleum convention that Jergins Corp., a family-controlled West Coast oil-and-gas company, was for sale. Several near sales had collapsed. Another major Wall Street house had been authorized to find a buyer, but had been unable to.

One hurdle was Jergins' half-ownership of the San Ardo field in

California, which had been virtually shut down because it contained thick low-viscosity oil for which there was no known market. Kennedy, taking a long-range view of the San Ardo field, figured that ways would be developed to use the oil. Moreover, he thought Lehman could realize a $9-million profit if it paid the $29-million asking price for Jergins and resold its marketable assets piecemeal. He presented an analysis to partner Fred Ehrman, who promptly went to work on the financing.

Ehrman raised $10 million from the partnership, Lehman Corp., and other Wall Street houses (e.g., Smith, Barney & Co.) and corporations (C.I.T. Financial Corp.), and borrowed $19 million from Chase Manhattan Bank. The Lehman group bought Jergins and rechristened it Monterey Oil. In the next eighteen months, by selling a Monterey-owned office building, a gasoline plant, and a minority interest in an electronics firm that was to become Beckman Instrument Corp., Monterey was able to reduce the bank loan to $14 million, and to pay back $5 million of the original $10 million to investors.

Other oilmen began to sense the long-range potential of San Ardo and offered Monterey a $5-million profit for its interest in the field. Ehrman declined. Within a year, General Petroleum, a subsidiary of Socony Mobil Oil, offered $18,200,000 and Monterey accepted. With the proceeds Monterey paid off the bank loan in full and virtually all of the $5 million remaining of the original investment. Thus within two years Lehman Brothers raised and paid out $29 million, recouped it, and had left in Monterey oil and gas assets valued at $28 million.

After 1953, Monterey acquired additional properties, mostly through the use of oil-payment-production loans—a profit-preserving, tax-minimizing technique Lehman has developed to a fine art. At the end of 1960, Monterey's assets were sold to Humble Oil for $119 million—which left $42 a share for its stockholders after payment of debts. At the time, Lehman Brothers, the Lehman Corp., and the Lehman partners still held most of the 200,000-odd shares they had acquired for 9 cents a share.

A good example of how Lehman Brothers helps corporations with which it has a long-standing association is its role in the growth of Hertz Corp. The present Hertz company was originally the Omnibus Corp. This firm owned subsidiaries that operated bus lines in New York, Chicago, and other cities. Lehman partner John Hertz became a director of Omnibus after selling his car-rental business to General Motors in 1933.

In 1952, Lehman's Industrial Department prepared a memorandum urging that Omnibus quit the bus transit field and get into some related but more profitable activity. While the Omnibus board approved the idea, officers of some of the operating subsidiaries—proud of their local prestige and importance—balked and reported it would be almost impossible to find a buyer for a city transit system. Lehman partners, however, went out and, with the consent of the board of directors, dug up buyers.

At about that time General Motors let it be known that it would sell its Hertz System to the highest bidder. As it turned out, Omnibus won the bidding. Its corporate name was changed to Hertz Corp., and under Lehman's guidance Hertz was launched on a program of buying back Hertz franchises. (General Motors had followed a policy of selling franchises to independent fleet operators.) In the past seven years the company has re-acquired about 50 Hertz franchises and created a continuous operating income. The market value of Hertz's common stock climbed from $7 million in 1953 to $183 million in 1961.

Litton common at 10 cents

A more characteristic example, perhaps, of Lehman's operating methods is its dealings with Litton Industries of Los Angeles. When Charles ("Tex") Thornton and several other electronics executives and scientists quit Hughes Aircraft to acquire and expand Litton Industries, they asked Lehman's Joe Thomas to help raise $1,500,000. Lehman rounded up the money and in return got 75,000 shares of common stock at prices of 10 cents to $1 a share. Early in 1962, after a two-for-one split, the stock was over $150 a share.

But Lehman does not grab at every underwriting opportunity that comes along. It passed up a chance to bid on the financing of Revlon, for example, largely because of Revlon's close dependence on TV advertising. Lehman reasoned that since no TV program remains permanently popular, Revlon's business might slide if and when the *$64,000 Question* lost its TV following. Lehman partners admit that in Revlon's case they "may have made a mistake." (The stock was offered at $11 a share in 1956; in 1961, after a two-for-one split, and long after the passing of the *$64,000 Question,* it sold for over $130 a share.) Lehman also turned down an opportunity to underwrite E. J. Korvette, Inc., the first discount house to become publicly owned: Lehman was unwilling to irk its big department-store clients by financing a price-cutting competitor.

Lehman buys Lehman

No feat of investment skill has been more widely acclaimed than Lehman's management of its closed-end investment trust, the Lehman Corp. Investment trusts, developed by the Scots in the mid-nineteenth century, grew fashionable in the U.S. around 1920. They became a craze at about the same time as the Charleston and bathtub gin.

In 1927—a year in which 140 investment trusts were formed— Lehman joined with Lazard Frères to underwrite a closed-end investment trust called General American Investors. Eighteen months later, Lehman was ready to underwrite an investment company bearing its own name. Lehman Corp., with Lehman Brothers partners owning 10 per cent, was launched in September, 1929. Its shares were sold to the public for $104, and were bid up to $136 within a few days.

But providence was kind to Lehman Corp.; the October crash came before much of its cash could be invested in securities. Then, when the first wave of selling ended in November, and reassuring statements about the 1930 outlook were being made by the Rockefellers and others, many Street experts rushed back into the market to buy just as the floors gave way a second time. Lehman's markets analysts, led by Monroe Gutman, did not rush in during the lull.

Instead they concluded that the best use for the money on hand, at a time when market values of most securities were fluctuating wildly, was to buy back Lehman Corp.'s own shares. They knew that Lehman Corp.'s assets in cash, bonds, and preferred corporates shares were worth considerably more than the market price of Lehman Corp. shares. Lehman's buying, moreover, provided a steady, healthy market for its own shares when markets were weak in other securities. By 1932 one-third of the original issue had been repurchased.

When the tidal waves of stock deflation finally subsided, Lehman Corp. was riding snugly at anchor. And to add to the luster of the record, Lehman-linked General American was was still seaworthy and soon emerged as one of the best-operated trusts on Wall Street.

The whole performance made quite an impression on New Deal Washington, which conducted long, searching investigations into the operations of investment trusts. The notable record of Lehman's trust management during the depression put the partners in a uniquely favorable position to make recommendations to the New Deal probers of Wall Street. Many of the reforms that Lehman recommended, including the requirement that trusts report stock commissions paid to brokers, the cost and market value of each security in their portfolios, and other details of operations, are now law.

Today Lehman Brothers benefits in several ways from its management of Lehman Corp. The partnership receives $225,000 yearly for guiding the corporation's investment policy. Moreover, many people confuse the corporation with the partnership and neither is harmed.

But the most convincing demonstration of the investment magic that surrounds the Lehman name came in the middle of the 1957–58 recession, when it was announced that the firm would sponsor an open-end investment company, or mutual fund. It was called the One William Street Fund, referring to the address of the partnership. The response to the fund was overwhelming. The initial offering was the largest underwriting of a mutual fund in financial history. Over 90,-000 individuals and institutions invested $183 million in the One William Street Fund. But even this was not all: coincident with the public offering, a private investment company, the Aurora Corp.—most of its stockholders were executives of the Ford Motor Co.— merged its $38 million of assets into the One William Street Fund. Thus overnight Lehman Brothers had launched the world's twelfth largest open-end company, with assets of $221 million.

But the One William Street Fund had its troubles. The huge volume of money that flowed into the fund could not be invested fast enough; and after that initial display of strength, One William Street wobbled around uncertainly for over two years. It suffered from several ailments. One was the lack of a sales force. While the Lehman name could draw money to the fund, it takes an aggressive sales force to keep selling a mutual fund's shares, and Lehman had no experience in this area.

Lehman had actually counted on its relationship with dealers and brokers to push sales of One William Street shares. The key factor in such a relationship is "reciprocity," i.e., when a dealer sells shares of an investment company, he expects to receive a proportionate share of the fund's commission business when it is buying or selling shares for its portfolio. The One William Street Fund and Lehman Brothers had little experience in working out these arrangements, and the dealer organization was consequently very weak. This fact, coupled with a mediocre investment performance, resulted in a long period in which redemptions were outrunning sales. However, the partnership reshuffled its counseling team and the fund operation has shown improvement in more recent months. Total assets have climbed past the $311 million mark. And Lehman Brothers' management fee for the fund is now running around $1,250,000 a year.

How to measure wealth

In investment banking it is difficult to rank houses precisely, because there is no single criterion of size. But it is notably fair to say that Lehman, even without counting the $500 million of underwriting it does annually, has more money continually under its *direct* influence than any other Wall Street house.

For one thing there's the capital of the partnership itself. As of January 1, 1961, Lehman ranked third among Wall Street houses with a capital of $35 million.

Then there is the personal wealth of the partners and associates, which must also be considered part of the partnership's financial strength. Back in 1924 the Lehman family fortune was estimated at $124 million. That money has since been hit by death taxes and split among Lehmans, some of whom have withdrawn their money from the firm's guidance. Yet it's unlikely the fortune shrank. Competent professional advice and normal accretion should have built it to at least $250 million. Robert Lehman's wealth is estimated at $60 million to $70 million (his art collection included). The personal fortunes of the other partners as a group probably match Robert Lehman's.

Quite apart from these sizable amounts—which other Street firms might match in many respects—there is Lehman's domination of the investment activities of Lehman Corp. with its $350 million of assets. This is a larger sum than is controlled by any other house. Then there is Lehman's sponsorship of the One William Street Fund (with $311 millions of assets in 1961).

The impressive sums above put Lehman Brothers in a commanding, or at least highly influential, position in the investment community—and they do not include the $1 billion of money guided by the Investment Advisory Service.

Wall Street patrician

The most authoritative voice in the House of Lehman today naturally belongs to the partner with the greatest capital in the firm. That is Robert Lehman. He controls perhaps 60 per cent of the partnership's capital.

Robert Lehman, cultivated in speech, lean and fit in appearance, is, at sixty-eight, a Wall Street patrician. "In the early days," says a former Lehmanite, "Bobbie was one of those fellows you'd wind up and he'd run at top speed for four months. Then he'd go to Europe for three months to buy art or something. He'd come back renewed, refreshed, and start again."

Robert Lehman always has an attentive ear for those inside or outside the firm whose opinion he respects. In recent years the chief outside influence on Lehman Brothers affairs has been Edwin Weisl, of Simpson, Thacher & Bartlett, who is Lehman's legal counsel. (He was for a time the special counsel to the Senate Preparedness Subcommittee when it was investigating the U.S. space program in 1959.) Weisl, sometimes called "Lehman's eighteenth partner," since he occasionally sits in on partners' meetings, has tremendous influence in the partnership, and sometimes steers business to the firm.

Lehman's hair shirt

After Robert Lehman, Paul Mazur and Monroe Gutman are the most important members of the partnership. Mazur is an energetic, distinguished-looking man in his late sixties. He is still the personality around whom the day-to-day work of the partnership revolves. He gave the firm its great reputation and prestige as a banker for merchandising firms. He also established the Industrial and Economics departments at Lehman. "He probably has the finest mind in the Lehman organization," says one of his former associates. But Mazur is also considered something of an intellectual hair shirt in the firm and the investment-banking community.

Occasionally he argues heatedly with a partner or client just for the exercise. Not that he is reluctant to put his personal convictions on the record. As long ago as the 1920s, Mazur was a stout advocate of the five-day work week as a device to spur consumption and lift the standard of living. Today Mazur devotes a great deal of his time to creating new business and improving Lehman's internal organization. He has turned over to partner Harold ("Jim") Szold the active supervision of the Industrial Department.

Monroe Gutman, a mild-mannered man of seventy-six, runs the Lehman Corp. Gutman looks more like a university professor than a Wall Street banker, but he has unsurpassed skill in evaluating market movements and financial trends. His alter ego in directing Lehman Corp. is Billy Glazier, a shy man who is one of the wealthiest of the partners. At 54, Glazier is generally regarded as the eventual successor to Gutman.

"New business" men

The other partners mostly work at developing new business. There is Joe Thomas, for example, a dynamic Texan who became a partner at thirty, after a master stroke that enabled Lehman interests to get control of American Export Lines for $1,500,000. There is Johnny Fell, friend of many wealthy and influential industrialists ranging from Henry Ford to Clint Murchison. He was responsible for Lehman's role in organizing the $330-million Trans Canada Pipeline Co. William Hammerslough devotes his time to the tobacco industry. Frank Manheim, Paul's younger brother, switched from teaching to finance in 1943, and is credited with helping build Hertz Corp.

THE RISE OF THE HOUSE OF LEHMAN

The firm of Lehman Brothers was founded shortly after Henry Lehman, twenty-two-year-old son of a cattle merchant, emigrated from Bavaria to the U.S. In 1845, Henry opened a general store in Montgomery, Alabama, and in 1850, when he was joined by his brothers Emanuel and Mayer, they formed the Lehman Brothers partnership. The Lehmans supplied cotton farmers in the area with clothes, utensils, and other merchandise. In return they often received raw cotton instead of cash. To get their money the Lehmans resold the cotton in bulk quantities, often making a profit on both ends of the transaction. Gradually the brothers moved into cotton brokerage and out of retailing.

Henry Lehman, an energetic but nervous man, became obsessed with a fear of yellow fever. When the disease broke out in Montgomery in 1855, his brothers agreed that he should go to New Orleans to set up a branch there. Henry departed for New Orleans where, ironically, he almost immediately contracted yellow fever and died.

In 1858, Emanuel opened an office in New York City, but the Civil War sent him hurrying back to Montgomery, where both he and Mayer served the South. Emanuel was in the Confederate Army when his son Philip was born. He also helped sell Confederate bonds in England during one of his trips abroad to sell southern cotton.

Mayer Lehman was on friendly terms with many of the leaders of the Confederacy. In December, 1864, he was appointed to a special committee to raise funds to aid Confederate prisoners in the North. The com-

Partner Morris Natelson, a tough-minded man, sold a chain of savings and loan banks to the public despite some stiff legal obstacles. Result: Great Western Financial Corp., whose launching produced a $1,500,000 profit for Lehman Brothers.

Partner Herman Kahn helped pioneer a new money source for airlines six years ago, when he persuaded nineteen life-insurance companies to grant a $90-million, forty-year loan to Pan American Airways for equipment financing. In the past, the limited life of planes has always restricted airlines to short-term borrowing on equipment.

The oil department has been one of the firm's most successful fields of activity for many years, though it has declined in importance recently. Edwin I. Kennedy, the man who brought many of the deals to the firm, remains in charge of it. But Francis Callery, who bossed Lehman's wild-cat ventures in the Southwest, has resigned from the firm and is pushing his own operations.

While there is only one partner of the Lehman name, there is a

---

mittee planned to send $500,000 worth of cotton through the battle lines for sale in New York. Jefferson Davis approved the scheme, but General Ulysses Grant ignored the committee's request for safe conduct. By April the scheme became a historical footnote. The war ended.

Within a year Emanuel was back in New York operating a cotton-brokerage business and he was joined by Mayer in 1868. The brothers worked together for the next thirty years, specializing in the cotton and commodity business. Mayer helped establish the New York Cotton Exchange, the Coffee Exchange, and later a Petroleum Exchange. In 1887 the partnership joined the New York Stock Exchange.

Toward the turn of the century the Lehman partnership cautiously began expanding its activities. The firm invested money in a number of industrial ventures: an early auto company, rubber manufacturers, etc. Only once in the nineteenth century, however, did Lehman Brothers lead a public underwriting of securities. In 1899, Lehman sponsored the sale of a stock issue for a combine consisting of the nation's five major producers of steam pumps. The combine didn't work out and in 1910 was reorganized in compliance with the antitrust laws; it emerged as the Worthington Pump & Machinery Corp.

These early ventures, while bringing the Lehmans into close relationship with the leaders of U.S. industry, did not make them underwriters or investment bankers. The firm was still considered essentially a commodity house and ranked far down the line in prestige and importance among the New York banking houses.

By 1900 the second generation of Lehmans had joined the firm (partner-

good supply of Lehmans and Lehman relatives coming along. Robert Lehman's son, Robert Owen (a great-grandson of William Jennings Bryan on his mother's side), represents the fourth Lehman generation in the U.S. He is now studying abroad, and as Robert's only son will undoubtedly inherit his father's majority interest in the firm. John Lehman, Herbert's son (Herbert Lehman and Robert Lehman are cousins), is very active and well regarded in the partnership. Robert A. Bernhard, a grandson of Arthur Lehman, is learning investment banking at Lehman Brothers.

But their careers depend, of course, on the future of the partnership itself and the outlook for investment banking in general.

Capital for consumers

As Lehman partners see it, the future role of the investment banker in the U.S. will be even more dynamic than in the past. "As great as

---

ship was limited by a family Salic law to blood relatives bearing the Lehman name), and the Lehmans had intermarried extensively with other New York banking families of German-Jewish origin. Eventually there were blood or marriage ties among a dozen or more Wall Street houses including Lehman Brothers; Goldman, Sachs; Kuhn, Loeb; Hallgarten; Wertheim; J. S. Bache; Loeb, Rhoades; and Ladenburg, Thalmann. Other houses once prominent in banking were also bound by similar ties, among them Lewisohn Sons, S. W. Straus, and M. Guggenheim Brothers.

The end of World War I saw these family relationships begin to dwindle in business importance, however, and today they are of little consequence in the highly competitive business of underwriting.

The Goldman, Sachs alliance

Lehman Brothers first got into underwriting in 1906 as a result of Philip Lehman's close friendship with Henry Goldman, dominant partner in the firm of Goldman, Sachs, the largest commercial-paper house in New York. Goldman wanted to get into investment banking and he sought the financial support of Lehman. Between 1906 and 1914 the two houses jointly underwrote fourteen security issues, most of them for clients of Goldman, Sachs.

World War I interrupted the partnership's underwriting activities (but the floating of Liberty Loans opened Wall Street's eyes to a whole new concept of selling securities to the general public). After the war new

have been the demands for capital in recent decades," says Paul
Mazur, "they promise to be enormously increased in the future." This
optimistic viewpoint, which also reflects the attitude of the other
partners, is largely based on the fact that the capital requirements of
the American consumer are burgeoning. The iceman has given way
to the refrigerator; domestic servants have been replaced by the wash-
ing machine, the dryer, and a host of other appliances; the home, in
short, is becoming a highly automated—and highly capitalized—
cconomic unit. And as the capital required to buy consumer durable
goods increases, so does the demand for investment banking. Since
World War II, for example, millions of dollars have been raised for
consumer finance companies.

Meanwhile the reservoirs of capital have been shifting into new
hands. Whereas the bulk of savings was formerly held by a relatively
few wealthy people, today much of the capital saved in the U.S. is

~~~~~~

faces and names began to appear in the Lehman–Goldman, Sachs ranks.
Philip's son Robert came out of the war a captain of artillery and plunged
into investment banking. John Hancock, Monroe Gutman, and Paul Mazur
were brought into the firm, and later became the first non-family partners.

Meanwhile, at Goldman, Sachs, the star postwar performer was Wad-
dill Catchings, a suave, literate man with an acute mind and a grasp of
the mood of investors in the early Twenties. Catchings took under his
wing Sidney Weinberg, who had worked his way up from office boy.

Catchings and Weinberg were impatient with the old arrangement
with Lehman. They saw no reason why Lehman should get a fifty-
fifty split on profits or deals originated by Goldman, Sachs.

Some of the young Lehman partners, for their part, didn't relish letting Goldman, Sachs take all the credit for underwritings that relied
heavily on Lehman money. As one banker who worked with the partnership puts it, "I guess both were too ambitious to stay married."

The Lehman Brothers partnership in 1925 consisted of six Lehmans,
with Philip, son of founder Emanuel, and Arthur, one of the four sons
of founder Mayer Lehman, the senior partners. Herbert Lehman, brother
of Arthur, resigned from the firm in 1928 to enter politics and has
since had no voice in its affairs. Arthur was the first president of Lehman Corp., and very active until his death in 1936. Philip Lehman, who
had been in the partnership sixty-two years, and dominated it from 1906,
gradually shifted more and more of his responsibilities to his son, Robert.

By 1925 the dispute reached a climax and Catchings, Arthur Sachs,
and Herbert and Arthur Lehman drafted a memorandum of agreement

held by insurance companies, pension funds, and other institutions that represent vast aggregates of wealth. And after years of talk about bringing Wall Street and Main Street together, the number of share-holders is finally expanding impressively. The task of collecting capital from this large group and funneling it out to productive enterprise has also created additional demand for the services of investment bankers. The new sources of capital—union pension funds, for example—are turning to the investment bankers for advice.

Indeed it would be a good bet that long before this second century in Lehman's history is completed, Lehman Brothers will have devel-oped many radically new investment techniques to keep pace with an era of profound technical, social, and economic change. For whenever the technical skill of the scientist creates some new tool for man's use, the banking skill of a Rothschild, a Morgan—or a Lehman—is required to bring it to economic life.

---

to guide the future conduct of the two firms. The memorandum listed sixty corporations that the firms had jointly underwritten including such names as Continental Can, Campbell Soup, and R. H. Macy—and each firm agreed to respect the other's primacy in specific corporations. Gold-man, Sachs was conceded a prime interest in forty-one companies, Leh-man in the others.

But after the Securities Act was passed in 1933, this memorandum had to be amended further. The negotiations between the two firms re-opened old wounds.

The reconciliation

It was not until 1956, in fact, that a full reconciliation was achieved. When Sears, Roebuck set up a sales-acceptance subsidiary, Sidney Wein-berg called on Robert Lehman and asked that Lehman Brothers reas-sume its historic place in the Sears financing.

From a long-range viewpoint, the breakup with Goldman, Sachs prob-ably benefited Lehman. One investment banker familiar with the whole sequence of events says:

"I think it's the best thing that ever happened to Lehman because they took off their coats, rolled up their sleeves, and went out to get some business. Lehman always had a lot of money, but that's different from being aggressive to get business. After the dispute they became real go-getters." The change, as the accompanying chapter shows, has benefited not only Lehman Brothers but investment banking and business in general.

6

The Case of the Irresistible Stockholder

Among the many recent fights for control of industrial corporations, the assault that overturned the management of Commercial Solvents several years ago is unique. The attack was not launched by raiders of dubious reputation, or by a brash newcomer to financial power, or by an ambitious empire builder. Here the attackers were members of one of the oldest, richest, most proper, and least-publicized families of the American business community. The moves and countermoves in the battle were not trumpeted in news stories of proxy fights; there were no public denunciations or taunts exchanged by the opposing parties. They confronted one another behind the closed doors of brokers' and lawyers' offices in downtown Manhattan, and in Commercial Solvents' headquarters on Madison Avenue. Here the sounds of struggle were completely muffled, and the contest was confined to the level of the board of directors, a distinguished group of businessmen, some of them bound by friendships of over half a century. The battle was not prolonged. The decision came after five days of hectic negotiation.

Despite the silence maintained by the principals in the brief but dramatic conflict, it was soon possible to put together the main outlines of the events that came to a climax in a terse announcement that the president of Commercial Solvents had resigned.

The prize at stake was control of a chemical-and-drug manufacturing corporation that, only fifteen years earlier, had been considered as promising as any company in its industry. Commercial Solvents had been the first mass producer of penicillin, the first to make the antibiotic bacitracin, and it had a headstart in the promising field of nitroparaffins. In 1946 the company had sales of $45 million and a very neat profit of $5,700,000. But in the late 1950s, Commercial Solvents was floundering, while its industry enjoyed a boom of gigantic proportions. By 1958 the company's sales had risen only to

$64,700,000, its earnings had dwindled to $1,400,000. The company was still sound—its assets were solid, its cash position good—but it ranked low in its industry and faced a rugged battle for survival.

"I'm not asking you . . . I'm telling you"

The battle for control of this troubled corporation was joined on Friday, January 23, 1959. That morning Harold H. Helm, chairman of New York's Chemical Corn Exchange Bank, which was the bank of deposit for Commercial Solvents, had an appointment to receive Jeremiah Milbank Jr. Helm and young Milbank were moderately well acquainted. Milbank was on the Chemical Corn's advisory committee. Both men were on the board of Commercial Solvents, and both were members of the five-man executive committee of the board.

Helm knew, of course, that his visitor watched over substantial family investments with his father, Jeremiah Milbank Sr., a name widely respected, though the image of its owner has always been a little blurred, even among some of the best-informed Wall Street financiers. One story about the senior Milbank has become part of the lore of the Street. In 1924, Milbank Sr. dropped into the offices of J. P. Morgan & Co. to call on partner Thomas Lamont. He found J. P. Morgan visiting Lamont when he entered. Milbank Sr. said he'd like to see some dividends paid on the common shares of the Southern Railway, for which the Morgans were the investment bankers. Lamont replied, in the firm Morgan manner, that the Southern board had decided not to pay out a dividend but to retain the company's profits for expansion.

Milbank, the story goes, said quietly: "I'm afraid you gentlemen misunderstand me. I'm not asking you to pay a dividend. I'm telling you. I own control of the Southern."

Lamont and Morgan jumped to their feet. How many shares did Milbank represent?

"Five hundred thousand shares," was the reply.

"Mr. Milbank, dividends will be paid on the Southern common," said Mr. Lamont.

And they were.

800,000 shares talking

The Jeremiah Milbank who walked into Mr. Helm's office in January of 1959 resembles his father in many ways. Both men are serious-minded, hard workers, soft-spoken, and reserved. If anything, young Milbank, according to acquaintances, is even more serious-minded than his father.

Jeremiah Milbank Jr. had brought with him a statement, and he read it to Helm. It was short. It was blunt. The Milbank interests, representing over 800,000 shares, or 30 per cent of Commercial Solvents' 2,700,000 of outstanding common, were opposed to the re-election of J. Albert Woods to the board of the company and were prepared to fight a proxy war to prevent it. Woods had been president of Commercial Solvents since 1950. Under the corporate bylaws the president had to be a member of the board.

Helm was staggered. There had been no unusual volume of trading in Commercial's stock to indicate that anyone was amassing a 30 per cent position. The Milbanks, Sr. and Jr., had been known to hold a substantial number of shares themselves. But in addition, they must have been quietly lining up the support of other stockholders— friends and business associates, and, no doubt, other members of the Milbank family. Helm read the statement himself while Milbank sat by quietly.

After Milbank left, Helm promptly started calling the directors, including Woods, and told them of the ultimatum. The news was received with shock and dismay.

This was the composition of the board, in addition to Helm, Milbank Jr., and Woods:

> Austin S. Igleheart, former chairman of General Foods.
>
> Henry V. B. Smith, head of H. J. Baker & Bro., a chemical export company.
>
> Harold F. McGuire, the company's legal counsel, a partner in Wickes, Riddell, Bloomer, Jacobi & McGuire.
>
> Harold W. Comfort, president of the Borden Co., one of Commercial's biggest customers.
>
> Arthur B. Lawrence, senior partner of the investment-banking firm of F. S. Smithers.
>
> James A. McConnell, former assistant secretary of the U. S. Department of Agriculture, now an agricultural economics consultant.
>
> Monroe C. Gutman, partner of Lehman Brothers, representing 31,000 shares of Commercial Solvents.
>
> William E. S. Griswold Sr., who at eighty-two was the sole surviving director who had been on the board when the company was founded in 1919.

Ernest W. Reid, former president of Corn Products Co.

Sydney T. Ellis, executive vice president of Commercial Solvents.

Maynard C. Wheeler, senior vice president of Commercial.

A number of these men were friends of Woods. Helm was on the committee that chose him for the presidency. A number of directors had come on the board at Woods' invitation. These included Smith, McGuire, McConnell, and Ellis.

But some directors had ties to the Milbanks. A Milbank was co-founder of the Borden Co., of which Comfort was president, and Milbanks had been prominent in the company over a period of eighty years. The Milbanks had also been large stockholders in Corn Products, among the largest, and were old friends of Reid. Jeremiah Milbank Sr. and Griswold had been friends for more than fifty years. Finally, board member Wheeler had been with Commercial since 1923 and many people had expected him to become president when Woods was brought in instead.

Woods, a native Tennessean, had started his career in 1919 as a salesman with the Armour Fertilizer Works. Ten years later he was a vice president and director. He went on to become president of the Chilean Nitrate Sales Corp., then moved to W. R. Grace & Co. as vice president. In 1947 he became president of the Wilson & Toomer Fertilizer Co. of Jacksonville, Florida, whence he had been hired away to take over the presidency of Commercial Solvents.

The man most voted against

The general reaction of the directors was natural enough: What did the Milbanks want? Why did they think it necessary to threaten a proxy fight?

To be sure, the board was aware, in a general way, that the Milbanks had not been entirely happy about the company's lack of progress—but then, no one was. Early in 1958 the Milbanks had persuaded management to hire a consultant to study some aspects of the company's operations. After three months the consultant had made some recommendations on how the company could improve its business. Woods followed up by hiring the management-consulting firm of Robert Heller & Associates to conduct a more extensive study. The Heller study was still in progress in January, 1959. Meanwhile, the proxy statement listing the candidates for election to the board at the next annual meeting, scheduled for April 2, was ready to be filed with the Securities and Exchange Commission. Why had the Milbanks chosen this moment to act so brusquely?

Phone calls and messages went back and forth among the directors and between Helm and the Milbanks. In the course of the day it became known that Paul Shields, who headed the investment-banking firm of Shields & Co., and who had been associated with Milbank Sr. in a number of projects, was in the Milbank camp. This information added a hardening note to the situation. At sixty-nine, Shields was still the tough-shelled, tough-talking, battle-scarred maverick of the financial community. He led the roughly waged campaign to reform the New York Stock Exchange in the Thirties, and in return received the most votes *against* his nomination to the exchange's board of governors in the first post-reform election. In the late Forties, at the request of Secretary of Defense Forrestal, Shields moved decisively into the noisy struggle being waged over Curtiss-Wright Corp. and took over.

Helm was anxious above all to prevent an open fight, and so took on the part of peacemaker. He was determined to persuade the Milbanks that they were being unfair to Woods. Helm set up a meeting with other board members to work out a reply to the Milbanks. On Saturday, January 24, 1959, the group convened at the Union League Club. Jeremiah Milbank Jr. was not present, of course; Griswold, Reid, and one or two others were also absent. The sentiment was strongly pro-Woods. The directors felt he had done a commendable job. There was also indignation over the abruptness of the Milbanks' ultimatum. Moreover, the ultimatum could be construed as a slap at the whole board.

Harold McGuire, the company's counsel, came prepared for all contingencies. He agreed, he said, that it was "in the best interests of the company" to conciliate the Milbanks. But he was not backing off from a fight. He talked about steps to be taken to fight the Milbanks if it came to that. He explained that he had set out to line up proxy soliciting firms and learned that some had already been approached by a representative of the Milbanks.

Were the shares there?

To most of the directors, the Milbanks' 800,000 shares seemed too big a block to buck. On the off-chance that the Milbanks might be bluffing, it was suggested that Helm verify that they did have 800,000 shares to vote.

Discussion then turned to the possibility of working out a compromise with the Milbanks. McGuire had a suggestion: if the Milbanks would agree to Woods' re-election to the board, the other directors would agree to institute a search for a new president. When the right man was found, he would become the chief executive officer and Woods would move up to board chairman. Woods agreed to go along with this approach.

What if this compromise were rejected? All the delaying tactics that might have been considered—postponing the annual meeting, which was set up for April 2, withholding the list of stockholders, etc.—were rejected as futile and costly to both management and stockholders.

Finally it was decided that the Milbanks be told it was the sentiment of the board that the issue should be settled peacefully; that all the weaknesses at Commercial Solvents were not of Woods' making and that consequently he should not bear sole blame; and that if the Milbanks remained adamant the board might feel impelled to resign en masse.

There was little discussion of this last suggestion, however. It seemed unthinkable that people like the Milbanks would not want a friendly, unpublicized settlement.

A directors' meeting was scheduled for the following Monday, January 26. At that meeting the directors were to approve the names of the directors to be filed with the SEC for election to the board.

On Monday morning Milbank Jr. was invited to meet with Helm and two other directors: Monroe Gutman, chosen for this meeting perhaps because he was a recent addition to the board and hence would tend to be impartial in an internal argument; and Harold W. Comfort, chosen perhaps because his firm was a key customer of Commercial. This meeting, too, took place in Helm's office. Milbank Jr. arrived accompanied by Paul Shields.

The Helm group tried to explain that it wished to get the dispute peaceably settled. A proxy contest could seriously damage the company by disturbing employee confidence, frightening customers, and encouraging competitors.

But Shields cut off this kind of argument. His side had already considered these points.

The Helm group brought up the compromise McGuire had suggested: re-election of Woods to the board and a quiet search for a new president. They argued that abrupt dismissal would be unfair to Woods, and that his personal contacts were responsible for some of Commercial's business.

Dismissing a hired hand

Shields replied brusquely. Looked at realistically, he said, Woods was a hired hand who had been well paid. Now a group of owners simply wanted to dismiss him. As for Woods' value in holding business, Shields argued that these days no company could afford to be the customer of another simply because of friendship among their executives.

Shields recalled that during his fight for control of Curtiss-Wright in 1949 he had made an arrangement similar to the one now proposed. The president stayed on while a new man was sought for the office, but it didn't work out; the president refused to carry out any of Shields' proposals and Shields had to replace him after all.

Memories of the Curtiss-Wright struggle seemed to flood back upon Shields and renew his zest for battle. He said he was prepared to spend $1 million to $2 million to buy Commercial shares for a proxy war.

When Helm, Gutman, or Comfort tried to draw out Shields or Milbank as to what changes "the Milbank interests" would like to see made in the company's operations, he got nowhere. Only one thing was clear: the Milbanks wanted Woods out.

That afternoon the board meeting was held as planned at the offices of Commercial Solvents. No action was taken on nominations for directorships to be elected on April 2 and the meeting was adjourned to February 16.

Afterward, Helm and other pro-Woods directors, including Woods himself, caucused. Helm reported that he had visited Milbank Sr. and was shown a list of the Commercial Solvents stockholders who were allied with the family. The 800,000 shares were there, all right.

As the discussion continued, a mass resignation more and more plainly seemed to be the effective way for the board to express its resentment of the relentless pressure the Milbanks were bringing to bear. However, McGuire, as general counsel, reminded the directors that they had responsibilities to the company and the stockholders.

No decisions were reached, but the next day, January 27, there were further conversations between Helm and the Milbank-Shields group. Shields had a compromise to suggest. He and the Milbanks would agree to re-elect Woods to the board and let him remain as president if: (1) Woods would give up his policy-making powers; (2) a policy committee would run the company, Woods to be excluded from its membership; (3) a selection committee (Woods again excluded) would hunt for a president; (4) McGuire and Reid would resign from the board.

Helm said only that he would pass the suggestion on.

The rich beginning

How had Commercial Solvents and its management come to such a pass that terms as stiff as these could be handed them as a "compromise"? We have already seen that the company's postwar record was dreary, but to appreciate just how dreary it could look to a big investor in Commercial Solvents one must go a little further back.

Commercial Solvents was founded just after World War I by American and British industrialists who acquired the patent rights to Dr. Chaim Weizmann's bacteria fermentation process for the manufacture of acetone. These patents enabled the company to prosper for several years, particularly after it was discovered that a byproduct, butyl acetate, made possible the production of a quick-drying lacquer with which autos could be painted in minutes instead of days.

By 1929, Commercial Solvents' profits were up to $3,700,000 and its stock reached $700 per share before a ten-for-one split, a record price for a chemical security. The company rode out the depression days, protected by its patent monopoly on the production of butyl and ethyl alcohol. After the repeal of prohibition it began to produce whiskey for wholesale buyers.

In 1936 the Weizmann patents began to expire and competition in industrial alcohol mounted. But the outbreak of World War II revived demand for acetone and ethyl alcohol. During the war, Commercial also built and operated an ammonia plant for the government, and enlarged its output of carbon black for the rubber industry.

The future glittered

As the first company to mass-produce penicillin and the first to produce a penicillin crystal, which permitted the drug to be shipped in bulk without refrigeration, Commercial seemed to have a glittering future in the postwar development and exploitation of new drugs. Another area of postwar promise for Commercial was in nitroparaffins for insecticides, fungicides, cosmetics, and scores of other products.

But the great promise didn't materialize. The company's research organization failed to deliver on the development of new biochemical products on which much store had been set. The big investment in penicillin production began to look bad as the price began to drop sharply. The company had been making a small but steady profit distilling alcohol for whiskey makers, but as the distillers built up their own stocks they relied less and less on Commercial's facilities.

The potential of the petrochemical end of the business remained in the test tubes. Union Carbide and du Pont were making cheap synthetic butyl and ethyl alcohol, and Commercial had hoped to underprice them with alcohol made from fermentation of corn or molasses, but the price of these two commodities remained at high levels, propped up by federal price supports and world demand.

When President Henry Perry died in 1950, sales had slumped from a peak of $55 million in 1947 to $33 million in 1949. Profits had fallen from $3.44 per share to $1.28 per share. It was at this low ebb that, after a search of several months, the directors brought in J. Albert Woods, from the Wilson & Toomer Fertilizer Co., to take over as chief executive officer. Woods was known in the industry as an energetic and effective salesman with a strong personality and a great deal of charm.

"Of course, we approved"

Jeremiah Milbank Sr. played no active role in selecting Woods, but as he admits, "Of course, we approved his selection, and he probably wouldn't have been selected if we had opposed him."

Woods moved quickly and aggressively in the areas he knew best. He revived the neglected nitroparaffin development program, and expanded rapidly in fertilizers. Woods started marketing solid ammonium nitrate and nitrogen solutions as well as anhydrous ammonia. He had new plants for ammonia and nitroparaffin compounds built in Sterlington, Louisiana.

In his first two years Woods got an assist from the outbreak of the Korean war. Demand for penicillin and other chemicals soared, and sales went up to $61 million for 1951, profits to $2.22 per share, almost double the 1949 earnings.

Well aware that this was a temporary boom, Woods sought to get some strength into the biochemical division. Seeing that $2 million to $3 million a year was sunk into research with no commercially profitable product forthcoming,* he began casting around for a merger with another drug and pharmaceutical company.

---

* Commercial did produce Dextran, a blood extender, but it had a small market in peacetime.

The most likely candidate was Sharp & Dohme, an old-line firm with an excellent research organization and established trade position, which needed more production facilities and a stronger sales organization. In 1951 its sales were $45 million and its profits $4,600,-000. But negotiations with Sharp & Dohme collapsed early in 1952, apparently on the point of the exchange basis for the shares.

In 1954, Commercial Solvents dropped out of the ethical pharmaceutical field and became a bulk supplier of antibiotics to the drug trade. By 1955 the company had virtually ceased its production of penicillin.

Fortunately, sales of methanol, and of nitrogen products, which Woods had pushed, continued to climb. As a result, the company's volume was over the $50-million level in 1954 and 1955. Earnings were $1.01 per share in 1954 and $1.31 in 1955. In both years the company paid out a dividend of $1. By 1956, however, competition in the nitrogen business had grown more acute and was causing price cutting. The same thing had happened in other areas of the company's operation.

Woods had been persuaded by an engineering-marketing study in 1955 that Commercial Solvents could get a good share of the fertilizer market in the northwest U.S. and in Canada's prairie provinces by investing $2,700,000 for a 53 per cent interest in Northwest Nitro-Chemicals Ltd., which had a plant at Medicine Hat, Alberta. This turned out to be a mistake.

In recent years, the bulk of the company's sales volume and virtually all of its profits have come from the petrochemical end of the business. This is, of course, the segment of the business that Woods expanded. However, one segment of the petrochemical business, the automotive division, has been in trouble. Commercial makes the methanol used in so-called "temporary" antifreeze, but does not make the glycol used in "permanent" antifreeze. Obviously, with ethylene glycol already in oversupply, it doesn't make sense for Commercial to build its own plant. Du Pont and Union Carbide, on the other hand, are integrated producers of all the elements for antifreezes (save for a few special additives) and are therefore the price leaders. Commercial buys glycol and packages an antifreeze of its own under the tradename PEAK, and also sells to Sears, Roebuck, Gulf, and others. While this antifreeze business is in the neighborhood of $10 million a year, it has not been profitable.

It has been argued that Woods should have sold off the automotive-chemical division, but his defenders contend that the present method of allocating overhead costs at Commercial does not permit a fair showing of the potential value of the division.

The impasse broken

When the pro-Woods group reconvened on Wednesday, January 28, 1959, Helm was accompanied by Chemical Corn's counsel, Maurice T. Moore of Cravath, Swaine & Moore. Helm explained to the directors that he had kept Moore informed of developments at Commercial Solvents, and thought that at this crucial meeting it would be helpful to have Moore's advice before they reached a decision.

Helm then presented the last-minute "compromise" proposal of the Milbank-Shields group, the formula that would permit Woods to stay

---

THE QUIET MILBANK MILLIONS

The Milbank family of New York controls what is probably the least publicized of the "mature" great fortunes of America. Its fortune has been building up through four generations of astute investment.

It is a tribute to the Milbanks' dislike of publicity, and their skill in avoiding it, that so little is known about them. When word got out in February, 1959, that the president of Commercial Solvents Corp. was resigning because of disagreements with "the Milbank interests," several newspapers erroneously identified the Milbanks concerned as descendants of the late Albert G. Milbank. Albert G. Milbank, co-founder of the law firm of Milbank, Tweed, Hope & Webb, was the best known of the family, but his heirs have no connection with Commercial Solvents. And Jeremiah Milbank Sr., whose holdings in Commercial Solvents were the basis for the thrust at the management of that corporation, as related in the accompanying article, was not even mentioned in the newspaper stories.

Wall Street, of course, has long been aware of the Milbanks as a wealthy family, but it has not fully appreciated the financial power the family could exert when it wanted to. The Milbanks, of whom Jeremiah Sr. is at present the most influential, have large stock interests in a wide variety of corporations, ranging from the Southern Railway to Commercial Solvents. A number of Milbanks have been considerable figures in the industrial history of the U.S., and the family has also left its mark on the educational and medical institutions of the country.

For medical and public-health projects the Milbanks contribute around $500,000 to $1,000,000 annually through family foundations. Characteristically, the family has avoided publicity in its giving as much as it has in its acquiring.

in office but without power. It was rejected. Woods was not willing to work under such restrictions and in such an atmosphere. To the other directors it was abhorrent that Woods should be put in a position where he might receive blame but no credit for what happened to the company thereafter.

At this point Woods broke the impasse by announcing that he was willing to resign. Now the question was whether or not the whole board would resign with him.

As bad as a proxy fight

Moore spoke on the various ramifications of a mass resignation. Such an action, he said, might have as deleterious an effect on the company as a proxy fight, the very thing the directors had sought to

---

"When you're interested in some project, really interested," one Milbank said recently, "it's more important that you get something done about it than whether your name is inscribed on a marble tablet or plaque."

Groceries, milk, railroads

The American family was founded by Samuel Milbank, who came here from England in 1794. A few years later he was in the brewery business in New York City. One of seventeen children, he himself sired twelve. The eleventh child and last boy, Jeremiah, was born in 1818. He went into the wholesale grocery business, married Elizabeth Lake, daughter of a substantial Greenwich, Connecticut, family, and prospered.

In the summer of 1857, Jeremiah Milbank took a fateful train trip. He had been visiting his in-laws in Connecticut. His seat mate on the train back to New York was a Texan who was looking for financial backing to launch a company to produce condensed milk. No one had yet succeeded with canned milk, and Milbank was intrigued. He suggested he might help out if the Texan failed to get the financial backing he expected in New York.

A little later, the Texan called on Milbank, who promptly put up $50,000, and Gail Borden and Jeremiah Milbank became equal partners in the New York Condensed Milk Co. (It was renamed the Borden Co. in 1919.)

Canned milk was used in great quantities in provisioning the northern armies in the Civil War, and by the end of the war Milbank and Borden were wealthy men. In 1864, Milbank opened shop as an investment banker and turned over to a son, Joseph, the management of the wholesale business.

avoid. Moreover, the stockholders were entitled to look to the directors to protect their interests by ensuring continuity of direction and management in the corporation. And on this score the outside directors might be considered to have a greater responsibility than the insiders.

Moore's words substantially changed the mood of the meeting. The Woods faction dropped the idea of a mass resignation. It was decided that the proxy statement to stockholders would contain the simple statement of fact that Woods had resigned in order to spare the company a damaging proxy contest.

McGuire than proposed that a statement be added to indicate how the other directors felt about the clash. This was finally made to read that "Each of the nine incumbent directors reserves . . . the right to retire from the Board" prior to the expiration of his term if he

---

In 1863 Jeremiah and his son led the organizing and financing of the construction of the Chicago, Milwaukee & St. Paul Railway. The road was later extended to the Pacific Coast, and in South Dakota a town that became a maintenance stop was renamed Milbank.

A disputed church merger

Jeremiah Milbank the First was the cause of a noisy church dispute in New York in 1862. He was a member and trustee of the Madison Avenue Baptist Church. The trustees voted to merge with the Baptist Church of Oliver Street. Milbank was opposed. He charged that under the plan of merger the Madison Avenue trustees were giving away property to the Oliver Street membership. His fellow trustees were horrified by Milbank's publication of his charges in newspaper advertisements and leaflets. They contended that he was disgruntled because the merged congregation had not elected him a trustee. But Milbank took the matter to court. After ten years of litigation his position was upheld and the merger never went through.

Jeremiah died in 1884, leaving an estate estimated at over $32 million to be divided equally between his son Joseph and his daughter Elizabeth, who had married Abram A. Anderson, a well-known portrait painter and friend of Teddy Roosevelt.

Around the turn of the century Joseph Milbank sold his 25 per cent stock interest in the Borden Co. But Mrs. Elizabeth Milbank Anderson retained her inheritance in Borden shares. She asked a cousin, Albert J. Milbank, who had gone to work at Borden and become treasurer of the company, to represent her interests there. After Albert J.'s death in 1912, she asked his son to serve in the same capacity. This was the attorney,

deems it proper. Since this was, of course, a right they had in any case, it presented no legal problem.*

Woods then asked for a brief recess while he left the room to confer with McGuire. Outside, he asked McGuire if it would be proper for Moore to represent him in negotiations with the Milbanks. Keenly aware of the Milbanks' hostility to himself, McGuire said it would be quite proper. Woods returned to the room, and asked Moore to represent him. Moore agreed.

Three more out

McConnell and Smith, who were on the board primarily because of their friendship with Woods, had announced that they too would step down, and Griswold had indicated that he was ready to yield his

* One SEC lawyer remarked after reading the proxy letter: "Hell, the Constitution has an amendment against involuntary servitude."

~~~~~~

Albert G. Milbank, who founded the famous Wall Street law firm of Milbank, Tweed, Hope & Webb. He served as board chairman of Borden's from 1917 to 1941.

"People's Palace" in Jersey

Elizabeth Milbank was an energetic, strong-minded woman with a wide range of charitable interests. She donated a library to Greenwich, Connecticut, and three blocks of choice New York City real estate to Barnard College, of which she was trustee and the largest benefactor at that time. With her brother Joseph she made possible a "People's Palace" in Jersey City, where the poor could enjoy sports and entertainment—but not hard liquor, which she opposed as much as she favored cleanliness. She had public baths built in New York's tenement sections. She also gave money for free lunches in the public schools, a project later taken over by the Board of Education. And she was the first donor to the National Committee for Mental Hygiene.

Mrs. Anderson's daughter Eleanor earned a medical degree and married Frederick Campbell. Dr. Campbell organized New York's Judson Health Center, which is today one of the oldest and one of the few remaining free health clinics financed by private donations. Until her death in 1959 at age 82, Dr. Campbell actively directed the center's experiments in new approaches to health service for low-income families, particularly in dental treatment.

Mrs. Anderson's largest donations went into the Milbank Memorial Fund established in 1905 in memory of her father and mother. It was originally endowed with $3 million. By the time of her death in 1921,

directorship. This would mean that the Milbank-Shields group would have to be consulted on four successor candidates, so Moore was asked to represent the whole board, not just Woods, in negotiations with the Milbank faction.

In the succeeding two weeks Moore negotiated the terms of Woods' retirement and the nomination of candidates to replace the directors not standing for re-election. Senior Vice President Maynard Wheeler was named "acting president."

The Milbanks supplied all nominees to be elected at the April 2 annual meeting. In addition to Jeremiah Jr., who was standing for re-election, they nominated Paul Shields, William W. Burch, a member of the Jeremiah Milbank organization, H. V. Sherrill, a partner in the Shields firm and a classmate of young Jeremiah, and Arthur E. Palmer Jr., a lawyer associated with the Jeremiah Milbank interests.

~~~~~~

Mrs. Anderson had given the fund $10 million. It is a tribute to the investment policy pursued by the fund directors, among whom there has always been a Milbank, that despite annual grants of approximately $500,000 to various social, medical, and educational projects, the fund, at last report, had assets valued at about $20 million.

Mrs. Anderson's brother Joseph retired from business in 1906. His two sons, Dunlevy and Jeremiah (the present Jeremiah Sr.), thereafter shared responsibility for management of the family estate. As a lawyer, Dunlevy specialized in estate work. During World War I he served on the War Industries Board. He died in 1960.

The family investments that Jeremiah handled included large real-estate holdings, particularly on the Lower East Side of New York. He was eager to branch out into other fields, much as the first Jeremiah had done.

In 1916 Jeremiah organized with his own money one of the first investment companies, Case, Pomeroy & Co. Walter Case had been an analyst with Ladenburg, Thalmann, investment bankers. Ted Pomeroy, Jeremiah Milbank's brother-in-law, had been a Chicago broker.

Case, Pomeroy was one of the first investment firms to set up an extensive statistical and engineering-research organization to study the prospects of a company or an industry. Among its most successful ventures was the development of the Northern Rhodesian copper fields. The firm formed a syndicate with British interests to finance a series of drilling ventures that became the Roan Antelope Copper Mines, Rhodesian Selection Trust, and other great properties. Case, Pomeroy investments in Rhodesian copper, the Southern Railway, and Corn Products (the large food manufacturer) added handsomely to the fortune Jeremiah Milbank had inherited.

The settlement

Woods remained a consultant to the company for four years at a salary of $50,000 annually (he had been getting $75,000 as president), and thereafter at $20,600 a year for ten years. In addition, he is eligible for an annual pension of about $9000, beginning in 1963.

The annual meeting on April 2 was a tame affair. All the candidates for the board were elected.

Acting President Wheeler announced that all the company's units except the Medicine Hat plant (whose losses were expected to continue for two or three years) were operating in the black. The petrochemical division, he said, was being helped by higher prices and a pickup in demand, and expansion of operations was indicated.

On April 8 the new board of directors met. It elected Wheeler president. The new chairman of the executive committee was Jeremiah Milbank Jr.

A cruise for the President

After 1928, when Milbank sold his majority interest in Case, Pomeroy to his partners, he continued to invest on his own account. He sat on the board of a number of companies, including the Chase Manhattan Bank, Western Union, and Allis-Chalmers. Usually his presence on a board meant that he held a substantial stock interest in the company. He became one of the big financial backers of the Republican party, heading or helping organize fund raising in New York State for every major campaign. In 1930, Herbert Hoover relaxed by cruising in Caribbean waters aboard Milbank's yacht *Saunterer*.

Jeremiah Milbank Sr.'s principal philanthropies have been in medicine. In 1917 he established the Institute for the Crippled and Disabled in New York City. During World War II the institute trained doctors and teachers in rehabilitation work. It operates on an annual budget of $1,500,000. While it relies for most of its funds on individual public contributions and investment income, Jeremiah Milbank Sr., through the J. M. Foundation, is the largest single benefactor.

In 1928 Milbank set up a grant of $280,000 for the International Committee for the Study of Infantile Paralysis. This was the first step in a long campaign that eventually drew upon many other donors and came to a triumphant climax with the development of the Salk vaccine.

Still good with figures

At seventy-nine, Milbank Sr. retains a quick grasp of, and a long memory for, figures; his associates are often impressed by his ability to recall the

The Milbanks' extraordinary power play reflected, among other things, a serene confidence in their own business acumen—in their ability to arrest the drift of Commercial Solvents and turn the company around. The events of the ensuing years suggest that their confidence in themselves was not misplaced. In 1960–61 their new management, headed by president Maynard Wheeler, made several major acquisitions, including the Stabilized Vitamin group of companies and a major interest in an Italian pharmaceutical and chemical firm, Istituto Chemioterapico; meanwhile, the automotive chemicals division was sold off. Sales volume declined from $70 million in 1959 to $64 million in 1961, but profit margins rose sharply. Earnings per share rose from $1.02 in 1959 to $1.70 in 1960 and $1.90 in 1961. In 1962, as this book was going to press, the company appeared to be involved, rather ambiguously, in the tangled affairs of Billie Sol Estes. But barring some sizable losses on this account, the 1962 prospects were for further gains. On balance, it would appear that the Milbanks still know pretty well how to take care of their investments.

---

exact price for which a stock was bought or sold many years back or the terms of a merger. He is an avid reader of corporate reports.

Milbank still maintains a large town house on East Sixty-seventh Street in New York, one block away from his late brother Dunlevy's residence, but he spends more and more time on his 25,000-acre estate at Ridgeland, South Carolina, which he acquired in the late Thirties. When in New York, he goes regularly to his offices at 44 Wall Street, where he maintains a nine-man staff. Most of the men in the office are graduates of the Harvard School of Business, as is Jeremiah Jr.

One Wall Street financier who knew Milbank during the Twenties says, "Milbank was a common-stock buyer all the time. He said a capitalist worthy of the name should ignore bonds and be willing to assume the equity risk." Milbank bought common stocks during the Thirties, too, and it was then that he took a substantial position in Commercial Solvents. He was attracted by the company not only as a good investment but as a potential producer of new drugs for the battle against disease. "The war against disease in all its forms," he said in the preface to the published report on the infantile-paralysis study he financed in 1928, "presents a stirring challenge and maintains a keen and never-failing interest. One of its satisfactions is that the battle line never retreats and, while progress may prove slow, each gain is held and forms the base for further advance."

But as time passed and Commercial Solvents' great promise failed to materialize either in business gains or in the development of new drugs, both sides of the Milbank personality, the investor-capitalist and the philanthropist, were antagonized. Then the Milbank power was forthrightly exerted to change the company's management.

7

Nine Powerful Individualists

The nine men described on the following pages are, by and large, unknown outside the Wall Street financial community. A few of them are not too well known inside the community, except to colleagues in their own specialized fields. But in the aggregate, these men may be the most powerful nine men on the Street.

Certainly better known than any of them are men like Robert Lehman, senior partner of Lehman Brothers, Henry Clay Alexander,

~~~~~~

NINE POWERFUL INDIVIDUALISTS

The Street's ablest bond trader

CHRISTOPHER J. DEVINE has been considered the ablest bond trader in the Street for more than twenty-five years. Now fifty-seven, he still works with a fierce intensity; few of his associates have ever seen him relax. His firm, C. J. Devine & Co., is the biggest dealer in U.S. government securities, records as much as $750 million a day in trades, carries an inventory of $200 million. Devine still supervises the day-to-day trading of his house, and says that nothing stirs him quite so much as "the thrill of gauging the market." The son of a Newark fireman, Devine got a job as a clerk in a bond house before he had graduated from high school. In 1933 he left to start his own firm, which now has 250 employees in 9 offices around the country. His advice is constantly sought by banks and institutions that have portfolios of government securities; it is also sought by Treasury officials who must estimate the coupon and maturity best suited to a new issue. Devine is one of the owners of the 1955 Preakness winner, Nashua.

chairman of the Morgan Guaranty Trust Co., or David Rockefeller, vice chairman of the Chase Manhattan Bank. But these executives, chiefs of great institutions, are not exactly powers in themselves. Their considerable influence depends to a great extent on the organizations they represent. Moreover, while their influence is spread over many fields, it cannot be said that they are preeminent in any single one, as is each of the nine. Robert Lehman exercises influence over his firm's vast underwriting activities, its huge investment advisory service, and two large investment companies that are associated with it—Lehman Corp. and the One William Street Fund. But up and down the Street, Albert Gordon exercises a larger influence on underwriting. The operations of the men described here are not unique. Most of them are individualists who exercise their power in a highly personal fashion; it is their personal opinion, not the collective wisdom of their firms, that the Street waits to hear.

Curiously enough, much of their power derives from the decline of individualism on Wall Street—and the concurrent rise in the influence of the great funds and trusts, and of the federal government. Where once the Street reverberated with rumors about the latest doings of various lone wolves ("Baruch is selling!"), today the big news

He advises the managers

RICHARD T. SHIELDS, fifty-four, is a vice-president of the Bankers Trust Co., which probably manages more money for more people than any other bank around. The thirty analysts and seven statisticians under Shields constitute the bank's Investment Research Division; its pronouncements guide the Pension Trust Division (which manages most of American Telephone's $3-billion pension fund, among many others), the Investment Advisory Division, the Personal Trust Division, and also the bank's four national divisions in charge of correspondents and out-of-town accounts. Thus Shields' reports determine the investment of an enormous amount of money in trust accounts of all sizes: not only of the A.T.&T. pension fund, but of the rural widow's inheritance, which is invested in line with a local banker's information from his New York correspondent, the Bankers Trust. Shields was born in Kansas City, graduated from Yale ('29) and the Harvard Business School ('31), and has been with the Bankers Trust ever since.

is apt to concern the investment decisions of the funds. And in this institutionalized, closely regulated world, these nine, with their special kinds of expertise, are strategically situated individuals.

Richard Shields of Bankers Trust, for example, heads a vast research operation whose findings affect the investments of the A.T.&T. pension fund and many other sizable institutions. Both he and Bernard Kilgore, the president of Dow Jones & Co., Inc., may be thought of as products of Wall Street's insatiable appetite for financial information and for careful research—of a kind quite different from the free-flying rumors that inspired investors in the 1920s.

Frank Weeden, the off-the-floor specialist, performs a special function for the big funds. The funds' transactions are so large that they often have the problem of buying and selling without distorting the price of stocks; Weeden and men like him trade directly with the funds, taking their only profit on a small price spread. George Garvin and C. J. Devine reflect the new and enlarged role of the U. S. Government on Wall Street. Through the unique kind of service Garvin provides, banks are able to meet the reserve requirements of the Federal Reserve Board, while at the same time keeping a minimum of their funds idle. Devine's business as a bond dealer has expanded

Dean of the commodity markets

JEROME LEWINE, the senior partner of H. Hentz & Co., might be described as the elder statesman of the commodity markets. Thirty-eight years ago he saw the possibilities of trading in industrial commodities, and was instrumental in the formation of the Rubber, Hides, Raw Silk, and Metals Exchanges. In 1933 he initiated the merger of these four exchanges into the Commodity Exchange, and then became its first president. He is still a governor of the exchange, and still keeps close watch on all its trading rules—e.g., when to suspend trading in a certain commodity, when and how to amend the terms of standard commodity contracts in the light of changing conditions. Lewine, now seventy-seven, seems very much a figure from a grander era on Wall Street: he wears a vest, sports a carnation in his button-hole, bears an uncanny resemblance to Bernard Baruch. He was born in Brooklyn, raised in Waco, Texas, went to work for Hentz in 1900 as an errand boy, and has been the senior partner since 1942.

steadily, largely because the growing national debt has brought forth a succession of new government issues (and also because of the tendency of the big funds to carry sizable quantities of government bonds in their portfolios).

Albert Gordon of Kidder, Peabody has had a unique success as an underwriter on the Street; much of his success hinges on his special relations to the big funds, with which he has repeatedly placed sizable private offerings. Andre Meyer of Lazard Frères has also been successful with such private offerings, but he is perhaps noted especially for his interest in foreign securities—an interest that has been taken up by many institutional investors. In 1958, Meyer and his firm launched their own Lazard Fund.

John Coleman, the senior partner of Adler, Coleman & Co., and Jerome Lewine of H. Hentz & Co. could be called "politicians" of Wall Street; in an age of endless federal regulation, both men have done a lot to keep the trading machinery of the big exchanges abreast of the times. Coleman is a power in the New York Stock Exchange, Lewine in the Commodity Exchange.

Policy-maker on the exchange

JOHN A. COLEMAN, senior partner of Adler, Coleman & Co., is one of the most influential specialists on the floor of the New York Stock Exchange, and is also a major influence on the policies of the exchange itself. His firm holds nine Big Board seats and makes markets in fifty-five leading stocks. Coleman's own views are sought not only on individual markets, but on the issues that affect the whole exchange—e.g., commissions, trading policies. In 1951 he was instrumental in picking G. Keith Funston, the president of Trinity College, to be president of the Stock Exchange. The son of a policeman, Coleman was born in New York in 1901, went to work for the exchange as a page boy at the age of fourteen, became a member eight years later. He was elected a governor in 1938, vice chairman in 1941, and chairman in 1943. He stepped down as chairman in 1947, but is still a governor. Coleman is also well known uptown for his activities in in Catholic charities; he is one of Cardinal Spellman's closest advisers.

The Street's men of breadth

What kind of men are they? Several of the nine are notably urbane men, very much at home in the erudite and wide-ranging discussions that go on in some of the private dining rooms of the Street's big institutions. Meyer, for example, prefers to hire men of breadth for Lazard Frères. "We need Renaissance men," he says. Gordon has made great efforts to raise the cultural level of his under-writing organization; recently he ordered his men to read *The Elements of Style,* by William Strunk, and to try writing more literate reports. But six of the nine did not graduate from college; indeed, while their contemporaries were still going to school the six were already on the Street, getting an education as runners, page boys, and clerks. None of them came out of an executive-training program. Of the three who went to college, two are Ivy Leaguers. (In the 1920s, graduates of Ivy League colleges descended on Wall Street in droves; during the depression they turned to other fields. Today they are rediscovering the Street; about twenty Merrill Lynch partners, who are now called "voting stockholders," are Ivy Leaguers.)

He knows where the money is

GEORGE K. GARVIN is the senior partner of a remarkable operation called Garvin, Bantel & Co., which keeps track of the deposit-to-loan ratios of 500 banks all over the country, and in general offers the investment community a "complete money service." He helps to bring banks that are overloaned together with banks that have money to spare; on an average day Garvin, Bantel & Co. arranges the transfer of $500 million (on which it takes a small commission), most of it in federal funds—i.e., in the excess of the deposits that member banks must keep with the Federal Reserve. Garvin's efforts to "educate banks on the most complete utilization of their capital" led, in 1958, to his censure by the New York Stock Exchange, which felt that he had contributed to speculation in government bonds by letting his customers buy them on thin margins. Garvin argued that the Stock Exchange rules on margin requirements were worded so vaguely that they could not be applied conscientiously. The Exchange later changed its wording.

None of the nine are poor by a long shot (it would be difficult for a poor man on the Street to make any pretense to the role of an expert). Some of them tend to be fairly secretive about the state of their finances, but it is probably safe to say that each of them has a net worth of at least $1 million, and a few—for example, C. J. Devine, the bond dealer—are obviously multimillionaires. But Devine's influence hinges on his ability to gauge the bond market, not on his millions.

One quality possessed by all nine of these men is an intent, and intense, drive; they all tend to "be in business" a lot more than eight hours a day, and to be endlessly preoccupied with small details. George Garvin usually has his pockets filled with memoranda and scraps of paper on which he has jotted down the outlines of business deals in which he has an interest. Andre Meyer is almost always deeply and personally involved in scores of deals in the U.S. and in Europe. John Coleman, who is a governor of the New York Stock Exchange, and perhaps the first man to be consulted when any change of policy is suggested for the exchange, is also personally active in making the markets for 55 different stocks.

Most of the nine are of mature age, and the oldest, Jerome Lewine,

---

International financier

ANDRE MEYER, sixty-three, the senior partner of Lazard Frères & Co., has always shied away from publicity, in the manner of European bankers, but in the field of international banking the Street can always feel his presence. When the Credit Foncier de France wanted to sell $50 million in bonds four years ago—its first such issue—it turned to Lazard and Morgan Stanley as underwriters, and to Meyer himself for pricing. Meyer personally supervises all the prestige underwritings for Lazard, which has handled bond issues for the European Coal and Steel Community and many European governments. Meyer also guides Lazard's venture-capital activities in the U.S., and has had a hand in developing such companies as Carter Products, Magma Copper, and Bestwall Gypsum. Meyer begins his working day at 6:30 A.M., usually does not quit until 11:00 P.M. He was born in Paris in 1898, went to work there as a messenger boy in the banking district, joined Lazard in 1925, became a partner in 1927, and came to the U.S. in 1940.

the dean of the commodities markets, is seventy-five. There are few "boy wonders" around the Street these days, at least in positions of real influence; in Wall Street, more than in almost any other part of the business community, power and influence are based on a long record of achievement. Indeed, the rather personal style of these men's operations would itself suggest that they have been around a while—specifically, that they were around in the freewheeling 1920s, when Wall Street produced more than its share of rugged individualists. All of the men shown here were working thirty years ago.

Although most of them got their training in the 1920s, many of them got their first real opportunities, oddly enough, in the threadbare 1930s. Al Gordon revived Kidder, Peabody in 1931 (the name itself, which he acquired from a firm that was on the verge of dissolution, was his only asset). C. J. Devine and George Garvin also founded their firms in the early 1930s. The fact is that the 1929 crash left a kind of leadership vacuum on the Street. The old order was discredited, and many of its eminent figures had departed; at the same time, the bright young men out of college who had been looking to the Street for their careers began looking elsewhere. All of a sudden, many of the men who had got their basic training during the 1920s found that they could rise to the top rapidly, with a minimum of competition.

Specialist off the floor

FRANK WEEDEN, a lanky Californian of sixty-nine, is an off-the-floor specialist whose firm makes markets in a wide variety of municipal bonds and stocks listed on the New York Stock Exchange. Currently Weeden makes markets in seventy-seven of the most active industrials and fifty-four rails and utilities; he does most of his business with large financial institutions. A fund that wanted to sell 10,000 shares of General Motors, for example, might fear that offering the lot on the floor would disturb the market; Weeden, however, takes it all at one price, perhaps only a half-point under the market. He charges no commissions, instead makes his income on the spread between the prices at which he can find buyers and sellers. Weeden sells from an inventory of between $10 million and $15 million that, he hopes, anticipates the appetites of the institutions. His typical deals involve middle-sized blocks of shares, largely bought and sold by banks and mutual funds. In 1961 his volume came to almost $900 million.

Instituting a change

The "institutionalization" of Wall Street began, of course, after the crash had convinced the investing public, a sizable number of Congressmen, and even some old Wall Street hands themselves that the Street had to be regulated in a big way. The Banking Act of 1933, which separated commercial and investment banking, was the beginning of reform on Wall Street. It was followed by the establishment of the Securities and Exchange Commission in 1934 (and by a steady broadening of commission powers during the 1930s), by the Investment Company Act of 1940, and by the establishment, in 1939, of the National Association of Securities Dealers—a kind of self-policing unit whose members include virtually all brokerage firms.

As the freewheeling operators on the Street were gradually fenced in by the new regulators, the business of the Street became increasingly impersonal. This tendency was reinforced during the 1940s and 1950s, as the purchase and sale of individual stocks by individual investors gave way to massive transactions involving mutual funds,

Man behind the ticker

BERNARD KILGORE, fifty-three; president of Dow Jones & Co., maintains (at least half seriously): "We could operate just as well from Chicago. I know hardly anybody on Wall Street, and I don't claim to know anything about the market." Nevertheless, the *Wall Street Journal* and Dow Jones' ticker service are important sources of the news upon which investment decisions are made. The ticker service operates in 600 cities in the U.S. and Canada, is watched on Trans-Lux screens in hundreds of banks, brokerages, and business offices. Kilgore has the final say on the stocks that are quoted on the ticker. Largely because of his efforts, the *Journal* has grown from a dry financial daily, which in 1940 had a circulation of 32,000, to a national newspaper noted for its lively style and feature stories; the *Journal* today has a circulation of 774,079, with 90 per cent of it in subscriptions. Kilgore became managing editor in 1941, president of Dow Jones in 1945. In 1961, despite the heavy costs incurred in the launching of a new national weekly, the *National Observer,* Dow Jones earned $6.7 million on revenues of $53 million.

closed-end investment funds, industrial pension funds, and insurance companies—all of whose purchases and sales indirectly represent millions of small investors. The insurance companies' investment decisions are perhaps the most important: the Prudential Insurance Co. and Metropolitan Life, each of which must invest at least $5 million daily just to keep their premium money at work, are likely to be told about any big deal on the Street from its inception. Their investment decisions, like those of the other big institutions, are likely to be based in large part on the findings of their sizable research departments. In general, research has been heavily bureaucratized, and firms pride themselves on the size of their departments. Some of the departments are crowded indeed: Merrill Lynch spends $10 million annually on all its research activities; the New York Society of Security Analysts actually has 2400 members today.

The next generation of powerful men on the Street will doubtless all be college men; they will doubtless come out of executive training programs; they will doubtless operate as "organization men," not as individualists. The men described on these pages are probably a vanishing breed.

Underwriter and salesman

ALBERT H. GORDON, sixty-one, has been one of the most aggressive and most successful investment bankers on the Street since he took over Kidder, Peabody & Co. at the age of twenty-nine. He is particularly noted for landing fat underwritings for Kidder, even when the prospective security issuer already has a cozy relationship with some other house on the Street. In dismissing the government's antitrust suit against the investment bankers, Judge Harold Medina mentioned Gordon's operation as proof of hard competition in underwriting. Thiokol and Collins Radio, for example, departed their bankers quietly and arrived at Kidder's hospitable door when they sold issues to the public. Gordon's sales staff has also enabled Kidder to become the top firm in mutual-fund sales in New York, as well as one of the country's top firms in private placements; last year the firm placed issues totalling $800 million. Gordon likes to walk at least half the seven miles between his Gracie Square home and Wall Street every day.

PART THREE

Some Men Who Broke the Rules

8

The World of Lowell Birrell

The American public, even that part of it that seldom reads the financial pages, has been hearing a good deal about two financial operators of exceptional reach and versatility. One is Lowell M. Birrell, who was indicted for swindling $14 million worth of stock in companies he had controlled, and who later turned up in Brazil, a country that had no extradition treaty with the U.S. The other is Alexander L. Guterma, who had been indicted for crimes that include stock manipulation, violation of the federal banking laws, and failure to register as an agent of the Dominican Republic.

What the public did not then realize about Birrell and Guterma —it emerged gradually from investigations by the SEC, the Justice Department, and half a dozen other agencies—is that they were by no means isolated figures. The paths taken by Birrell and Guterma repeatedly cross the paths of other men who shared with them a flair for certain kinds of bizarre financial transactions. All of these men, it now appears, constituted a kind of demimonde within the U.S. financial community. Investigators on their trails were continually obliged to broaden the scope of their inquiries; and it is fair to regard the Birrell and Guterma cases of the late 1950s as the real beginnings of the large inquiries into the stock exchanges undertaken in 1962 by the SEC (see Chapter 12).

Among the names that have turned up in the investigations of Birrell and Guterma are these:

• The late Serge Rubinstein, who made an estimated $10 million in devious and gamy deals, and who was strangled in 1955 at the age of forty-six. He was involved in deals with Birrell as far back as 1944.

• Virgil D. Dardi, fifty-six, a bearlike, backslapping man whose worst sin may have been his unfortunate choice of associates. He was taken to the cleaners by Rubinstein in an oil deal in 1954, and has been used as a front man by both Birrell and Guterma. It is Dardi's contention that he never knew until too late the kind of company he was keeping.

• BenJack Cage, forty-four, a huge Texan convicted in 1958 of embezzling $100,000 from an insurance company, who joined Birrell in Brazil to avoid going to jail. Cage once had an almost worthless company palmed off on him by Guterma—to whom Cage was introduced by the ubiquitous Virgil Dardi. (The theme of the swindler swindled often recurs in the affairs of these men.)

• Earl Belle, thirty-one, a jobber of watered stock who ran off to Brazil leaving three U.S. banks short $825,000. One was the Security National Bank of Huntington, Long Island. Belle is accused of having swindled $475,000 from this bank after he had been introduced to bank officials by an alleged associate of Guterma.

Investigators believe that Birrell, Guterma, Rubinstein, Cage, Belle, and others who were associated with them at various times had a hand in wrecking seventy-five or more corporations, and in causing losses to investors that may have amounted to $100 million. Their schemes were imaginative, bold, and frequently characterized by a brain-numbing complexity. Now and then they could expect their maneuvers to be questioned by stockholders, or by the respectable front men they induced to sit on their boards; in that event, some fast double talk—e.g., about "tax savings"—often served to silence the questioners. And even if SEC lawyers or perspicacious stockholders should see through one of their devices, Birrell and the others could usually count on the fact that prosecuting attorneys would be reluctant to take on a case that would be about as bewildering to the average juror as a problem in nuclear physics.

Many of the inhabitants of this financial demimonde had achieved success at a very early age. Rubinstein was running a bank when he was still in his early twenties, Birrell was a highly paid corporation lawyer at twenty-nine, and Earl Belle had already made his pile and fled to Brazil by the time he was twenty-six. They often indulged a passion for expensive nightclubs, expensive restaurants, and expensive girls. BenJack Cage once listed on a single expense voucher the names of five girls on whom he claimed to have spent a total of $3100 in individual amounts ranging from $32 to $1200. And many of them displayed ferocious gall. Paul Windels Jr., who ran the SEC office in New York from 1956 until 1961, recalls the first time he met

Guterma, just after he had been appointed. Guterma condescended to congratulate him on the appointment, and added gravely that he hoped to maintain the good relations he had always enjoyed with the SEC's New York office.

Fun in Bucks County

Lowell Birrell was undoubtedly the most gifted of all this predatory crew. In the opinion of many who have officially investigated his activities, he has wrecked more corporations, duped more investors, and engineered the theft of more money than any other American of this century. At the peak of his career he maintained a 1200-acre estate in Bucks County, Pennsylvania, where he threw lavish parties that went on for days. He drank heavily, and he liked to have a pretty girl handy at all times. He once offered a model $1000 if she would strip off her clothes in front of newspapermen and take a shower in oil gushing from one of his oil wells. To Birrell's astonishment, she refused. Sometimes he stayed up all night for two or three nights in a row, refreshing himself with catnaps on nightclub tables.

He could also act the part of the sound (though imaginative) financier. He dressed conservatively, belonged to New York's Union League and Metropolitan clubs, and saw to it that his boards of directors were frequently adorned with men of spotless reputation. His charm, when he chose to exert it, was often irresistible. Paul Whiteman, who was a Bucks County neighbor of Birrell's, has said, "He took some of my friends but I still can't find it in my heart to hate him." (Whiteman added thoughtfully, "I suppose I'd feel differently if I'd lost money.")

Yet at times Birrell was crude and brutal, particularly when stockholders in the enterprises he was looting began asking sharp questions. He once called the annual meeting of one of his companies for a date certain to inconvenience most stockholders—July 3. When a sizable group of rebellious stockholders showed up anyway, he denounced them as stooges and jerks, and threatened his chief critic, an elderly man, with eviction and a poke in the jaw. At another annual meeting held in midsummer, a stockholder later charged, Birrell's lieutenants had the air conditioning turned off in order "to sweat us out." Actually, such tactics were seldom necessary. Before he grew greedy and careless toward the end, Birrell's financial maneuvers were so cleverly conceived and executed that stock-

holders failed to ask the right questions at the right time. An SEC
spokesman has described him, in fact, as "the most brilliant manipulator of corporations in modern times." Even allowing for a
natural tendency on the part of SEC officials to regard with awe a
man they were nearly twenty years catching up with, the statement
is not likely to be challenged.

The all-American boy

The record of Birrell's early years reads like the beginning of
countless American success stories. Born in 1907, the son of a
small-town Presbyterian minister, he was a model boy, hard-working
and precocious. In 1925, when he was only eighteen, he earned a
B.A. from Syracuse. That same year he went on to the law school of
the University of Michigan. At Michigan he worked his way, served
on the *Law Review*, and graduated near the top of his class. Like
many a young lawyer with brains and ambition, he set his sights for
Wall Street, and landed a job there with the law firm of Cadwalader,
Wickersham & Taft. He stayed with the firm for five years and then, in
1933, opened an office of his own. Soon afterward, he was hired to
work on the reorganization of the Bush Terminal Co. in Brooklyn. He
earned around $75,000 in fees—the first real money he had made—
and on the strength of his performance got an offer to work for another big company, Munson Steamship Lines, which was also being reorganized. Munson's chairman, a man named Cecil Parker Stewart, was to play an important part is some of Birrell's earliest business
ventures.

Birrell's business career began in 1938, when he borrowed some
money from Mrs. Ruby Schinasi, the widow of a rich New York
cigar manufacturer, and got control of a Brooklyn brewery that
made something called Fidelio Beer. Fidelio was pretty terrible stuff,
but Birrell was more interested in the company's stock than in its
beer. He began issuing the stock in large batches and selling it to a
group of holding companies. Some of these companies were controlled by Stewart and his friends, and in several Birrell himself had
an interest. Although the purchasers ostensibly were buying this stock
for investment, they appear to have soon unloaded a good deal of it on
the public—without filing the registration statements required by the
SEC when public offerings are made. (SEC staff members regarded
this as a violation of commission rules but there was no prosecution.)

These transactions enabled Birrell in 1945 to set in motion an ingenious plan that involved, among other things, loading the investment portfolios of a group of insurance companies with overvalued securities.

Birrell himself was no insurance expert, but he was able at this time to draw on the experience of a man named Stewart Hopps. Hopps, a highly successful, though unorthodox, operator in the insurance field. Birrell had met him through Cecil Stewart, who had been associated with Hopps for many years in a number of business ventures. One of these was Rhode Island Insurance, an old casualty company, and after Stewart died in 1945, Birrell took his place on the Rhode Island board, of which Hopps was also a member. It is Hopps' contention that in all his dealings with Birrell—which have been numerous—he was not a collaborator but a victim. "Yes, I knew him," he says. "He left me wiser and a good deal poorer." Hopps' style of living does not suggest, however, that he was completely impoverished by his association with Birrell. His house overlooking San Francisco Bay is said to have cost $500,000, and has been described by an awe-struck biographer as "the most expensive four-room home ever built in America." Hopps also has a house in Palm Springs whose outdoor accessories include a swimming pool with a floating telephone.

The scheme that Birrell put into operation in 1945 was, like all his later schemes, both complicated and ingenious. With money received from the sale of stock in his brewing enterprises, he had bought, in late 1944, control of a little holding company called Claude Neon. The chief attraction of Claude Neon was that its stock was traded on the Curb Exchange (now the American Stock Exchange), and was therefore easy to market. Birrell had Claude Neon issue hundreds of thousands of shares of its stock, and used these in a series of deals that gave Claude Neon (and therefore Birrell) control of several small insurance companies.

Rhode Island Insurance and the other companies were useful to Birrell in two important ways. First, he and Hopps set up a firm to manage the companies as a group (and to select their investments for them). For this service Birrell and Hopps collected in fees 25 per cent of their net income. Second, Birrell was able to use the insurance companies to conceal for a time the fact that he was actually engaged in watering Claude Neon's stock.

He did this by using the companies as a repository for certain securities he was buying for Claude Neon. In many cases Claude Neon was actually buying these securities from Birrell himself, who unloaded them on the company in roundabout transactions at outrageously high prices. He then had the securities transferred to the investment portfolios of the insurance companies, where the SEC, which does not have jurisdiction over insurance companies, could not question their valuation. An additional virtue of this arrangement, from Birrell's point of view, was that the insurance companies used the overvalued securities to inflate their reserves. This enabled them to take on more business and thereby earn more income—of which Birrell and Hopps, of course, got their cut.

For a while things went swimmingly. True, the other directors of Rhode Island Insurance balked at some of the cats and dogs Birrell offered it for its investment portfolio. When they did, Birrell simply slipped them into the reserves of one of the other insurance companies, where his control was unchallenged.

The same old cats and dogs

But he could not continue this deception indefinitely. For the main business of these other companies consisted of reinsuring risks underwritten by Rhode Island. And by 1948, Rhode Island's directors were acutely aware of the fact that when they called on the companies for cash or securities to help meet loss claims, they got the same overvalued and often quite unmarketable securities that they had turned down for their own portfolios.

At this point, the directors indignantly canceled the company's agreements with Birrell's insurance firms. But their action came too late. Rhode Island's financial strength was badly impaired and the company was soon in court custody. It is now defunct.

Claude Neon survived Birrell's regime, but not without suffering heavy damage. He relinquished control of the company in 1949 and withdrew from the management of its affairs. Suspecting belatedly that Birrell had been stealing the company blind, a group of stockholders had already begun legal action against him. In 1958, after nine years of litigation, a federal court ordered Birrell to pay Claude Neon $3,256,639.40 for frauds committed against the company. So far the company hasn't collected a cent.

Although the Claude Neon affair might seem sufficiently complex to have demanded Birrell's undivided attention, the fact is that he had been simultaneously engaged in other and equally complicated dealings. He was becoming more and more adept at selling trashy securities to publicly held corporations he controlled, and at concealing his part in such transactions by the use of dummy nominees, interlocking holding companies, and foreign bank accounts. He was not averse to pulling the same trick more than once, and his success at Claude Neon in using insurance companies to bilk stockholders encouraged him to attempt a second major coup of the same kind.

Next victim: United Dye

This time the company selected for the Claude Neon role was United Dye & Chemical Corp., a manufacturer of logwood dyes. In 1951, at the invitation of the company's controlling stockholder, David S. Fischman, Birrell went on the board of United Dye. Two years later he acquired Fischman's interest.

Birrell then began looking around for a man to put in nominal charge of the company's affairs—someone who would be amenable to suggestions (from Birrell) but who would also exude an air of respectability. The man Birrell settled on was Virgil Dardi, a native Californian who for many years had been associated with the Bank of America. At this time Dardi was president of a very substantial company, Blair Holdings Corp., but he was not happy in his job. The cause of his unhappiness was Birrell's old friend, Serge Rubinstein. In making a deal with one of Rubinstein's companies, Blair had unwittingly overvalued certain Canadian oil properties, and Rubinstein was demanding huge penalty payments. Blair seemed likely to lose several million dollars in the deal, and its directors were making no secret of the fact that they held Dardi responsible.

Birrell, who had been watching this situation develop, realized Dardi might soon be in the market for a new job, and in 1953, after the two men had met at a cocktail party, Birrell offered him one. As Dardi recalls the conversation, Birrell spoke enthusiastically about his plan to make something really exciting out of old United Dye, and said he would like Dardi's help.

Dardi now insists that he was completely taken in by Birrell. To begin with, although Birrell himself was involved (somewhat remotely) in the Rubinstein-Blair Holdings deal, Dardi says he was unaware that Birrell even knew Rubinstein. Furthermore, he argues, he had no reason to suspect a man who was vouched for by Blair's own counsel, Thomas A. Halleran. Halleran, a member of the distinguished old Wall Street law firm of Cravath, Swaine & Moore, was also counsel to one of Birrell's companies, and when Dardi mentioned Birrell's proposal, Halleran said he thought Dardi might provide just the kind of stabilizing influence Birrell needed at United Dye. Dardi soon agreed to become chairman.

The tax-savings bait

United Dye had recently acquired a subsidiary, Camden Forge, which was earning around $2,500,000 a year before taxes. Two-thirds of its earnings, however, were being paid out in regular and excess-profits taxes. Birrell pointed out to Dardi and the other directors that United Dye could realize big tax savings if it would set up or acquire some insurance companies, which have a special status under the tax laws, and transfer into their reserves the earnings of Camden Forge.

The board was delighted with this notion. United Dye organized one insurance company, Guardian Insurance Co., and acquired another, Central Standard of South Dakota. Birrell then arranged to have these companies linked by reinsurance agreements to certain other insurance companies that he himself controlled. Most of these were currently inactive companies Birrell had picked up during his years at Claude Neon. One, however, was a flourishing concern, control of which Birrell had just acquired from his old associate Stewart Hopps. This company was Inland Empire Insurance of Boise, Idaho. Inland Empire and Central Standard were to play the role that had been assigned to Rhode Island Insurance in the Claude Neon scheme —that is, to generate new business, which the other companies would then reinsure.

From Birrell's standpoint, these arrangements had some familiar advantages. Cash and good securities in the reserves of Inland Empire and Central Standard (some of which United Dye had contributed as capital) were transferred to companies that were simply corporate fronts for Birrell himself. In exchange, Inland Empire and Central Standard received the same sort of trash that had wrecked Rhode Island Insurance.

But there were a few new ingredients in the mixture this time. Rhode Island's difficulties had given state insurance commissioners an insight into Birrell's methods, and he had to take special measures to divert their suspicions. Good assets were temporarily substituted for bad ones when a state examiner was due to look at the books. Securities that would not pass muster in South Dakota, and were therefore no good to Central Standard, were parked in the reserves of companies in other states where standards were laxer, or where no examination was imminent. Officers of companies controlled by Birrell further confused the examiners by altering the minutes of directors' meetings, hiding important documents, and, on one occasion, hastily transferring all records to another state.

Virgil Dardi's slow take

While all this was going on, Virgil Dardi was serving as chairman of Central Standard, as well as of its parent, United Dye. Nevertheless, Dardi claims it was many months before he suspected what Birrell was up to—i.e., watering the assets of United Dye through its insurance operations.

But evidence of Birrell's misdoings was mounting. By the summer of 1955, it was clear to United Dye's other directors that the company had dropped nearly $2 million on its insurance venture, and that Birrell was responsible. Birrell agreed to resign from the board. He further agreed to buy out United Dye's insurance interests, but later he defaulted on the payments and United Dye took a $1,500,000 loss. In 1955, Birrell also abandoned Inland Empire. Claims against the company were piling up, the assets Birrell had foisted on it were proving to be nearly worthless, and before long the company was in receivership. Inland Empire's receiver later sued, for a total of $2,600,000, two companies formerly controlled by Birrell; the chances of recovery seem rather slim.

Some time in mid-1955, Birrell sold most of his United Dye stock. Dardi's version of this transaction, in which he again casts himself as the innocent dupe of predatory financiers, has a special interest. As Dardi tells it, Birrell had just resigned from United Dye's board, and Dardi, in the interest of economy, had decided to sublease some unused office space at United Dye's headquarters in New York. One of the prospective tenants who showed up, an owlish-looking man of about forty, was interested not only in the space, but in Dardi's desk —an imposing mahogany piece that he said looked very much like his own. The two men chatted a while, and Dardi mentioned the trouble he had been having with Birrell and said he was eager to find somebody who would buy Birrell out. The visitor said he himself might be interested in acquiring Birrell's United Dye holdings. A few days later he did so, and Dardi had a new boss. His name was Alexander Guterma.

Like Birrell, Guterma got a lot of mileage out of United Dye, but in a different way. Guterma's operations will be described in the next chapter.

Slot machines in exurbia

In 1955, Birrell's career was in full and brilliant flower. He moved in an atmosphere of big money and big affairs. He had a suite at the Park Lane in New York and a flat in Havana. Sometimes he chartered a 100-foot yacht. He employed nearly forty people on his Bucks County estate, Echo Falls Farm, which he had recently enlarged by buying up adjoining property from such prominent exurbanites as Moss Hart and Budd Schulberg. (Before Stewart Hopps moved to California in 1951, he was also a neighbor of Birrell's.) The amenities at Echo Falls included a swimming pool, riding horses, and slot machines. One visitor of this period recalls that the machines didn't seem to pay off very often.

Birrell's business activities were extensive and richly complicated. In furtherance of his schemes, he constantly shifted assets from one corporate or financial pocket to another. At one bank alone, a branch of the Manufacturers Trust Co. located in midtown Manhattan, he controlled (directly or indirectly) nearly a hundred accounts. He devised his own legal stratagems, and continued to list himself in *Who's Who in America* as a lawyer; he was a partner in the law firm of Birrell & Larson, which was in fact Birrell himself (Larson was in semi-retirement), and which had for its principal clients companies that Birrell controlled.

All in all, there were twenty or more such companies. Some, like Greater New York Industries, Inc., the successor to the old Fidelio Brewery, were holding companies. Others, like Echo Falls Oil Co. or Royal Pharmacal Corp., were used by Birrell to generate the dubious securities he liked to sell at such big markups. But in 1955 Birrell was also in control of two substantial publicly held corporations. These companies were to command much of Birrell's attention during the next two years. One was Doeskin Products, a manufacturer of facial tissues; the other was Swan-Finch Oil Corp.

Buying Doeskin with Doeskin

Birrell had actually been in control of Doeskin since 1947. He had acquired this control in a characteristic Birrell deal: he had used the company's own assets to buy control of it. Specifically, he had contrived to sell Doeskin certain securities, and then used the proceeds, amounting to just under $2 million, to buy out the previously controlling stockholders. Certain other stockholders, however, complained that some of the securities Doeskin had acquired in the deal —e.g., debentures of a mysterious enterprise called the Beverly Hills Cemetery, located in Peekskill, New York—were much overvalued, if not actually worthless. These stockholders sued Birrell and others associated with him in the deal (including Hopps), and in 1951 Birrell agreed to pay Doeskin some $200,000. Birrell had meanwhile given Doeskin's operating executives a free hand with the business, and between 1947 and 1955 Doeskin's sales rose from under $12 million to almost $19 million.

Swan-Finch, when Birrell got control of it, was a much smaller company than Doeskin. Established in 1853 to distribute fats and sperm oil, its product line in later years had consisted of industrial oils and greases. In 1954, when Birrell paid $240,000 to buy 40 per cent of the company's outstanding stock, Swan-Finch had a sales volume of only about $3 million a year, and it was losing money. But from Birrell's point of view, Swan-Finch had one great attraction: it enjoyed unlisted trading privileges on the American Stock Exchange. That is, its stock was traded there, but it was not required to furnish the exchange with the detailed financial information required of fully listed companies. (When a Swan-Finch stockholder naively suggested at an annual meeting that the company's stock be fully listed, Birrell asked rhetorically: "What the hell do you want to do? Have us tell our secrets to everybody?")

Birrell's designs for Doeskin and Swan-Finch were on a grand scale. His plan, it now appears, was this: to issue secretly to himself hundreds of thousands of watery new shares of Doeskin and Swan-Finch stock, theoretically worth tens of millions of dollars, and to unload these shares on the public.

"From Fish-Oil to Fission"

To whet the public's appetite for Swan-Finch stock, which was not so well known to investors as Doeskin, Birrell took two important steps. First he prevailed upon a widely known business executive, Robert F. Six, to serve as chairman of Swan-Finch; Six, who was president of Continental Air Lines—and, incidentally, the husband of Ethel Merman—seems to have been quite unaware of Birrell's real intentions. Next Birrell initiated a legitimate program of expansion and diversification. He negotiated mergers that gave Swan-Finch ownership of gas fields in Pennsylvania, uranium mining leases near Grants, New Mexico, and a grain-storage terminal in Olean, New York. Swan-Finch also acquired some 200,000 shares of Doeskin stock, representing control of Doeskin. These shares had been owned by Birrell's Greater New York Industries, and in exchange for them Swan-Finch issued 500,000 shares of its own stock to Greater New York.

To acquaint investors with these developments, Swan-Finch ran a series of five-column advertisements in the financial section of the New York *Times* in the spring of 1956. One of these advertisements carried a headline reading "In 103 years . . . we've expanded from Fish-Oil to Fission" (that is, from whale oil to uranium-mining leases). The company's leap into the atomic age was illustrated by drawings of a spouting whale and a mushroom-shaped cloud.

All this had the desired effect of stimulating a brisk demand for Swan-Finch stock. To satisfy this demand, Birrell now initiated certain transactions intended to give him possession of large blocks of new Swan-Finch stock. He also acted to get his hands on a lot of new Doeskin stock. Birrell achieved these aims in his usual complicated fashion—and apparently without the knowledge or consent of most of the other directors of Doeskin and Swan-Finch.

There were three principal transactions:

▶ In May, 1956, Birrell had Swan-Finch issue 300,000 shares of stock to acquire the capital stock of Equitable Plan, an industrial-loan company in California. From the point of view of Swan-Finch stockholders, there were at least two things wrong with this deal: (1) the 300,000 shares of stock went to Birrell, who controlled the Panamanian corporation from which Swan-Finch acquired Equitable Plan; and (2) Birrell was getting roughly $2 million worth of stock for a property he had picked up for an investment of $250,000.

▶ In December, 1956, Birrell had Doeskin issue 700,000 shares of its stock. The stock was ostensibly issued to a subsidiary of Swan-Finch, in exchange for the stock of another Swan-Finch subsidiary called Keta Gas & Oil. But the 700,000 shares of Doeskin never reached the treasury of Swan-Finch, or of the subsidiary, Swan-Finch

Gas Development Corp., which supposedly had been the owner of Keta Gas. Instead, the shares ended up in Birrell's possession.

▶ In January, 1957, 700,000 shares of Swan-Finch, with a market value of over $2 million, were issued by a roundabout route to a Birrell-owned company called County Equities, Inc. In exchange, Swan-Finch received all the outstanding shares of Rockton Drilling Corp. This was a company whose capital stock Birrell had acquired at a sheriff's auction for less than $1000. Rockton had subsequently acquired some substantial assets, but they had been pledged as collateral for loans to Birrell.

All together, these transactions gave Birrell possession of 700,000 newly issued shares of Doeskin stock, worth around $8 million at the market price then prevailing; and one million shares of newly issued Swan-Finch stock, theoretically worth about $4 million. Obviously, Birrell could not make a formal public offering of this stock, for which an SEC registration statement would be required. If the stock were to be sold to the public, he would have to sell it indirectly, and one way to do this was to disguise the origin of the stock and sell it through brokers.

The compliant admiral

That is what Birrell did, for instance, with many of the 700,000 shares of Doeskin stock that were issued in the Keta Gas deal. He did it this way: First, in his capacity as chairman of Doeskin, Birrell instructed Doeskin's transfer agent, Manufacturers Trust Co., to issue the stock to Swan-Finch Gas Development Corp. At the same time, counsel for Doeskin—it was actually Birrell's own firm, Birrell & Larson—notified the bank that the shares were being acquired for long-term investment, not for public sale, and that consequently they need not be registered with the SEC. The bank issued seven certificates, each representing 100,000 shares of Doeskin, and Birrell asked the president of Swan-Finch Gas Development, a lawyer and retired rear admiral named Roy Callahan, to sign a receipt for the shares. Callahan, who has since admitted that he usually signed anything Birrell put in front of him, did what Birrell asked. Three days later, also at Birrell's request, he endorsed the certificates over to Birrell. He never saw the shares again.

Less than ten days after the stock was first issued, Manufacturers Trust was instructed to reissue the shares in certificates of smaller denominations and to transfer them to various Canadian nominees. It struck one of the officers of Manufacturers Trust as a little odd that shares supposedly acquired for long-term investment should be broken up into relatively small packages. But when he consulted the bank's law firm, he was told there was no ground for refusing to comply with the instructions. The shares were accordingly reissued, and the new certificates were sent up to Canada. Later, acting through intermediaries, Birrell had the stock shipped back to the U.S. for resale by New York brokers. These moves were designed to conceal the fact that the stock was newly issued: for all the New York brokers could tell, the certificates they received represented long-outstanding shares of Doeskin for whose sale no registration was required.

Birrell disposed of most of his Swan-Finch stock by a different and less devious route. He (or his nominees) simply posted it with a group of moneylenders as collateral for loans totaling $1,500,000. Then he defaulted on the loans, and the lenders began unloading the stock.

Off to Havana

It was the cascade of Swan-Finch stock which began pouring onto the U.S. market in December, 1956, that got Birrell into his principal legal difficulties. In April, 1957, the SEC moved for an injunction to halt the public sale of this stock. At this point the SEC was not contending that the stock had been improperly issued, or that it might not have belonged to Birrell. Whatever suspicions the commission may have had on this score, all it was claiming was that Birrell was using moneylenders as middlemen in an illegal transaction: i.e., to circumvent the law requiring the controlling stockholders of a company to register with the SEC any stock they offer to the public.

After months of legal skirmishing, Birrell was served with a subpoena, calling for his appearance as a trial witness in New York on October 7, 1957. The subpoena was handed to him at La Guardia Airport on the morning of October 4. (He had just flown in from Canada.) Later that day Birrell left by plane for Havana to begin a long period of self-imposed exile.

The peripatetic exile

Birrell's departure from the U.S. by no means signified his retirement from business affairs. He made his headquarters in Cuba, where he had interests in a racetrack and an oil company. He seemed to have plenty of money. In Havana he was frequently seen in nightclubs and casinos. He made a bewildering number of quick trips out of Cuba. At least once he flew to Canada and drove down to Echo Falls for a short visit. Although a bench warrant had been issued for his arrest in the U.S., he was not picked up. He was often in Europe, moving restlessly from country to country. In October, 1958, he was in Paris on the ninth, London on the eleventh, Geneva on the twelfth, London on the fourteenth, Paris on the fifteenth, Montreal on the sixteenth, and Paris again on the seventeenth. He ran up huge telephone bills. During a three-day stay at the Ritz-Carlton in Montreal he put in more than a hundred long-distance calls. He made several trips to Brazil, and in the spring of 1958 he was granted a permanent residence permit there. He listed an obscure local weekly as his employer; the publisher later admitted he got $50 for signing an employment certificate.

In the U.S. it was finally becoming clear that Birrell had done more than just evade SEC registration requirements. In California, state authorities belatedly discovered that Equitable Plan had loaned at least $5 million, on virtually worthless collateral, to other companies controlled by Birrell. Equitable went into bankruptcy.

In New York, stockholders of Swan-Finch started legal action to recover for the corporation such assets as Keta Gas & Oil Co., which Birrell, to put it politely, appeared to have given away to Doeskin. (The controlling stock in Doeskin that Swan-Finch had once theoretically held also disappeared; it had all been pledged as collateral for loans to various Birrell companies and then sold out when the loans were defaulted.) Swan-Finch went into bankruptcy. Its trustees, convinced that Birrell had been stealing right and left, pressed the authorities to prosecute him on criminal charges. This seemed the only way to get him back in the country, and to find out what he had done with Swan-Finch's property. In July, 1959, a New York County grand jury indicted Birrell for grand larceny. The indictment contained sixty-nine counts, and charged him with misappropriating in various ways some two million shares of Doeskin and Swan-Finch stock.

Birrell's whereabouts in July were not known to the New York police. (He was actually in Paris.) Later they learned that he was in Rio de Janeiro, and at their request the Brazilian police arrested him for questioning. Since Brazil and the U.S. had no extradition treaty, and since Birrell had a Brazilian residence permit, there seemed at first to be no grounds for holding him. Then the police found that Birrell had entered Brazil on an invalid Canadian passport made out in the name of Lowell McAfee—McAfee is his middle name—and they decided to hold him for possible deportation.

At first, Birrell spoke of going back to the U.S. voluntarily. He was quoted as saying he was "broken, broken, broken." But he quickly recovered his nerve and hired the same Brazilian lawyer, Jorge Chaloupe, who had previously blocked the deportation from Brazil of the precocious Earl Belle.

With Chaloupe's help Birrell began a vigorous legal and propaganda campaign to keep from being thrown out of the country. In talks with Brazilian newspapermen and politicians, Chaloupe hammered away at the notions that Birrell had used a phony passport only to "save his life from Castro firing squads in Cuba"; that Birrell was wanted in the U.S. only in connection with some trifling tax matters; that he had really come to Brazil to invest $14 million (sometimes it was $20 million) in new industries; and that powerful U.S. interests were bent on thwarting this project. Birrell and Chaloupe even seized the offensive against the SEC momentarily. When an SEC investigator, Edward Jaegerman, showed up in Rio de Janeiro, Chaloupe filed a criminal slander suit against him on the ground that he had made slighting remarks about Birrell to reporters. The suit was tossed out of court, but not without causing the SEC a good deal of embarrassment.

Prison can be fun

Birrell remained in prison in Rio de Janeiro until October 1959, when he was released. Even while he was in jail, he lived in style. He paid fellow prisoners to take care of his room and clothes, dressed elegantly, had his own innerspring mattress and bedding, and had his meals sent in from expensive restaurants.

It is possible that even in jail Birrell was living a good deal better than some of the stockholders of U.S. companies he once controlled. It might be noted, however, that Claude Neon, now renamed Dynamics Corp. of America, has recovered nicely; it makes electronic equipment and household appliances, and in 1961 it earned $1,922,-714 on sales of $47,517,284. United Dye changed its name to Chemoil Industries and Virgil Dardi, struggling to salvage something of his reputation as a banker, managed to show some profits in Chemoil before merging it in early 1962 into Szabo Food Service, Inc.

The situation at both Doeskin and Swan-Finch is rather ambiguous. Right up until November 1960, over a year after his flight to Brazil, it appeared that Birrell continued to control Doeskin's affairs. But its sales continued to decline, hitting $12 million, a drop of one-third in a four year period. In November, 1960 the court appointed a fiscal agent to run Doeskin's affairs. Prospects improved almost at once, and in 1961 sales bounced back to $15 million and the Union Bag-Camp Paper Co. stepped forward with an offer of $5.6 million to buy all Doeskin's assets. The offer was turned down by the court on the grounds that, following such a splendid improvement, the present management should have a longer period to run the company. The bankrupt Swan-Finch was deeper in trouble. In April, 1962, the court-appointed trustees, with no solution of their own, invited reorganization suggestions from any source—an offer that must have sounded like a challenge to Birrell's fertile imagination and sense of fun, even from a distance. Particularly since Swan-Finch still claims it is the legitimate controlling stockholder of the recuperating Doeskin Corp. Stockholders of another Birrell corporation, Greater New York Industries, the first real company Birrell ever got hold of, are also in a baffling fix. One stockholder recently spent a couple of days trying to find the company. It wasn't at the address listed by the New York Department of State, and diligent research failed to locate its officers, lawyers, books, records, or corporate seal. Apparently it had vanished without a trace.

Birrell's name still pops up in the newspapers from time to time, usually in connection with some newly discovered swindle. In 1960 he was indicted again, this time for embezzlement. In 1961 he was indicted a third time, for having defrauded Doeskin of the proceeds of the 1957 sale. This last indictment may be the most dangerous of all for Birrell, since it came *after* the U.S. had finally signed an extradition treaty with Brazil. (The treaty was signed on January 13, 1961.) Lawyers are not entirely clear as to his jeopardy in this new situation. But if there is any possible means of avoiding retribution, Birrell is certain to find it.

9

Who Is Alexander Guterma?

During the last several years, the U.S. financial community has heard a lot about a bespectacled, egg-bald man in his forties who says he comes from Irkutsk. Most of the time, he has been in a great deal of trouble. He has been under four separate indictments, and is charged with such varied offenses as violating the laws relating to securities trading; inducing an officer of a federally chartered bank to "injure and defraud" the bank; and failing to register as an agent of the Dominican Republic. In February, 1960, he was sent to prison for withholding required financial reports from the SEC and he was in prison as this book went to press. He has loudly averred that these indictments are frame-ups, and he has been working hard to have all the charges dismissed. Nevertheless, it is hard to foresee the time when the man who calls himself Alexander Guterma will be out of trouble.

Elementary facts about his background are unknown to the officials who have been prosecuting him and even, it appears, to men who have been in business with him for years. They are not at all clear as to when or where he was actually born, or what his real name is, or what he was doing before 1950—the year he appeared on the U.S. financial scene. Reporters who pressed him for biographical data were consistently rebuffed. The press was persecuting him, he bitterly complained. The complaint was delivered in an odd-sounding drawl that sometimes suggested the Deep South, sometimes New York's Lower East Side.

One thing is clear about Guterma: in the past decade he has transacted a great deal of business with men who subsequently got into trouble with the law. Guterma once bought a company from Lowell Birrell, the swindler and stock manipulator. Guterma once sold a company to BenJack Cage, a Texan subsequently convicted of embezzlement and now, like Birrell, residing in Brazil. Guterma crossed the path of Earl Belle, another recent émigré to Brazil, at the Security National Bank of Huntington, Long Island. Belle is accused of taking the bank for $475,000; it is the opinion of some government investigators that he had been introduced to the bank president by a man named Irving Pasternak, who was an associate of Guterma's, and who was named as co-conspirator in a stock fraud case. At the very least, it may be said, Guterma has had remarkably bad luck in picking the company that he moves in.

Guterma did not begin to make the headlines until after he was in trouble, and the extent of his empire before that trouble began is still not widely realized. But the fact is that at one point in 1956 he controlled the stock, and was the chief executive officer, of three corporations that were listed on the New York Stock Exchange. (Officials of the exchange can recall no other individual who ever approached this record.) All of them were old, established companies. One of them, United Dye & Chemical Corp. (now called Chemoil Industries, Inc.), had taken a severe mauling from Birrell before Guterma acquired it, but the extent of the former's depredations—he had got United into the insurance business, then invested the funds held as insurance reserves in his own cats and dogs—was not known to the public. Another Guterma company was Bon Ami, whose cleaning compounds had been famous household products since the turn of the century. The third was F. L. Jacobs, a manufacturer of automobile parts.

The man with pine paneling

These Big Board enterprises were by no means the only irons Guterma had in the fire when he was at his peak. His other interests in the mid-1950s included these:

• Shawano Development Corp., of which he was the founder and controlling stockholder. In 1955, Shawano's diverse assets included land in Florida, cattle, a textile mill, a uranium concentrating mill, a mercury mine, and oil reserves.

• McGrath Securities, a brokerage firm that he had founded in 1953 (McGrath was his wife's maiden name). The firm became a major dealer in over-the-counter securities, especially those of Guterma-organized companies.

• Micro-Moisture Controls, Inc., founded by Guterma in 1953. At first it made special electronic controls, later diversified into steel scrap, aluminum awnings, and appliance manufacturing.

• Chatco Steel Products, Ltd., an established company with two plants in Canada. Guterma acquired virtually all its stock in 1956, and used his "corner" to drive the price up from $3.30 to $16.75 a share. This tactic understandably infuriated a group of Canadian investors who had sold the stock short; and, as we shall see, their reprisals played an important part in Guterma's later troubles.

While he was on top, Guterma lived the way a mogul is supposed to live. He owned an English Tudor establishment in Greenwich, Connecticut, and had two or three Cadillacs and a Dual Ghia sports car, a ninety-foot yacht on which he frequently cruised along the Florida coast, and a Convair plane. An official of the Securities and Exchange Commission recalls that Guterma once terminated an interview with him by remarking that he was rushing off to Palm Beach in his plane. The official asked what kind of plane it was, but Guterma couldn't remember. "I really don't know," he said, with an impatient gesture. "It has pine paneling."

Sandy McSande from Siberia

The Guterma of the mid-1950s was an overwhelmingly self-confident man who had a wide circle of friends, and enjoyed taking them on pleasure trips aboard his yacht and also to obscure little coffeehouses and restaurants on New York's Lower East Side—for a man who was supposed to have arrived in the U.S. only a few years earlier, Guterma had a remarkable fund of information about New York. In fact, he knew a lot about a great many different subjects, including professional baseball and boxing, and the works of Shakespeare, and was accustomed to doing most of the talking. One former business associate recalls that "He didn't listen much to what *you* said and he spoke as though *he* were omniscient." He spoke at least six and possibly nine languages; the number is uncertain, but in addition to English, he spoke Chinese, Russian, Spanish, German, and the Tagalog of the indigenous Filipinos, and he had a command of obscenity, breath-taking in its explicitness, in several of these languages. Now that Guterma's background has been called into question, and he has pretty much stopped talking, his friends of the mid-1950s are acutely aware of the fact that they never really did know much about him.

What they did know—or what, at any rate, he was then telling people —was that he had been born in 1915 in Irkutsk, in Czarist Siberia. He said that his father was a general in the Russian Army, and that his mother was of Polish origin. It is unclear what happened to his father, but Guterma has referred at times to childhood trips with his mother to Poland, then to Germany, then back across Siberia to Harbin, in Manchuria, and later to China. Guterma says that he received his elementary education at a missionary school in Tsingtao, China, and, very plausibly, cites his cosmopolitan childhood as the reason for his linguistic virtuosity.

Thus far the story is unverifiable but not suspicious; after all, there were thousands of stateless refugees from Russia in the Far East in the 1930s. But the story of his life takes an odd turn when it comes to the year 1935. Immigration officials found him in that year working in Honolulu, which he had entered illegally. At first he told them that he was an American named Sandy McSande. ("Sandy" has been his nickname much of his life.) When the officials checked up on him, they found that he was working in a radio-repair shop and using the name Alexander Guterman—with an "n." At different times he had told his employer different stories about his age—sometimes he was eighteen, sometimes twenty. He had also told his employer that he came from Brooklyn. There were never any formal deportation proceedings brought against him, and he slipped out of Honolulu by stowing away on a boat bound for China.

Tales of the Far East

His activities over the next six years are largely unknown. Many of the wildest rumors about Guterma relate to the years 1935–41—when he was presumably in his early twenties. According to one intriguing story, Guterma had a remarkable familiarity with the operations of pirates off the Chinese coast in the late 1930s—a familiarity he had acquired in the course of backing some of these pirates, much as English investors in the sixteenth century used to back the freebooters who prowled the Spanish Main. (Questioned about this story a few years ago, Guterma retorted that this was a smear invented by his enemies.) At one point during the Sino-Japanese war, he is supposed to have been operating a fleet of fishing vessels out of Shanghai, apparently with the permission of Japanese officials—who let his ships pass through the blockade of the port after they were registered under the Czechoslovakian flag. Another rumor has it that he was in New York during the latter 1930s, and was again using the name Guterman, with the "n."

His tracks through the 1940s are a bit clearer. He was caught in the Philippines at the time of Pearl Harbor and was at first placed in a concentration camp. But later he established to the satisfaction of the Japanese that he was not an American, and they released him and allowed him to conduct several business operations in Pasay, south of Manila, during the war. One of these seems to have been a fairly posh gambling establishment, another a commissary store, which catered to Japanese servicemen. At the end of the war he was moderately prosperous.

In 1945 he was accused by U.S. counterintelligence of being a collaborationist. A good deal of mystery still surrounds the details of these charges, and their final disposition; but it is at least clear that Guterma was never convicted on them. In the postwar years he turned up as a manager of several companies controlled by J. Amado Araneta, a wealthy and powerful Filipino industrialist. He was also speculating in several commodities, and possibly in currency too. By 1950, Guterma was worth perhaps $450,000.

Meanwhile, he had married an American woman named Anita McGrath, the daughter of Robert McGrath, whose family owned a shoe-manufacturing company in the Philippines. In August, 1950, the Gutermas came to the U.S., and Guterma applied for citizenship. (He was finally naturalized in 1956.) They bought a house in Los Angeles, but stayed only a few days. Then Guterma decided that there were bigger opportunities in the East, and he sold his house (at a profit of $8000) and moved to New York.

The kenaf and ramie game

His first business move was to organize a holding company called Western Financial Corp., whose assets consisted of Guterma's cash and a few small items in his portfolio. Although he had broken with Araneta, he now had backing from other Filipino businessmen; using their money and some of the resources of Western Financial, he bought a large tract of land in Florida, some forty miles northwest of Palm Beach. It was his plan to use the land to grow kenaf and ramie, fibers that have several special advantages but are hard to process. The principal problem is the high cost of decorticating the fibers; this is what has made both of them uneconomical in most Western nations.

At first the venture enjoyed a limited success, and some of the ramie produced was sold to a Japanese company. Within a year, about 920 acres of land were under cultivation, and a processing mill was in operation. All together, some $860,000 had been invested, of which $140,000 was Guterma's. But in 1952, Guterma appears to have decided that the project involved too heavy a risk and two small a return, and he pulled out. The Filipino investors tried for a while to maintain the property, but they found it impossible to supervise from abroad. Finally, in early 1953, Guterma offered to find an American investor willing to buy them out.

The investor he came up with was Foremost Dairies, of Jacksonville. A deal was worked out whereby Foremost got 1400 acres of grazing land; the Filipino investors were released from all mortgages and other obligations; and Guterma himself got the ramie-processing mill and the 920 acres of land that were under cultivation. This property became the principal asset of Shawano Development Corp., a company that Guterma organized in November, 1953, establishing himself as president.

Like many companies Guterma founded or got control of, Shawano was to play the leading role in a stock-promotion plan. To equip Shawano for the part, he recruited some fairly well-known people to serve on its board. They included John K. Colgate, a director of Colgate-Palmolive; and the Honorable Charley E. Johns, who was governor of Florida at the time Shawano was organized. Guterma also took steps to establish a market for Shawano's stock. The required offering circulars were filed with the SEC, and 116,000 shares were sold over the counter, mainly on the representation that ramie had a great past (according to one circular, "the ancient Egyptians used it to wrap mummies") and a greater future.

Oil, milk, and uranium

This trickle of shares was only the harbinger of a mighty torrent of Shawano stock. In 1955, Guterma went on a merger kick, issuing new shares in wholesale lots in exchange for a heterogeneous assortment of properties. In less than six months Shawano acquired a dairy herd in Florida; mercury-mining claims in Nevada and Oregon; a Miami resort hotel called the Isle de Capri; uranium deposits in an area of Wyoming called Poison Basin; and sixty-three oil wells in Kansas and Wyoming. The oil wells were acquired in a merger with a company called Garnak Drilling, whose principal stockholders, Samuel Garfield and Irving Pasternak, were to do business with Guterma on several later occasions. Both men have been questioned in a federal investigation of organized gambling, and Garfield was once fined $500 and costs for running a gambling establishment in his offices in Evansville, Indiana.

All these acquisitions were part of a process whereby millions of shares of Shawano stock, none of which had been registered with the SEC, were funneled into the hands of the public. Actually, stock issued to effect a merger, or to acquire the assets of another corporation, need not under certain conditions be registered—even if it is later sold to the public. So far as the SEC could tell at the time, the deals engineered by Guterma met these conditions, the principal one being a requirement that a merger or acquisition must not be simply an intermediate step in a public stock distribution. Nevertheless, most of the businessmen whom Guterma persuaded to accept Shawano stock in return for hotels or uranium leases took the stock only on assurances that there would be a market for it.

Stoking the boilers

Distribution of this stock to the public was effected mainly by high-pressure salesmen working the telephones in New York boiler rooms. Guterma himself helped to stoke the fires by writing optimistic reports and letters, one of which noted that over a five-month period "the book value of our stock has more than quadruplicated [sic]." He was also successful in inducing other people to talk up Shawano. On August 31, 1955, the financial editor of the New York *World-Telegram and Sun,* Ralph Hendershot, devoted a whole column to Shawano and to Guterma's "careful and expert handling" of its affairs. (A year later Hendershot left his job to become chairman, at $25,000 a year, of a company controlled by BenJack Cage.) Shawano stock was also rhapsodically touted by Pierre DuVal, the proprietor of a market advisory service called *DuVal's Consensus.* In a report marked "for confidential use of subscribers only," DuVal noted that "THIS STOCK IS READY TO MOVE—NOW," and he went on to praise Shawano's "dynamic program of carefully planned expansion and diversification"; its "miracle" fiber, ramie ("strong enough for tarpaulin, yet sheer enough for a negligee"); its "fabulously valuable uranium claims"; and its "oil 'sleeper' which alone is worth *several dollars on every share.*"

The rich prose lavished on Shawano had the desired effect, and some 15,000 Americans invested in the company. All together they may have bought nearly 18 million shares of its stock, most of it at from $1 to $2 a share. Unfortunately for the investors, it turned out that many of the claims made on behalf of Shawano had been greatly exaggerated. Guterma, for example, had widely disseminated the notion that Shawano had oil reserves totaling 20 million barrels. The correct figure, the SEC later held, was more like two million barrels. In 1956, Shawano's oil properties were placed in a separate company, Diversified Oil & Mining, whose stock was then distributed to Shawano's shareholders. In 1957, Diversified lost $562,000, and by the end of 1958 its stock, which had once sold for $2.50 a share, was quoted at 8 cents bid. Meanwhile, Shawano had disposed of its Florida properties, and was dissipating its remaining assets in an unsuccessful attempt to develop its uranium deposits. In 1957, Guterma abandoned Shawano and it later went into bankruptcy. A last echo of Guterma's efforts for Shawano was sounded late in 1961, when Edward McCormich resigned as head of the American Stock Exchange. It was revealed at the time that McCormich had earlier allowed Guterma to pick up some of his gambling debts—at a time when Guterma was trying (unsuccessfully) to get an A.S.E. listing for Shawano.

People like Garfield and Pasternak, to whom Shawano stock was issued in the first instance, and who then resold it to the public, were not the only ones to profit by Guterma's scheme. Guterma himself had a lot of stock to sell. When Shawano was organized, he got several hundred thousand shares for virtually nothing, and later he got a few hundred thousand more by selling to Shawano (for stock) land and other properties of which he was the principal owner. (This stock was later split four for one.) Moreover, the mergers provided huge batches of stock that could profitably be retailed by McGrath Securities, the over-the-counter firm Guterma had founded in 1953, which the SEC has characterized as "essentially . . . a boiler-room operation from its inception." In 1955, Guterma sold his interest in McGrath to the firm's president, Robert C. Leonhardt. But McGrath continued enthusiastically to peddle watery stock in companies Guterma had organized.

Shares for BenJack

One of these companies, Diversified Financial Corp., has an intriguing corporate history. It was founded by Guterma in 1950, but he did little with it until 1955. Then he had more than a million shares of its stock issued in exchange for certain properties owned by Ben-Jack Cage. Soon afterward, Cage took over control of Diversified

...l, changed its name to Consolidated American Industries, ...alled himself as president and Ralph Hendershot, the ex-newspaperman, as chairman. (Hendershot later turned up running something called the Stock of the Month Club.)

McGrath's salesmen, who had been plugging the company's stock for months, spoke warmly of its fine new management and of a diversification program that included flyers in Panamanian oil and Mexican sulfur. But while McGrath and other dealers sold millions of shares of Consolidated American at prices as high as $2 a share, Cage was in fact looting the company. By October, 1957, when Cage was convicted of embezzling $100,000 from a Texas insurance firm, Consolidated American's assets had mostly disappeared, and the company was in bankruptcy.

Another company that Guterma organized, and whose stock was peddled by McGrath Securities, was Micro-Moisture Controls. Micro-Moisture was founded in 1953 to manufacture electronic controls, among them a device to make the top of a convertible go up automatically at the first drop of rain. Between 1954 and 1957, several million shares of Micro-Moisture stock were sold to the public at around $1 a share. Most of this stock was issued in mergers. In 1957 the SEC accused McGrath of violating the securities laws by selling stock generated in one of these mergers, which the commission held was simply a ruse for distributing stock to the public without filing a registration statement. The SEC also accused McGrath of making false representations about Micro-Moisture—e.g., that it had big contracts with Ford and General Motors. The following year the SEC revoked McGrath's registration as a securities dealer, and the firm went out of business. By this time Micro-Moisture, which had consistently lost money, was bankrupt.

Moving up in the world

In 1955, Guterma took a step that improved his standing in the financial community. While continuing to promote the stock of obscure, jerry-built enterprises like Shawano, he took over an established company that was listed on the New York Stock Exchange and installed himself as its chairman.

The company was United Dye. Guterma got control of it by buying, for himself and a small group of associates, 38,500 shares of United Dye stock owned by Lowell Birrell. According to Guterma, the price was just under $400,000. On the face of it, this was not a very good buy, particularly since Birrell had just stripped the company of some $2 million worth of its assets. But Guterma nevertheless managed within a few months to dispose of his United Dye stock for several times what he had paid for it.

According to one of the indictments later brought against him Guterma did it this way: First, with the help of United Dye's compliant president, Virgil Dardi, who had been chairman of the company when Birrell was in control, Guterma contrived to withhold from the public any hint that United Dye had been looted by Birrell. Then he enlisted the aid of Pierre DuVal of *DuVal's Consensus* (who was later indicted along with Guterma) to spread the word that United Dye was under aggressive new management and was about to make some exciting acquisitions. There were only 153,000 shares of United Dye's common stock outstanding, and with so scanty a supply it was easy, by touting the stock, to send its price soaring on the Big Board. Within a few months the price rose from $9 a share to a high of $38.25 on October 27, 1955. By this time, the government later charged, Guterma had profitably disposed of most of his holdings. As an officer of United Dye, he was legally obligated to report such transactions to the SEC and the New York Stock Exchange. But presumably he was not eager to have the news get around that United Dye's aggressive new management was unloading its stock in the company, and he kept the information to himself.

A pipeline for United Dye

Having sold the stock he had acquired from Birrell, Guterma made plans to get his hands on a fresh supply. He was still chief executive officer of United Dye, and he arranged to merge the company with Handridge Oil, a company that had been organized by Garfield and Pasternak, in which Guterma himself had a substantial interest. Handridge's assets, at the time the merger went through, consisted mainly of $750,000 in cash and a pipeline in Wyoming, which Garfield and Pasternak had picked up for less than $1 million. In return for these assets, Guterma had United Dye issue 575,000 shares of new common stock.

The deal was concluded in May, 1956. United Dye had belatedly made public the $2-million loss it had suffered under Birrell's regime, and the market price of its stock was dropping rapidly. But even at, say, $10 a share, the United Dye stock issued in the Handridge merger would fetch nearly $6 million.

No such sum could be realized, however, simply by offering the new United Dye stock for sale on the New York Stock Exchange; the appearance of some half-million shares would give the price of the stock a further downward shove. Arrangements were therefore made to have the stock sold by McGrath Securities and other over-the-counter brokers to small investors who would not be likely to offer it for resale on the exchange. According to the government, Guterma was at the same time acting through intermediaries to buy small amounts of United Dye stock on the New York Stock Exchange. His objective was to maintain the quoted price—or at any rate to keep it from declining precipitously. His efforts were reasonably successful, and in the late spring and summer of 1956, several hundred thousand shares of United Dye stock were sold over the counter, many of them at more than $10 a share. (By the end of 1957 the price had fallen to $1.)

The Handridge deal did more than simply provide Guterma with some United Dye stock that could be resold at a profit. It was also an important link in a chain of events that gave Guterma control of F. L. Jacobs and Bon Ami.

First he took over Jacobs. For $300,000, he brought 28,000 shares of Jacobs stock from a man named Frank Howard, a former associate of Birrell and Serge Rubinstein. Then he used his control of Jacobs, as well as his command of the assets of Handridge, to take over Bon Ami.

Control of Bon Ami was held by a group of investors active in the grocery-products field, and Guterma made arrangements for United Dye to buy them out for $2,250,000. United Dye needed some cash to put down on the purchase; this was provided by the $750,000 in cash the company had acquired in the Handridge merger. The rest of the $2,250,000 was borrowed. Guterma had Jacobs lend United Dye $300,000 and arranged for United Dye to borrow $950,000 from banks. An additional $250,000 was needed to swing the deal, and Guterma borrowed it from Garfield and Pasternak. According to charges later brought by a group of Bon Ami stockholders, the two men were well rewarded for making the loan. Bon Ami had nearly $3 million in liquid assets, and as soon as Guterma got control of them he had Bon Ami invest $1,250,000, as an accommodation to Garfield and Pasternak, in debentures of a tottering oil company in which they were interested.

Carved jade and pep pills

By the summer of 1956, Guterma was at his zenith. His net worth was probably well over $1 million, and he owned securities—most of which, however, were pledged for bank loans—worth several times that amount. He controlled companies with assets of around $25 million. He made his headquarters at 430 Park Avenue in Manhattan, where he had a huge office adorned with carved ivory and jade. While he could on occasion be very ingratiating, his manner with associates was notably brusque. "At board meetings," a former employee recalls, "only Mr. Guterma's voice came through the door." He worked long and hard, gambled heavily, and dosed himself alternately with pills to pep himself up and pills to quiet his nerves.

It was toward the end of the year that Guterma accomplished a feat all speculators dream of. He cornered the market in a listed security when other traders had sold it short. This coup should have made him a fortune. But in fact he appears to have suffered a setback from which he never entirely recovered.

The company whose stock Guterma cornered was Chatco Steel Products Ltd., a Canadian firm listed on the Toronto Exchange. Initially, Guterma was interested in Chatco simply as a good source of stock to be merchandised by boiler-room operators. In June, 1956, one of Guterma's associates, acting as an underwriter, bought 100,-000 shares of new Chatco stock at $4.50 a share. This was more than Chatco had been selling for on the Toronto Exchange. But the floating supply of Chatco stock was small—including the 100,-000 shares just issued, there were only 160,000 shares outstanding—and Guterma and his confederates had no difficulty in running the price up. As the price rose, the boiler rooms began selling the new shares of Chatco stock to U.S. investors.

The wolves of Bay Street

This maneuver attracted the attention of certain speculators on Toronto's Bay Street. According to Guterma and the SEC, their leader was the Canadian stock promoter, Louis B. Chesler, who was associated with General Development Corp., the largest Florida land company, as its principal financial backer and promoter. The Toronto speculators knew that Chatco had no real prospects as a company, and as Chatco's stock doubled and then tripled in price, they began selling it short. But they seem to have overlooked the fact that only 160,000 shares were outstanding. And when it came time to cover, they found that Guterma had secretly bought up all the shares.

Theoretically, Guterma was sitting pretty. The short-sellers owed him 40,000 shares, and he was legally entitled to name the price at which he would permit them to settle. "The wolves of Bay Street," he told a reporter, "have learned that the wolves of Wall Street can still teach them a trick."

But Guterma's position was not unassailable. The fact that most of his personal assets were pledged for loans did not escape the notice of the Bay Street wolves. They reportedly threatened that if Guterma pressed his advantage, they would retaliate by staging a bear raid on United Dye and Jacobs stock—that is, they would sell these stocks short and force the market price down to a level at which the banks, to protect their loans, would sell Guterma out. In the end, Guterma allowed the shorts, according to a version he himself has given, to settle for only $400,000. It had cost Guterma an estimated $1,600,-000 in cash to acquire his corner and to provide Chatco with some badly needed working capital. But trading in Chatco had been suspended indefinitely by the Toronto Exchange, and all he had to show was 160,000 shares of stock for which there was virtually no market.

Guterma's losses in his Chatco venture, which amounted to perhaps $1,200,000, did not make a pauper of him. But from late 1956 on he seems to have been hard-pressed for ready money. He needed a lot simply to live in the style to which he had become accustomed. He bet large sums on football games and other sporting events, and he regularly sat in on pinochle, gin-rummy, and poker sessions at which tens of thousands of dollars changed hands. In any case, after the collapse of his Chatco scheme, Guterma's business dealings took on a certain air of desperation. He began to run risks he had avoided before, and his maneuvers grew bolder.

Bon Ami gets the business

At first, Bon Ami was his principal theatre of operations. A federal grand jury has charged that toward the end of 1956 he contrived to have Bon Ami buy some of his Chatco stock at $15.40 a share, far above its book value; and that soon afterward he raided the company's treasury by selling it television time at a tremendous markup. Bon Ami was spending well over a million dollars a year on advertising, most of it in TV. In March, 1957, Guterma had the company make a loan of $115,000 to a distributor of television films, Matthew Fox. Fox happened to own contracts giving him control of television time—it was in the form of spots for commercials—and as collateral for the loan, he posted a portion of this time that had a nominal value of $500,000. Fox defaulted on the loan, thereby putting Bon Ami in a position to take over his collateral. But without apprising the company's other directors of their rights, Guterma paid Bon Ami the $115,000 Fox owed and took over the television time himself. Next, for $200,000 in cash, he bought from a company called Guild Films an additional block of television time theoretically worth $750,000. This gave him control of time with a nominal value of $1,250,000, for which he had paid $315,000. Guterma sold this package to Bon Ami for $830,000, realizing a profit of $515,000.

In mid-1957, Guterma became uneasy about the attention his activities were attracting from the SEC, which had started investigating a number of companies in whose affairs he had figured. United Dye was under particular scrutiny, a fact that made it highly risky for Guterma to engage in any further shenanigans with the company's assets or stock. He consequently agreed to sell Virgil Dardi 43,-000 shares of United Dye stock, representing control of the company, and resigned from its board.

The films of Sonny Fassoulis

By this move Guterma also divested himself of control of United Dye's subsidiary, Bon Ami. But this did not stop him, according to the SEC, from setting in motion one last scheme for milking the company. Dardi and the other directors of United Dye were eager to sell Bon Ami, which had begun to lose a good deal of money, and Guterma obligingly came up with a purchaser. He was Sortiris G. ("Sonny") Fassoulis, a blond, wavy-haired young man who was later indicted for forging bonds.

On August 20, 1957, Fassoulis purchased from United Dye, for $1,700,000, 90,000 shares of Bon Ami stock, and thereby got control of the company. The very next day he concluded a wonderfully profitable deal with Bon Ami. (Guterma himself helped set up the deal by arranging for Fassoulis to borrow the money he needed to buy Bon Ami; the chief lender, in fact, was a Swiss bank of which Guterma was an important stockholder.) Fassoulis, through a Panamanian corporation called Icthyan Associates, owned television rights to

170 old films, many of them British. The rights were narrowly limited: none of the films could be shown in the U.S. or Canada, and many could not be shown in the United Kingdom, the Middle East, South America, or Asia. Fassoulis apparently had acquired the rights for $150,000; he now palmed them off on Bon Ami for $1,323,000.

Guterma next turned his attention to F. L. Jacobs, the auto-parts manufacturer he had acquired in 1956. He began a program of diversification that was reminiscent, in its headlong speed, of Shawano's early days. In six months Jacobs got control of Chemical & Rubber Corp., a maker of pads and carpets; Scranton Lace, whose chief attraction was more than $2,100,000 in net current assets; Storm-Vulcan Inc., a machinery manufacturer; Hal Roach Studios; Symphonic Electronic Corp., a manufacturer of high-fidelity sets; and the Mutual Broadcasting System.

The three-percenters

Guterma was at this time apparently in desperate need of money. As chief executive officer of Jacobs, he had control of large blocks of Jacobs' own stock and of stock in Scranton, a partially owned subsidiary. The government later charged that he began pledging some of this stock, without notifying Jacobs' other directors, as security for loans to himself or to holding companies he controlled. He tried to get such loans from banks. But banks, alerted by now to the fact that Guterma was being investigated by the SEC, were getting more and more wary of dealing with him. He had to turn to private lenders, borrowing from them at rates that sometimes were as high as 3 per cent a month. By late 1958, Guterma owed moneylenders an estimated $3 million, on which he was paying interest at a rate of around $1 million a year.

A company listed on the New York Stock Exchange is required to file an annual report with the exchange within ninety days after the end of its fiscal year. Jacobs' report for its 1958 fiscal year was due on October 31, and Guterma presumably hoped that by this time he would have managed to get the company's assets out of hock. But when October 31 came around, he had not done so. So he simply failed to file the required report. Five weeks later the report still had not been submitted, and on December 4 the exchange suspended all floor trading in Jacobs stock. (It could still be traded over the counter.) This alarmed Guterma's creditors, who began threatening to sell him out.

Trujillo comes through

Guterma was now more than ever in dire need of money with which to shore up his financial position. The source to which he turned was General Rafael Trujillo, dictator of the Dominican Republic. He wangled $750,000 from Trujillo—and made it look easy.

Guterma contends that when he first went to the Dominican Republic in January, 1959, he was acting on a tip that he might be able to borrow some money cheaply there. But on learning that Trujillo was extremely interested in getting some favorable publicity in the U.S., Guterma suggested that Mutual Broadcasting, with its 450 affiliated radio stations, was just the medium Trujillo needed. He offered to establish a special news bureau to feed Mutual material on the Dominican Republic. Trujillo accepted the offer, and agreed to finance an eighteen-month publicity campaign. On February 5, Guterma left Ciudad Trujillo by plane with an attaché case containing $750,000 in cash. In New York he set aside some of this amount—reportedly it was $150,000—for commissions to various people who had helped arrange the deal with Trujillo. (They included Porfirio Rubirosa, the noted Dominican ladies' man and a former son-in-law of Trujillo.) Guterma then rushed the rest of the money to the offices of Reldan Trading Corp., one of the moneylenders to which he was indebted.

But this transfusion of cash came too late to bail him out. Under the direction of a lawyer named Eileen Evers, the SEC had begun an intensive inquiry into the affairs of F. L. Jacobs. Guterma's creditors, fearing the SEC might step in and halt all sales of Jacobs stock, had already begun selling shares of Jacobs and of Scranton that Guterma had put up as collateral. In February, 1959, the SEC suspended over-the-counter trading in Jacobs stock, and asked for an injunction to prevent further dissipation of the company's assets.

Guterma's reaction was to resign in an elaborate huff as president and chairman of Jacobs. He complained that the SEC was persecuting him for minor technical irregularities, and in talking with reporters he worked hard to project an image of outraged virtue and sober rectitude. On February 14, Guterma suffered the indignity of arrest. The charge was failure to file reports required by the SEC, and the commission said it was acting on information that Guterma and a close associate named Robert J. Eveleigh had booked passage by

plane for Istanbul and were planning to leave the country.* Guterma
was furious. "This is a lie," he told reporters. "This is getting a man
for spitting on the sidewalk."

Where are the assets?

But Guterma's legal troubles were only beginning. Dozens of investigators were by now poking into the affairs of companies he had
once dominated. Shawano, Micro-Moisture, and Chatco Steel were
already bankrupt or defunct. United Dye and Bon Ami, their treas-
uries depleted, had been delisted by the New York Stock Exchange
and both were losing money. Jacobs and Scranton went into receivership. There soon were claims of $6 million against Jacobs alone, and
its receivers were able to locate only $1 million of the $6 million in
assets the company had when Guterma got control. By September,
Guterma had been indicted for fraud, stock manipulation, violation
of federal banking laws, and failure to register as an agent of the
Dominican Republic. For what it is worth, Trujillo later said he didn't
get a penny's worth of propaganda for the $750,000 he put up.

In the next few months, just before he finally went to prison,
Guterma understandably put in a lot of time with his lawyers. But
there were hints that his spirit was far from crushed. Late in the summer, for instance, the SEC looked into the sale of stock in a company
called Anaconda Lead & Silver. Although the company had only
a little over $1000 in the bank, kept no records, and hadn't worked
any of its mining claims for years, its stock was suddenly being sold
by boiler rooms at $4 a share. One of the principal sources of the
stock turned out to be an attractive young woman named Patricia
Kelly. When an SEC investigator questioned her, she said, "Oh, I
didn't own those shares. They belonged to Alexander Guterma, and
he was just using my name."

* Reservations had in fact been made, but Guterma has suggested they were
made for the purpose of embarrassing him.

10

The Looting of H. L. Green

One of the most bizarre episodes in modern business history took place a couple of years ago in a warehouse belonging to H. L. Green Co., then one of the biggest variety-store chains in the U.S. The warehouse, a gloomy and cavernous affair, was in Chrichton Corners, on the outskirts of Mobile, Alabama; it was serving at the time as a central depot for all the stores in Green's Olen Division. In February, 1959, a search of the warehouse was begun by a team of auditors working for Scovell, Wellington & Co. What the chief auditor suspected, and what two Green-Olen executives with him knew to be all too true, was that someone had seriously falsified the Olen Division's inventory accounts.

This fact was also known to a third Green official, who was then in New York, and who was anxiously awaiting the outcome of the audit. He had good reason for anxiety. For he was Maurice Olen, the president and chief executive officer of H. L. Green—and the man principally responsible for the deficiencies in the Olen Division's accounts. He was also one of Green's principal stockholders, with some 150,000 shares; the stock was then selling for about $43 a share. Exposure of the deficiencies would bring to an abrupt end the truly extraordinary career of Maurice Olen, who, at thirty-four, was riding high on a reputation as the *Wunderkind* of retailing.

At this time, Olen had been running H. L. Green for four months. He had found it a plodding, woefully mismanaged enterprise, desperately in need of fresh blood. The company's sales, which were running around $110 million in 1957, had scarcely risen at all during the booming 1950s; and earnings had declined steadily, from about $5,300,000 in 1950 to about $3,200,000 in the year ending on January 31, 1958.

This deterioration was, in fact, the reason Olen had been able to soar to power at Green. Beginning in 1946, when Maurice Olen took over two small retail stores owned by his father in Pensacola, Florida, and Mobile, Alabama, he had proved that he was a born retailer. By 1958 the two stores had grown to 123, scattered all through the southeastern U.S.; their combined sales were over $20 million, and annual profit was almost $500,000. Thus Olen had little difficulty persuading the Green directors to merge with his hot company; and what they had liked best about the deal was that Olen himself came with it, bubbling over with plans for further expansion. H. L. Green thought it had, at last, an energetic and imaginative chief executive. In the year ending February, 1959, when the auditors arrived in Chrichton Corners, the value of the Green stock doubled.

The little black book that wasn't

Though the merger had been in effect for four months, this was the first time that Scovell, Wellington & Co.—which had done Green's auditing for twenty-seven years—had been requested to inspect fully the physical assets described in Olen's financial statements; thus far, Olen's statements, as certified by the Alabama auditing firm of Lewie F. Childree & Co., had been subjected only to a limited review. But in January several Green directors had grown curious, then concerned, about the sizable inventory shown in the Olen Division's year-end reports. Before Scovell, Wellington's chief auditor, Charles Nielsen, went to Chrichton Corners, he had been warned to expect some discrepancies. With a great show of candor, Olen had acknowledged that he had, at times, juggled his accounts somewhat in order to comply with the terms of a loan—which required him to maintain his working capital at a certain level. He had, he blandly informed Scovell, Wellington, overstated his inventories by something like $1 million and understated his fixed assets by about the same amount. But the matter could be straightened out easily if Nielsen would just consult with Margaret Mandeville, assistant controller of the Olen Division, and Herschel Harris, a vice president and director of Green; these two would assist Nielsen in every way possible. Nielsen was advised to ask them, before he began the audit, for a special black book in which Olen had recorded the true expenditures for inventory and for fixed assets.

Nielsen has some vivid recollections of his stay in Chrichton Corners. When he arrived, he went directly to Miss Mandeville, a pleasant woman of matronly appearance, and asked for the little black book. After some preliminary skirmishing, Miss Mandeville reported sadly that there was no such book. Nielsen then called Olen in New York and demanded an explanation. Olen suggested that, even without a black book, the auditor could get a true picture of the division's assets quickly enough by checking alterations that had been made on the inventory tags. Nielsen started checking, but soon discovered that on some tags it was just about impossible to make out the original figures; on others, he was able to read through the erasures and altered figures. Nielsen now realized that Olen's suggestion was wildly impractical. Accordingly, he called his home office and asked for another crew of accountants to assist him in making a complete new physical inventory.

Eventually, the auditors confirmed Olen's claim that the fixed assets were undervalued. But Nielsen discovered almost immediately that the inventories were *overvalued* by far more than Olen had admitted. In addition, Nielsen made the alarming discovery that the records of merchandise received did not jibe with the accounts payable. He demanded an explanation from Herschel Harris, who got on the telephone to Olen in New York. Olen asked to have Miss Mandeville put on, and after she had listened for a few minutes, she hung up and walked rapidly into the rear of the warehouse, where she momentarily vanished. She reappeared bearing a shoe box on which was inscribed "Olen—personal," and handed it to the auditors. Inside was approximately $250,000 of bills from suppliers—bills that were unpaid and unrecorded on the division's balance sheet.

Several times in the next few days this skit was repeated. Nielsen's team would find a discrepancy between the books and suppliers' invoices; the auditors would demand an accounting from Harris and Miss Mandeville; the latter would check with Olen on the telephone, then disappear into the warehouse and return with another box full of unrecorded accounts payable. Each time Miss Mandeville would sweetly inform the auditors that now, at last, they had all the figures. The only variation in the routine occurred near the end of the audit, when Harris, after several hours of wrangling with the auditors and denying that he had any more invoices, suddenly and wordlessly reached into his own files and produced another boxful.

At last, after ten days, when Nielsen had finished his preliminary work in Crichton Corners, he felt that he had a pretty good idea of what was wrong with the Olen Division's balance sheet. The division's inventories were short of the amount stated by about $1,700,000; its total liabilities were at least $600,000 greater than the amount stated. Thus H. L. Green had got at least $2,300,000 less than it had been led to believe at the time of the merger with Olen; and there were strong indications that still more unrecorded accounts payable might turn up.

It seems incredible that Maurice Olen was able to bamboozle H. L. Green so easily. How did it happen? Olen's accounts had been audited and approved by the Childree company, an established, respectable firm. Many of Olen's fictitious figures had also gone unchallenged by the SEC, when the Olen Co. went public in 1958. And Olen's elaborate fantasies had been undetected by the H. L. Green directors, most of whom were experienced businessmen. Indeed, the performance of the board all through the disaster has raised some large and complex questions about directors' responsibilities—and thus far, at least, the questions have not really been answered.

The glider

The questions are hard to answer because Maurice Olen has always been a hard man to keep up with. His career has been marked by some fast operating, and years before the Green episode, he had shown his adeptness at gliding on thin ice. He was born in 1924, in Pensacola. His grandfather had been a pack peddler moving through the southern states; his father, Harry Olen, had run stores in North Carolina and Tennessee before he settled down in Pensacola and opened a junior department store, specializing in low-priced soft goods. Maurice, a second child, ten years younger than a sister, seems to have been bothered by a bitter notion that he was "unwanted." At an early age, he showed an almost unbelievable drive to learn all there was to learn about merchandising. Even while he was in grammar school, he worked after classes in the store, checking inventory and making deliveries; occasionally, he was allowed to accompany his father on buying trips to New York.

In 1942, when he left Pensacola to attend the University of Chicago, he remained active in his father's business, and made buying trips in the Midwest and to New York, Philadelphia, and other cities. He graduated from Chicago in two years and then took special courses in mathematics and industrial engineering at the University of Michigan. He did well at both. Then, in 1946, he returned to work in the family store.

Pensacola was a booming town then, and the elder Olen's store prospered. Business was so good, in fact, that Harry Olen decided to open a second store in Mobile. The site he picked was composed of two vacant stores with a hardware dealer separating them. The dealer would not sell out, but Harry Olen went ahead with the store anyway. Within a month he knew he had made a big mistake. Maurice was summoned to Mobile to tackle the problem. He was persistent, glib, and sincere and the hardware dealer finally succumbed to his arguments. This success persuaded the family that Maurice, at twenty-two, should take charge of the company. By 1947 Maurice had opened five more stores.

He then set about touring the Southeast, looking for medium-sized towns that had been avoided or overlooked by the big chains. Olen applied a lot of the most modern theories of retailing, and began introducing self-service, pre-packaging, and modern sales-promotion techniques. He grew adept at finding soft goods that could be purchased at distress prices. In ten years he opened over sixty stores. In 1953 he moved into the big time by opening his own New York resident buying office. He also introduced the very sophisticated I. B. M. Dennison inventory-control system, which, he said, would keep the company's money working at capacity.

In 1956, Maurice Olen pulled off a major coup when he purchased the Yellow Front stores, a forty-four-store soft-goods chain. In a way, this deal may be regarded as the beginning of his troubles. To swing the deal, he had to borrow $500,000 from the Jefferson Standard Life Insurance Co. of Greensboro, North Carolina. The terms of the loan required that the Olen company maintain a two-to-one ratio between current assets and current liabilities, and have at least $1,500,000 of working capital at all times. Olen appears to have begun cheating on these terms almost immediately. After the disclosure of the Green inventory shortage, a banker asked him confidentially one day when he had first "gone wrong." Olen calmly replied that it had been years ago.

Big names for Olen

Early in 1957, Olen decided that he was big enough to go public, and he began to shop around for an underwriter. Finding one seemed to present no great problem. By this time the Olen company had about a hundred outlets and a volume of over $12 million. In addition, Olen himself had achieved some distinction in the Southeast. He was a director of an Alabama insurance company, a member of the Mobile Opera Guild, and a conspicuous leader in several Mobile charity campaigns.

The underwriter Olen found was R. S. Dickson & Co. of Charlotte, North Carolina. In the fall of 1957, Dickson began serious negotiations to bring out an Olen stock issue. Dickson saw no reason to question Lewie Childree's auditing of the Olen books. However, Childree's firm had no familiarity with SEC procedures, and Olen's special counsel—he had managed to retain the prestigious law firm of Dewey, Ballantine, Bushby, Palmer & Wood to help with the offering—suggested that another auditor be brought in. Specifically, the special counsel suggested the nationally known firm of Lybrand, Ross Brothers & Montgomery. Olen seems to have been delighted with this idea: the more big names surrounding him, the better he evidently liked it. L.R.B.&M. read the financial statements Childree had prepared, and helped to get them into a form suitable for the registration. Later the firm reviewed certain of Childree's working papers and discussed the scope of his audits with him. Then the firm sent Olen a letter noting that, while it had not made its own audit of his financial statements, and so did not certify them, it saw no reason to believe that the company's net assets and net income were overstated. L.R.B.&M. asked Olen not to show the letter to anyone except underwriters and their counsel, but there is no doubt that Olen worked the letter hard in his subsequent approach to H. L. Green.

Dickson then went ahead with the offering, in which 100,000 shares of Olen Class A common stock were put on the market at $10.50 per share. The prospectus said that in the year ended January 31, 1958, the Olen company had earned $450,957.89. This figure, which went unchallenged by the auditors for the underwriters, and by the SEC, later proved to be largely fictitious. Just before the offering the Olen board declared a quarterly dividend of 18 cents per share, payable in June, and indicated that the company intended to pay regular quarterly dividends on the Class A stock. (In addition to the Class A stock, the company's capitalization included 225,000 shares of non-dividend-bearing Class B stock. Most of this was retained by the family.)

The proceeds of the sale served to reduce Olen's short-term debt and to boost the company's working capital to $2,200,000. In addition, the sale had an important indirect effect: it sharpened the image of Maurice Olen as an aggressive young comer in the retail field. Bankers and business brokers began to cultivate him. Many of his 1400-odd employees invested in the company.

Olen lapped up all the attention. He got into the habit of coming to New York and dropping in on his Wall Street friends to discuss his problems—and his urge to expand his thriving business. He indicated he was looking for new acquisitions: on one occasion, he tried to buy control of the Wieboldt Department Stores in Chicago. This failed, and so did a later attempt to gain a sizable stock position in S. H. Kress, when control of that company was being contested by several different groups of directors. Then, one day in May, 1958, Olen dropped in to talk with a partner of a small brokerage firm. The partner mentioned to Olen that H. L. Green might be interested in getting together with a new chain that had some bright, experienced young men in it. He added that the key man at H. L. Green was Jules Freed, the controller; and then he called up Freed to tell him about the bright young man who was in his office.

Olen comes for lunch

Freed was indeed a key man. He had started with the old F. & W. Grand Stores, the variety chain, and had stayed with the company all through its reorganization in the early 1930s. He had served for almost twenty years under Harold L. Green, who was brought in as president by the Chase Bank—by an eerie coincidence, he was a former Scovell, Wellington auditor—and who bestowed his own name on the reorganized company. Green never put Freed on the board of directors, however, and even after Green died in 1951, and the directors became heavily dependent on Freed for their knowledge of the company's finances, he was not brought onto the board.

Olen found him to be the epitome of the corporate financial man. Dressed in banker gray, his eyes expressionless behind rimless glasses, Freed seemed remote and forbidding, and at first he brushed the young Southerner aside. But Olen was a persistent caller, and worked hard at getting to know H. L. Green and its controller. Freed mentioned the calls to the company's chairman and president, H. R. Boynton, and said that Olen seemed to want to make some sort of merger deal. Boynton suggested that all three men lunch together at the Fifth Avenue Club.

At lunch Olen gave the two H. L. Green executives a quick run-down on his own company. When they returned from lunch, Freed suggested that he submit a formal merger proposal to the H. L. Green board. Olen promised to do that, and said that meanwhile he was leaving on a six-week European tour; while he was gone, Freed could get any information he might want from the Olen Co. by calling on Herschel Harris, the executive vice president.

The formal merger proposal, accompanied by a beautifully bound brochure on the Olen Co., arrived in Freed's office a week later. Meanwhile, Freed asked the southeastern regional manager of the H. L. Green chain to look over the Olen stores and give him a report. The report was favorable, and in mid-July Freed called Harris and said he was flying down to take a quick look at the Mobile headquarters. When he arrived at the Mobile airport, Harris said he had a surprise for him. The surprise was Maurice Olen, waiting at the company offices to greet Freed; he had cut his vacation short when he heard about the visit.

At the H. L. Green board meeting in July, Freed submitted the Olen proposal. The board, it should be noted at this point, had four outside directors (out of nine), and all of them were men of substance and distinction. They were C. M. Boyce, vice president of Baltimore's Mercantile–Safe Deposit & Trust Co.; J. M. d'Assern, head of his own Wall Street brokerage firm; Percy J. Ebbott, retired president of the Chase Bank; and James M. Nicely, senior vice president of the First National City Bank of New York. These men questioned Freed closely, but the controller, with figures supplied him by Olen, was able to present the proposal capably.

Olen's figures suggested that a merger would bring H. L. Green an additional $30 million in volume, and $1 million in profits, by the end of 1959. It would also give the company an opportunity to penetrate areas in which it had little or no representation. And Freed was able to argue the advantages of getting Olen's aggressive young management. The directors appointed a committee headed by Boynton to make a check on Olen and his company.

In Mobile they found nothing but praise for him. To be sure, he seemed to be slow in paying bills, but Olen himself had warned the directors about that, explaining that he needed money to finance his expansion. Anyway, both the Chemical Corn Exchange Bank and the Hanover Bank & Trust had extended substantial lines of credit to the Olen Co., a reassuring fact.

A premium for Olen

In August, 1958, an Olen-Green merger agreement was signed. The H. L. Green directors agreed to accept roughly two shares of Olen stock for one of their own company. The Olen stock then had a market value of about $13 per share, and the H. L. Green stock of about $31.50, but the latter's book value per share was over three times that reported by Olen, and so there is no doubt that H. L. Green was paying a premium in order to swing the merger.

The terms of the merger agreement called for a full audit of the Olen Co. After the signing, Maurice Olen questioned whether the full audit had to be done by H. L. Green's firm, Scovell, Wellington. He told Freed that Childree was just then making a midyear audit, and that it would save time and money if Scovell, Wellington reviewed Childree's working papers instead of undertaking another full audit. Freed and Boynton assented to this procedure. After all, they told themselves, Childree himself had a good reputation; some of his papers had already been read by Lybrand, Ross Brothers & Montgomery; Childree's audit had then gone unchallenged by the SEC—and there were those loans to Olen by the big New York banks. Freed knew that H. L. Green's own staff had looked over some of Olen's inventories and stores—and seen nothing untoward. On top of everything else, the directors knew that the merger would make Maurice Olen H. L. Green's largest stockholder, and they regarded this fact as strong evidence that he would do nothing to damage the company.

The Scovell, Wellington auditors went ahead with their "limited review" and on October 21, 1958, sent the H. L. Green board a letter describing what they had done. The letter pointed out that they had not examined Olen's books and had seen only the working papers used in inventory tests of six stores. In addition, the letter noted that Childree's papers did not indicate how closely his firm had examined Olen's internal controls; therefore, Scovell, Wellington could not determine the adequacy of Childree's testing.

This letter never reached the board. When Freed saw it, he brought the letter to Olen. The latter argued with Scovell, Wellington that there was no reason, under the circumstances, for an auditor's letter to call his company's practices into question; anyway, Childree would immediately answer any questions that Scovell, Wellington cared to raise. Childree did, in fact, supply some supplementary information that day; and on the following day, October 22, Scovell, Wellington submitted a new letter. This one omitted many of the qualifications in the previous letter, and it stated that the limited review had turned up nothing wrong. Freed took this second letter to the board, which proceeded to seek stockholder approval of the merger.

The Olen-Green merger further reinforced the image of Maurice Olen, then thirty-four, as an ornament of the retailing business. Parties and dinners were given in his honor. Commercial bankers were soon scrambling to lend him money. Olen relished all this attention —and made good use of it.

In his early tour of Wall Street, one of the investment houses Olen had visited was the old and respected firm of Wertheim & Co. While the Green merger was being worked out, Olen went back to Wertheim and said he wanted the firm to give him financial advice. Specifically, he wanted help in expanding a small, family-owned commercial finance company he had launched in Mobile in 1957, named Commercial Investment Corp. Impressed by Olen's rapid rise, Wertheim & Co. agreed to work with him. As it happened, Wertheim knew that another finance company, the U. S. Loan Society of Philadelphia, with $1,500,000 in assets, was then in need of an aggressive management. Wertheim helped arrange a merger between the two finance companies, and it went into effect two weeks before the Olen-Green merger.

As soon as the Green merger was completed, Olen accelerated his expansionist plans. He prepared to open twenty, possibly thirty, new H. L. Green stores in the following year. In November, 1958, he started negotiations to acquire the thirty-two-store D.&C. chain in Michigan. In December he quietly slipped down to Philadelphia to see Albert M. Greenfield, the controlling stockholder of United Stores Corp. Olen told Greenfield, a wily veteran with years of experience in finance, retailing, and real estate, that H. L. Green wanted to purchase control of United. Olen was obviously thinking big. For United held 39 per cent of the stock of the recently merged McCrory-McLellan stores, which had 450 outlets and a sales volume of $170 million. Olen's ultimate goal, it appears, was a giant merger that would put him in control of a chain that had 835 stores, a volume of over $300 million, and profits of more than $7 million. But Greenfield told Olen that he was not interested.

Undaunted, Olen returned to Wertheim & Co., and told its partners about his interest in United. As Wertheim partner George Jones recalls it, he and his associates told Olen that he was moving too fast, and suggested that he spend more time with Green before blossoming out. Olen insisted that he wanted United, and said coldly that if Wertheim would not handle the discussions, he would get someone else. The Wertheim partners then approached Greenfield. He suggested that they get from Olen a certified resolution of the H. L. Green board, approving the purchase of United Stores stock. A copy of the resolution arrived promptly, and Wertheim successfully completed the deal with Greenfield. The latter received $7 million for shares he had purchased two years earlier for $3,500,000. Olen disregarded Wertheim's comment that he was paying a high premium, and he immediately set about pushing for a merger between H. L. Green and McCrory-McLellan. But by this time Olen had a sizable problem in his own organization.

The stunning of Jules Freed

The problem concerned Jules Freed. Olen repeatedly acknowledged that he was dependent on Freed to show him the ropes, and Freed was soon elected a director. When the Value Line Income Fund sold its own H. L. Green holdings in December, 1958, Olen arranged for Freed to acquire 3000 shares, at $37 a share, for two trusts set up for his relatives. Freed had also purchased 3000 shares of C.I.C. at $1 a share—although Olen had offered him the stock free.

Freed became disenchanted, however, as Olen began to move on to other projects at a furious pace. Freed also noted the strong bond between Olen and Herschel Harris; after eight years of working together, Harris and Olen had what seemed like a father-son relationship. Freed was disturbed when he heard that Harris would become an "executive vice president" of the corporation after the merger with McCrory-McLellan. Freed earlier had blocked a suggestion that all of H. L. Green's bookkeeping be handled in Mobile.

These were relatively minor matters. But in January, 1959, Freed made a discovery that really shook him. He noted that some $2,500,-000 of H. L. Green cash had been transferred to the Olen Division and he asked Olen when it would be transferred back to the parent company. Olen told him that it would not be for some time. Freed asked for an Olen Division balance sheet. Olen explained that, because of confusion stemming from the merger, there would be a short delay in obtaining the balance sheet.

Finally, however, Olen did produce a report. Freed was stunned when he saw that the report showed Olen Division inventories of $8 million, of which $3,200,000 worth were stored in the Chrichton Corners warehouse. A year before, this depot had been reported as holding only $112,000 worth of Olen Co. merchandise.

Double talk for the auditors

Freed says that he was not, at this point, suspicious of Olen; he also says that his sale of 800 shares of H. L. Green later that month had nothing to do with the startling figures he had seen on the Olen Division balance sheet. He prepared a report for the January 28 directors' meeting, calling attention to the sudden rise in Olen Division inventories. It aroused the outside directors' curiosity—as Freed had intended—and it also aroused Olen's wrath. The outside directors instructed Freed to find out what was happening.

Early in February, Freed asked a Scovell, Wellington auditor to make an unofficial visit to the Chrichton Corners warehouse. The auditor took a fast look at the warehouse and reported by phone that he seriously doubted the existence of $3,200,000 worth of inventory there. Freed now began to press Olen for a fuller explanation. On February 15, Olen admitted for the first time that there were some minor irregularities in the Olen Division's bookkeeping.

Freed still did not confront Olen with his suspicions of hanky-panky. Instead, he asked Olen to explain the matter to Scovell, Wellington auditors, so that they would be able to help him reconstruct an accurate balance sheet. Olen agreed, but it appears that there was a fair amount of double talk in his presentation, for neither the auditors nor Freed could completely grasp what he said. In any case, Olen reluctantly consented, on February 18, to a full investigation of the warehouse inventory. When Lewie Childree learned of this decision he rushed to New York, claiming that this was unnecessary. But by this time, no one at H. L. Green was taking Childree's word for it. Scovell, Wellington's Nielsen went down to Chrichton Corners, and began his strange tug of war with Herschel Harris and Miss Mandeville.

On March 11, 1959, after the auditors had returned from Chrichton Corners, there was a board meeting. The Scovell, Wellington auditors and Freed reported at the meeting that the Olen Division had an inventory shortage of over $1 million; and that, moreover, there were substantial amounts of unpaid bills representing unrecorded liabilities. While the directors were trying to absorb this startling information, Olen argued swiftly that the deficiency was nothing to be concerned about. He said that Scovell, Wellington's reports were not accurate. He said he was confident that the final adjustment would not be much over $1 million, and he pledged that he would make full restitution.

At this point, the outside directors had to face the question of how much information should be disclosed to stockholders—and how soon. Obviously, the H. L. Green stockholders and the securities markets had been misinformed at the time of the merger with Olen the previous fall. In every day of trading that passed without the information's being fully disclosed, some new stockholders would be exposed to unknown risks. The directors might be liable to personal suits for failing to force prompt disclosure. On the other hand, it was important to minimize the loss by getting back as much money as possible from Olen himself. As soon as the public was informed of the Olen deficiency, anything might happen. Olen might be arrested. His assets might be attached or put beyond the reach of H. L. Green. And so immediate disclosure involved some risks, too.

The board adjourned its March 11 meeting without coming to a decision on disclosure. But after consulting with their counsel, and with Scovell, Wellington, the directors met again, on Friday, March 13. At this meeting they formally decided to wait for more information before disclosing what they already knew. The delay was contingent, however, on Olen's demonstrating good faith by producing $1 million in cash. Meanwhile, Freed had sold his entire remaining holdings in H. L. Green—some 3000 shares.

In the next two weeks Olen was still talking confidently of his plans to merge with McCrory-McLellan. Indeed, it seems probable that the merger was now more important to him than ever—if only because it would confuse and complicate the company's financial picture further. But Olen's plans were thwarted at a board meeting called for March 25. This time, Nielsen's detailed report was read to the board.

As soon as it was read, Nicely demanded that Olen immediately transfer that $1 million in cash to H. L. Green. Olen did that, and also agreed to put up the stock of his family holding company, Industrial Development Inc., as collateral against a larger deficiency, if one should develop. I.D.I. held title to over 123,000 shares of H. L. Green. However, Olen made a last effort to prevent a complete blowup. He asked the board to give him one more week to raise enough money to offset all the losses he had caused H. L. Green—he still would not concede that they were more than $1,250,000—and then to undo the whole merger. Olen and H. L. Green would break up and go their separate ways again. The board agreed to give him more time.

The doubting director

But the next day, it appears, d'Assern was stricken by doubts. Around noon, he phoned Nicely to say that he could not stay silent any longer and was going to inform the SEC. Of all the directors, d'Assern was in the most awkward position. For as a member of the New York Stock Exchange he was bound to disclose any material information about a security that a client might want to buy. Nicely assured d'Assern that he understood the broker's position, and suggested only that he wait until the market closed. D'Assern agreed; he went to the SEC that afternoon. On the day after that, March 27, Nicely, d'Assern, and Freed held a press conference in the SEC offices and disclosed an "apparent deficiency" of $3 million in the net assets of the Olen Division. Olen and Harris promptly announced their resignations from Green.

Freed was at first the directors' choice to succeed Olen as president, but several of the directors were unhappy about his sale of H. L. Green stock during the waiting period. They finally voted to give the presidency to Joseph Unger, who had headed the Metropolitan Stores Division for six years.

Olen's departure from H. L. Green did not, of course, end the misfortunes he had brought it. The net deficiency in the Olen Division's accounts was later put by the company at $4 million, not $3 million. Several men stepped forward with plans for retrieving the company's fortunes.

• The first of these was Jack Wolgin, who headed a small finance company in Philadelphia, Atlas Credit Corp. One of the bankers who had extended credit to C.I.C. suggested to Wolgin that it might be a good idea for him to take over that company. Wolgin was indeed interested, and arranged to meet Olen. Their negotiations concluded with Wolgin and two associates, Raymond Perleman and Sylvan Cohen, deciding to purchase, not C.I.C., but all of Olen's stock in H. L. Green. When he made the purchase, Wolgin was unaware that this stock had already been posted as collateral for the deficiencies in the Olen Division. There followed an infinitely complex three-way fight, involving Olen, Wolgin, and H. L. Green. Olen came out of the fight without any stock, or any of the proceeds of the sale—but with a promise from the directors that they would not press any damage suits on him. Wolgin came out of the fight with 9 per cent of H. L. Green stock, and the right to nominate three board members. H. L. Green came out of the fight with $600,000 of the proceeds of the sale, in addition to the $1 million it got from Olen—and with a new fight on its hands.

• This was initiated by a second bidder for power, Maxwell Gluck, the chairman of Darling Stores, Inc. (Gluck had hitherto been famous chiefly because, when he was appointed U. S. Ambassador to Ceylon in 1957, he was unable to tell the Senate Foreign Relations Committee the name of that country's prime minister.) Gluck now offered to buy $4 million worth of H. L. Green unissued common. The H. L. Green management learned about the offer from the newspapers, before Gluck's letter arrived, and at first did not regard it seriously. Then the directors arranged some meetings with Gluck, at which he asked that he be named to the executive committee and later permitted to nominate two members of the board. The company rebuffed this proposal when it made its agreement with Wolgin. Gluck threatened a proxy fight at the annual meeting in April, and criticized the board sharply for the agreement it made with Olen and Wolgin. However, he never developed enough support to make a serious bid for control.

In the end, the McCrory-McLellan merger that Olen had dreamed of did take place—but with McCrory's top man, Meshulam Riklis, coming out in charge of the merged company. Before the merger took place, H. L. Green sold off its Canadian subsidiary, Metropolitan Stores, and also sold thirty-one stores of its former Olen Division. Then, in May, 1961, H. L. Green's remaining stores were swallowed up in Riklis' McCrory Corp.

A man with a future

Olen himself is back in Mobile, working in the family business, which includes a retailing venture called Shopper's World. Olen has also been involved in the management of the King Dollar Stores, a small chain of drygood stores in the Mobile area. His exact position in the operations of these chains is unclear. He pled no contest to the charges of violating securities regulations, when his case came before the U. S. District Court in 1961, and he was fined $2500. It is an indicator of Olen's talents that many of those who have known him, and been burned by him, nevertheless believe that he will be back in the retailing big leagues before long.

PART FOUR

Protecting the Stockholders' Rights

II

What Good Are Annual Meetings?

In the spring of 1961, the Olin Mathieson Chemical Corp., a giant enterprise (1960 sales: about $700 million) headquartered in New York City, invited its 73,000 stockholders to attend its annual meeting in Saltville, Virginia (population: 2800). Olin Mathieson has a plant in Saltville, where the old Mathieson company was started, and both the old and new companies have held their meetings there in every year except one. As the site of a modern annual meeting, however, it does pose some problems. To get there, stockholders presumably begin by flying or taking a train to Bristol, Virginia. At Bristol they change to a train for Glade Spring. This community is nine miles from Saltville, but there is no train or bus service, so the stockholder must strike a deal for chauffeuring service with someone in town, or possibly just hike it. When he gets to the meeting, he ordinarily finds that it is over in less than an hour, and no lunch is served. Olin Mathieson discovered over the years that the turnout at Saltville was not likely to be overwhelming: stockholders who worked at the local plant came, and perhaps a few security analysts too. The company said it was eager to improve attendance at its meetings, and expected to begin holding them somewhere else in the future, as soon as it changed a provision in its charter that required meetings in Virginia.*

Stockholders of International Business Machines Corp. have had an easier time of it in recent years. One day in April, 1961, they boarded commuter trains at New York's Grand Central Station and rode to Mount Kisco, New York. They were met there by chartered buses, which took them to the company's new research center at Yorktown. Solicitous guides showed them to their seats in a tent adjacent to the research center. They had a two-hour discussion of the company's operations and prospects, asked questions of President Thomas

* The 1962 meeting was held in New Haven.

J. Watson Jr., and then adjourned for a box lunch and a tour of the research center. Late that afternoon they were driven back to Mount Kisco and their train for New York.

These two episodes in the annual trek of investors to the multitudinous meetings of U.S. corporations illustrate the degree of enthusiasm that corporations have for them. I.B.M. could be said to feel very enthusiastic; Olin Mathieson's feelings could be called tepid. A large number of companies are distinctly cold. Some go so far as to insist that annual meetings are a nuisance and expense, a travesty of democracy, and an unmitigated pain in the neck. As the case was succinctly (but privately) stated by a public-relations adviser to many large corporations, "The main purpose of an annual meeting is to adjourn."

No one seriously argues that such meetings can or should be "democratic" in the same sense that a town meeting is; after all, at a town meeting everyone has an equal vote, while at a corporate meeting everyone's vote is determined by his shareholdings, which probably means by his wealth. Antagonists of annual meetings can often point to situations in which even the controlling stockholders don't bother to attend, and to situations in which the audience's time is consumed by stockholders whose interests are trivial. (At the 1960 U. S. Steel meeting, for example, virtually the entire question period was taken up by three stockholders whose aggregate holdings were around 100 shares.) The stockholders may ultimately decide, or at least ratify, the corporation's policy, but they certainly don't do it at the annual meeting.

The room on the twelfth floor

Before looking further into the case for and against annual meetings, or examining the corporation's legal obligations to the stockholder, consider the actual practices of some firms.

Among others that have not tried very hard to attract many stockholders to their meetings: F. W. Woolworth, which still meets in Watertown, New York, where it was founded; the Cudahy Packing Corp. of Omaha, Nebraska, which in recent years has met in Portland, Maine (at the 1959 meeting the company's representatives and the visitors to the meeting added up to *five* persons); Cities Service Corp., which meets in Dover, Delaware (one train a day), and often finds that the directors outnumber the other stockholders.

Delaware, incidentally, is a favorite meeting place. Many corporations justify holding their meetings there by noting that their charters were issued in the state. But this contention is not entirely valid. Actually, one of the reasons so many companies incorporate in Delaware is the freedom it allows them, e.g., the freedom to meet wherever they like. New York is not so liberal: it requires corporations it charters to hold at least three meetings out of five within its borders. The Corporate Trust Building in Wilmington is the address of hundreds of corporations, though many of them do not even have a desk there. For those who want to hold meetings in the building there are the facilities of a room on the twelfth floor, capable of seating a hundred persons; more often than not the room is partitioned into two sections in which ceremonies can be run off quickly, and more or less privately.

Some corporations discourage stockholders from attending, though probably not always intentionally, by putting on a show of stupefying dullness, following elaborate rules of parliamentary procedure, and insisting that even completely noncontroversial matters, like dispensing with a reading of the minutes of last year's meeting, be moved and seconded from the floor and put to a vote. Some companies actually insist on reading the minutes of last year's meeting; and at others the president reads the entire annual report to the stockholders, even though they had got the report long before they came. (The Securities and Exchange Commission insists that annual reports go out to stockholders at least as early as the proxy statement.) In the course of waging war for their rights, a fair number of stockholders have become as knowing about parliamentary procedure as corporate chairmen. At the annual meeting of Cuban-American Sugar Corp. in January, 1961, Chairman David M. Keiser hurried through the announcements in only twenty minutes, and then suggested that the meeting adjourn, after which, he said, he would answer questions informally. But a recalcitrant stockholder pointed out that once the meeting was adjourned, Keiser would be under no legal obligation to answer questions, or even to stay in the room. Keiser finally agreed to answer the questions first.

Lunch as a weapon

Lunch is used artfully by many companies. While some announce that lunch will be provided, and hope the announcement will induce more stockholders to attend, others refrain from saying anything about it until the time that stockholders begin asking questions—at which point the chairman may inform them that lunch will be served "as soon as the meeting is adjourned." Chrysler employed this tactic at one recent meeting, and while the lure of early refreshment did not succeed in stopping the flow of questions, it probably made the questioners less popular than they might have been otherwise.

One way of keeping things under control in large rooms is simply not to provide microphones. Professional meeting-goers like the Gilbert brothers often counter this tactic by bringing portable battery-powered microphones of their own. But at a recent Standard Brands meeting in New York, it appeared that many of the stockholders, with no portable microphones at hand, failed to make themselves heard, could not hear what was going on, and suffered other frustrations as well. The management had announced before the meeting that it would answer only questions submitted in writing. It stuck to this rule, permitted no rejoinder to the management's answer, and refused to consider a raft of complaints about the whole procedure. Possibly in retaliation, some stockholders descended on an exhibit of Standard Brands products and stripped it clean; they were discomfited, no doubt, to find that the exhibition bottles of Fleischmann liquors, which are distributed by Standard Brands, were empty.

Though they are doubtless still a minority, the companies that follow the I.B.M. approach to annual meetings, make them easy to attend, and try, within obvious limits, to tell the stockholders what they want to know, are growing rapidly. A.T.&T. has gone from small auditoriums in New York City to ballrooms to armories, in an effort to accommodate its interested stockholders. In 1961 the company met in Chicago, at the McCormick Place exhibition hall, where it drew about 20,000—the record for annual meetings up to that time (and 4000 more than the Chicago Cubs drew the same day). A number of big corporations with large numbers of stockholders have been using closed-circuit television; these include General Mills, I.B.M., General Electric, and American Machine & Foundry. One company recently tried to work out a deal to go on an *open* circuit, on a nationwide ABC-TV network. At the last minute the network's programing difficulties made the show impractical.

The case for the big, informative annual meeting has to do with public relations, principally. However, the public-relations staff—or stockholder-relations staff, as it is now likely to be called in companies that take the meetings seriously—can argue that the meetings offer some unique opportunities to management. For one thing, the meeting is an occasion when the president's pronouncements are especially apt to be printed in the financial press. He can get all kinds of publicity for a new sales campaign: in fact, corporations with widely dispersed ownership have come to view their stockholders as important consumers, and may use the annual meeting to introduce them to a new product (as Borden did one year with its instant mashed potatoes) or demonstrate a new technical development (as Polaroid did with its color film in 1960). The management has a chance to exult over the figures if they're good or explain them away if they're bad, to quash rumors, to insist that it is too early for the expansion program to be paying off, etc. It is true that annual meetings will also provide opportunities for attacks on, say, the high salaries the officers are getting, and the low dividend payout, and possibly the management's rejoinders will not be very persuasive. But the increased scale of the professional stockholders' operations makes it likely that such attacks are going to take place anyway when management is vulnerable; and so management might as well be prepared for them, and make its own pitch for the stockholders' loyalty.

An afternoon at the filling station

There was a time, in the nineteenth century, when the typical annual meeting really was a meeting of the corporation's owners. These would be a small group of people that very likely ran as well as owned the corporation, and that met, not to ratify what its directors had proposed, but to decide dividend policy and the basic direction the corporation should take. The growth of public corporations with hundreds, and then thousands, of stockholders tended to make this kind of annual meeting seem rather unrealistic, and there was a period, early in this century, when only curiosity seekers went to them. The rights of small stockholders were more or less nonexistent in those years, especially since the proxies they signed over to management gave it broad general powers and were often good for years. In 1934, Standard Oil of New Jersey showed pretty much how the business community viewed annual meetings when the company held one in a room above a filling station in Newark, New Jersey. The modern annual meeting as an institution really came into being in the mid-1930s when the newly formed Securities and Exchange Commission began to limit the use of proxies—a proxy today signs away only one vote on certain stated issues and is good only for a single meeting—and in other ways to clarify the rights of stockholders.

What rights do stockholders actually have at meetings today? Since these rights derive from different state laws, from the requirements of different stock exchanges, and from a variety of SEC rulings, there is considerable confusion on this score. However, there are some rights that are now pretty well established all over the U.S. and apply to virtually all corporations. It is clear, for example, that stockholders are entitled to know the salaries of all officers of a corporation. They are entitled to know the purpose of all extraordinary expenditures, and to have detailed breakdowns of corporate assets. It is a rule in practically all states that corporations must have the minutes of the last meeting at hand, and must allow stockholders to examine them. Moreover, stockholders have a right to examine lists of their fellow stockholders for ten days *before* the annual meeting. The only limitation on these rights is that they must be exercised for a "proper purpose"; a G.E. stockholder who ran an investment advisory service, for example, could not demand the stockholder list for the use of his direct-mail operations.

What the Big Board says

Certain other rights are also coming to be recognized. The April, 1961, issue of *The Exchange,* official publication of the New York Stock Exchange, contained a summary of basic information that stockholders in all public corporations—not just those on the Big Board—should be entitled to:

1. The current trend of sales and earnings.
2. Any major operating problems that may be facing the management.
3. The prospects of any nonrecurring profits or losses.
4. The management's plans for expanding its plants and products.
5. The company's dividend policies.
6. Research-and-development policies and programs.
7. Any major litigation that is pending by or against the corporation.
8. Any unusual financial matter that the company's independent auditor may have brought to the board's attention in the past six months. (Stockholders are entitled to have the auditor present at the meeting and available for questioning on such matters.)
9. Any pending moves importantly affecting the corporation's executive personnel, and the status of its labor relations.
10. The management's intentions, if any, to seek new financing.

There are also some clear-cut limitations on the stockholders' rights. One limitation, which comes as a rude blow to stockholders on occasion, concerns stock that they hold in a broker's name; if they forget to get a proxy signed by a partner in the brokerage firm they have no rights at the meeting—and, in fact, are not even supposed to be attending it. Stockholders have very few rights to economic data that might give valuable information to a competitor or a union. They cannot, for example, expect to be told about divisional profits or the profitability of individual products or stores, unless the management wants to tell them (which it seldom does).

In the uncertain area, there is much confusion as to the right, if any, of stockholders to examine the minutes of the meetings of boards of directors. At the annual meetings of some companies, these minute books are brought in by management, and are available for stockholders to examine. Their right to inspect the minutes of directors' meetings sometimes becomes an issue when the directors request stockholder approval of insider transactions—e.g., of acquisitions of supplier companies. Sophisticated stockholders ordinarily counter such requests by demanding to look at the minutes.

Making the stockholder sue

The foregoing recitation of stockholders' rights is not intended to suggest that they are easy to exercise. Actually, the stockholder who stands up to demand some of the information he is entitled to may well be told to sit down and mind his own business—perhaps because the chairman doesn't know his own obligations, or perhaps because he suspects the stockholder isn't going to court over the issue. Sometimes, of course, the management would actually like to have the stockholder go to court, where he will be obliged to show that he has a "proper purpose" for wanting the information. In some situations the management may frustrate the stockholder's purpose by making him disclose it. Several years ago, a major stockholder dissatisfied with the performance of the White Motor Co. sought to acquire the stockholder list so that he could make tenders for additional shares. But the management forced him to go to court, where he was obliged to reveal his plan, including the proposed tender price. When the proposed offer was printed, White Motor common promptly jumped to that price, which made the tender offer impossible.

On the other hand, there are some situations in which the stockholder seeking information is better protected if he sues for it. The court will insist, for example, that any stockholder list he gets be kept up to date. And the court will make the management supply the petitioning stockholder with transfer sheets, so that he can learn who is buying or selling stock right up to the last moment.

In theory, the principal business of an annual meeting—the only business that *all* corporations take up at their meetings—is the election of directors. At meetings of corporations in which a family or management group owns over 50 per cent of the stock, this business is not much more than a ritual, of course. Such companies are not required by the SEC even to solicit proxies, so that stockholders who want to register a protest against the directors proposed for election can do so only by going to the meeting and sounding off. (The New York Stock Exchange recently ruled that any of its listed companies that do not solicit proxies now—e.g., Canadian Pacific—must do so by the end of 1962.) Even in companies where there is no majority interest, the election of directors may not be terribly meaningful. Many companies have bolstered the management's position by offering staggered elections of directors—i.e., a different group is elected each year to serve, say, a three-year term; thus no insurgent group can ever topple the management slate in one year. Loud minority protests at annual meetings have led more and more companies—including American Can and American Radiator & Standard Sanitary recently—to announce that they would abandon this system.

Right now cumulative voting is probably the major change being demanded by minority stockholders who want to organize the election of directors more democratically—or at least more to their own advantage.* Under cumulative voting each stockholder is entitled to multiply each of his shares by the number of directors being elected;

* The late Robert R. Young favored cumulative voting when he was in the minority during the fight for the New York Central. But when Young won control of the Central, he refused to introduce cumulative voting there.

FOWSAB AND THE U.S.A

Though the Gilbert brothers (see page 180) are still preeminent among professional stockholders, two other professionals have enlivened a lot of annual meetings over the years. One is a voluble blonde and relentless feminist, Wilma Soss, who in 1944 organized the Federation of Women Shareholders in American Business, Inc. (or FOWSAB, as it is actually called). The federation is based on the arguable notion that, because most of the nation's corporate wealth is recorded in the names of women, women should have a louder voice in industry and should grace the boards of directors of more major corporations.

Mrs. Soss is frequently the scourge of secretive managements, but she has never revealed the membership of her own federation; even her own directors do not know how big it is. A New York membership costs $15, an out-of-town membership $10.

Federation members have investments in scores of corporations, and they often give their proxies to Mrs. Soss, who seems to enjoy kicking up a rumpus at the big meetings. Though most of her crusades are for purely feminist objectives, the federation is now working for a secret ballot at annual meetings, so that stockholders who are employees will not be in-then he can either cast his total vote for one candidate or spread it among any number of candidates. The point is to give minority stockholders a chance to combine and get at least one minority representative on the board. The system is a variation of proportional-representation voting in political elections. Today twenty-three states require cumulative voting.

Should auditors be elected?

The right to elect auditors at the annual meeting is another issue being pressed by some stockholder groups. According to the latest report of the Securities and Exchange Commission, some 676 listed firms elected auditors in 1961, vs. 608 in 1959; and the practice, which is mandatory in some states, is still expanding rapidly.

The auditors themselves are all for being elected by stockholders, because it strengthens their hands in dealing with management, particularly with a management that wants to have a specific item or transaction recorded so as to put itself in the most favorable light. The stockholders' feelings about the issue were illustrated in several incidents in Pennsylvania in recent years. In 1959, Pennsylvania amended the corporation law under which the election of auditors by stockholders had been required. Several corporations, including Westinghouse and Jones & Laughlin, thereupon dropped the practice at

~~~~~~

fluenced by management—an objective the Gilberts have also worked for on occasion. U. S. Steel and A.T.&T. fought her proposal, but both have had to put it in the proxy letter to stockholders.

Lawyer Benjamin Javits is another conspicuous figure at annual meetings most years. He planned to attend about fifteen in 1961. Javits wants stockholders to unite in his United Shareholders of America, which he formed in 1949 and envisages, ambitiously, as an influence upon national economic legislation, and as a force for educating the public on business and finance. Recently the U.S.A.'s influence has been limited, however. Its membership is listed at 6000 (as of 1961), but Javits admits that only some 1200 pay the dues, which are $10 a year. (In 1960 he paid $50,000 to a public-relations firm in an effort, thus far unsuccessful, to boost the membership to 25,000.) Members who pay dues get a pamphlet about the U.S.A. and a monthly newsletter about its activities. The organization promotes itself by giving out 300 or 400 awards every year to corporations with good managements or good stockholder relations.

Ben Javits is a peppery, fast-talking man, often credited with having made enough money to finance the political career of his brother, U.S. Senator Jacob Javits of New York. Both brothers made their legal reputa-

their 1960 meetings. Stockholders protested to both companies, and both had their stockholders elect the auditors in 1961.

The auditors are also pushing another reform in the holding of annual meetings. Along with many of the brokerage houses and some stockholders, the auditors would like to see more corporations break away from the widespread practice of holding annual meetings in March, April, or May. The practice grew up because of several legal requirements. An annual report must be in the hands of listed-company stockholders no more than three months after the close of the business year, which means by March 31 for companies that operate on a calendar year, as most companies do. The report must also be available to stockholders *before* they are asked to cast a proxy vote on any particular item. Since it takes at least two months to prepare, print, and distribute the annual report, companies normally begin meeting in March; companies that want to give themselves a bit more leeway usually set their meetings for April, which is actually the most popular month. Two hundred and forty-eight companies met on April 25, 1961, and 550 or so met on other days that same week.

The auditors have several reasons for wanting corporations to meet at different times. Stockholders will be able to attend more meetings. Brokers will not have to cope with a flood of proxy material descending on them all at once. And, of course, auditors themselves will not have so much of their work bunched in the first eight or ten weeks of

tions in stockholder derivative suits back in the 1930s. Their partnership was broken up only in 1959—in part because Ben wanted to take cases before federal regulatory agencies.

One likely reason for his problems in getting U.S.A. off the ground is his past and present identification with stockholder suits—and not always on the side of oppressed minority stockholders. In 1953, for example, Ben Javits received $100,000 from Twentieth Century-Fox for helping it get rid of cumulative voting when there was a threat of a proxy fight.

The relations between the annual-meeting "professionals" are not always friendly. Lewis Gilbert supports many of Mrs. Soss' proposals, but he has been critical of Javits for helping managements defeat cumulative-voting proposals.

THE MAN WHO'S BEEN TO 2000 MEETINGS

The busiest "professional stockholder" in the U.S. today is Lewis D. Gilbert, who has probably attended 2000 annual meetings in his life, which is almost certainly the world's record. In 1961 he planned to attend 117 annual meetings. His younger brother John attended another forty-six, and some dozen fellow stockholders who have joined their cause attended

the year. To spread annual meetings around, the auditors propose, more companies should switch from a calendar year to a "natural business year." This is a fiscal year geared to the annual cycle of activity of a corporation—i.e., it ends when inventories, receivables, bank loans, etc., are at their lowest point. Among the advantages of the natural business year: The company does not have to take stock of itself during its busy season, but rather when it is most liquid and most relaxed. Tax returns show fewer expenditures for inventories, thereby reducing a chronic source of argument with Internal Revenue, and income statements tend to show results of operations during one full business cycle. Most department stores, for example, are now on a fiscal year ending January 31, when the hysterics of Christmas selling and post-Christmas returns have subsided. Auditors would also like auto manufacturers to end their business year in September (when the model change is completed), and companies in other industries to follow suit.

New uses for annual meetings

There have been indications in recent years that annual meetings can be used by some stockholders to publicize causes that have not traditionally been on the agenda. Wilma Soss (see page 178), for example, has seemed at some meetings to be speaking less as an investor

~~~~~~

perhaps thirty others. At that, the Gilberts were missing the meetings of most of the corporations they try to follow; all together they and several relatives hold shares in some 800 corporations—up 200 from a few years ago.

Their purchases are usually in lots of five, ten, or twenty shares, and they hardly ever sell. This practice has served them well financially. Their original family fortune was considerably more modest than the "$2 million to $3 million" Lewis says their stock is worth now. His own dividend income is about $25,000 a year.

The brothers work together in Lewis' Park Avenue apartment, from which they keep track of all their corporations. In the den of the apartment they correspond with some 5000 other sympathetic shareholders, who send them proxies to be voted at annual meetings, and contribute a few dollars apiece to help pay for an annual report on their activities. The report is now in its twenty-second year. In 1960 it ran to 295 pages, crammed with details of the meetings the Gilberts and their associates attended.

The real flavor of the Gilbert operation is hard to convey to someone who has not seen Lewis or John on his feet at an annual meeting, exhorting the management to adopt cumulative voting (at Merritt-Chapman & Scott),

 a crusader for women's rights. A member of the Committee on
 Equality appeared in 1960 at meetings of F. W. Woolworth
and W. T. Grant (he had one share of each) to make a case for
lunch-counter integration. Union representatives have increasingly
made the annual stockholders' meeting an occasion for demanding
better working conditions. At the 1960 meeting of Crucible Steel,
representatives of the Steelworkers came to protest the closing of the
old Park Works in Pittsburgh.

Union representation at annual meetings is bound to grow more important as time goes on. For one thing, the total shareholdings of employees and the proportion of employees who own some stock continue to grow. On the basis of several different stock-purchase plans
General Electric has operating, the company expects that by 1965
over two-thirds of all employees will own some stock. At Varian Associates, the West Coast electronics firm, some 40 per cent of all the
stock is held by employees. (Varian is one of the very few corporations that hold their meetings at night—so that they can be attended
by people who hold jobs.)

urging that a ceiling be put on executive salaries (at General Motors and
du Pont), demanding that an auditor tell whether or not he checked inventories to assure the stockholders there was little chance of pilferage
(I.T.T.). They get excited when they are crossed by management, which
is often, and their shouting matches with executives sometimes exhaust
the patience of other stockholders, who clamor for them to sit down. In
turn, they are likely to denounce such critics as management stooges, paid
to disrupt their presentations. (Sometimes they are.) Several years ago
there was a spectacular comedy of errors at a Twentieth Century-Fox
meeting, when Lewis tangled with Spyros Skouras, the ebullient, fractured-
English-speaking president, who kept trying to agree with him, but kept
on being misunderstood and denounced more furiously than ever.

It is obvious that the Gilberts thrive on publicity, but also obvious that
they use it artfully in fighting for the rights of stockholders. They keep in
touch with the financial reporters, and often exchange tips with them.
They also get a lot of tips from disgruntled employees who are stockholders, but feel inhibited from raising issues at a meeting run by their
employers.

The Gilberts' influence on corporate practices is hard to assess. Many
of their "triumphs" are on trivial issues—e.g., brother John recently got
the president of a real-estate corporation to stop charging voice lessons to
the corporation. But there is no doubt that the knowledge that a Gilbert
will show up is a pressure on many top executives to respect the rights of
their stockholders. And they have some solid achievements to their credit.

Perhaps the main reason the annual meeting is being subjected to all these new influences is simply that the modern corporation, increasingly "public" in fact as well as in law, is being subjected to them too. Some corporations, facing this prospect realistically, have opted for bigger and more elaborate annual meetings, dealing with a wide range of issues. General Electric, for example, agreed in 1961 to a proposal by James B. Carey's electrical workers' union (whose pension fund owned twenty-five shares) that stockholders vote on the question of employing any executives convicted of violating antitrust laws, and on other issues relating to the company's recent antitrust problems. G.E. is even thinking of staging "post-annual meetings." These would be held after the regular meeting in New York at perhaps thirty or forty G.E. plants. They would be presided over by the plant manager, and stockholders, employees, and other people in the community would be invited to attend. It is still hard to believe that corporate meetings will ever be democratic in any strict sense of the word. But it is beginning to seem likely that the meetings will become a lot more important to stockholders—and, no doubt, a lot more interesting too.

Industrial corporations almost always get their annual reports to stockholders before their meetings, but banks, which are not regulated by the SEC, sometimes hold their meetings *before* they publish their reports. This sequence of events obviously handicaps bank stockholders who want to ask some searching questions at the meetings. When Lewis made an issue of it, a number of banks changed the sequence.

Lewis has often scored his point even when he has been outvoted. When the late George Coppers was head of National Biscuit Co., Lewis kept introducing a motion to put a ceiling on the executive-pension program. The motion never won over more than 10 per cent of the stockholders, but Coppers finally decided that he did not want to ignore the views of this minority. He consulted with Lewis and the company put a ceiling of $45,000 on executive pensions.

Lewis has probably done as much as any one man to further the stockholders' rights to information. Not all stockholders are grateful, however. At a meeting of Unexcelled Chemical Corp. in 1961, Lewis rose in outrage to note that the annual report did not even indicate whether the corporation had operated at a profit. Ordinarily, a corporation must show its operating figures separately from its capital transactions, but Unexcelled's auditor argued against Lewis, contending that for the past year the capital transactions *were* the only real operations of the company. Lewis was attacked by other stockholders who were present. "Are you trying to drive the price of the stock down?" one of them demanded.

12

The SEC: Caveat Emptor

According to Keith Funston, president of the New York Stock Exchange, the expansion of American industry in the immediate years ahead may be so great as to demand new equity financing of about $7 billion per year between now and 1965. Since Mr. Funston is given at times to hyperbole, this may be an extravagant prophecy, but there is no doubt that the capital market of the U.S., centered in Wall Street but operating, too, in most larger cities of the country, has been growing rapidly. In 1961 corporate securities offered for cash ran to some $12.7 billion, of which about $3.1 billion was in the form of stocks and $9.6 billion in bonds. This was a $2.4 billion increase in total corporate financing over 1959 and a $5.8 billion increase over 1951. Meanwhile, in the decade after 1951 the value of all stocks quoted on the exchanges of the U.S. tripled, rising from $111 billion to some $327 billion, or about $30 billion more than national debt of the U. S. Government. And in early 1962, with the Dow-Jones averages at all-time highs, it was understandable why gentlemen operating in the vicinity of Broad and Wall streets should be paying more attention to the question of whether stocks can eventually hit 1000 than to the question of how the abuses of the last "New Era" can be avoided.

But while active capital markets are in general good news for a capitalist economy, they also place a growing and fearsome responsibility on that unique American institution called the Securities and Exchange Commission. Set up twenty-eight years ago to administer the famous "truth in securities" act of 1933, the "full disclosure" act of 1934, and a mass of subsequent legislation, the commission modestly defines part of its activities as follows: "supervision of the registration of securities for sale to the public by use of the mails and in interstate commerce, the surveillance of the exchange and over-the-counter markets in securities, regulation of the activities of brokers and dealers, regulation of registered public utility holding company systems and investment companies, and litigation in the courts." Considering that in 1961 alone the commission as a matter of course handled some 1507 registration statements covering some $19.1 billion of securities, and that at the end of that year there were some 5446 brokers and dealers registered with the SEC, this is to say the least quite a job.

"All that we are is educated lie detectors caught between the investing public and the issuer," sighs a veteran of a quarter-century on the SEC. But even in a day of "truth serum" tests and intricate psychiatric analysis, lie detection is not proving an easy task. And for the SEC, the cop on the corner not just of Broad and Wall streets, but of Pine Street, San Francisco, and La Salle Street, Chicago, and Exchange Place, Salt Lake City, and dozens of other streets where securities are actively traded, lie detection is proving an onerous, exacting, and ever more expensive task.

It was the widespread and growing feeling about the SEC's inadequacy in coping with the liars of the securities markets that led Congress, in mid-1961, to press upon the commission $750,000 for a full-scale, intensive investigation of the stock markets. This investigation will not be concluded until early in 1963; but it is already apparent, from the zeal with which it was undertaken, that it will lead to major reforms in the securities markets. Somehow or other, it is clear, the SEC will be tightening its regulation of the over-the-counter market, the American Stock Exchange, and even the Big Board. The market for new issues is being examined with special thoroughness. Conceivably, the investigation may even end in legislation requiring a separation of the broker and dealer functions— i.e., forbidding stock brokers to buy and sell securities for their own accounts.

The chairman of the "Kennedy SEC," William Cary, was an enthusiastic supporter of the investigation from the time it was proposed, but it is significant that the proposal came from *outside* the SEC, principally from Congress. The fact is that by 1961 there was a widespread feeling that the commission, which ordinarily spends between $5 million and $7 million a year on the detection of financial lies, had been dozing on its beat. True, the number of its investigations into shady security transactions rose from 1117 in fiscal 1955 to 1527 in fiscal 1961. During this period, a young attorney by the name of Paul Windels, Jr., head of the SEC's New York regional office, came to be known as "Pistol Paul" for his savage attacks on boiler-room operators (high-pressure salesmen of nearly worthless securities), his vigor in hauling phony stock dealers into court, and his obvious fondness for such legal firearms as injunctions, stop orders, and suspension orders. Yet despite all this the number of shady stock deals and weird corporate manipulations seems to keep on mounting.

The rapid rise and then collapse of the stock of the Bellanca Corp. back in 1956; the strange doings of Leopold D. Silberstein in the case of the Penn-Texas Corp., disclosed in 1957; the ease with which investors were fleeced in Great Sweet Grass Oils and Kroy Oils; the baffling trail left by Lowell Birrell in the rape of the assets of the Swan-Finch Oil Corp.; the dizzying manipulations of Alexander Guterma in several different public corporations; the charge of the SEC itself that raider Louis Wolfson was something less than frank with the public in the matter of American Motors stock; the fantastic career of Maurice Olen, whose largely fictitious financial statements, passed by the SEC, figured in the H. L. Green fraud; the gyrations of Artloom Carpet, U. S. Hoffman Machinery, and Canadian Javelin—all these alarums and excursions have tended to cast doubt on the SEC's efficacy as even a detective outfit. Add in the congressional investigation of Bernard Goldfine, which showed that his East Boston Co., while listed on the Boston Stock Exchange, had gone for six years without submitting a financial report to the SEC, and it's obvious why members of the commission and their staff have been occupying some uncomfortably warm seats. When Commissioner Cary gave up his law professorship at Columbia to head up the SEC in 1961, he made it clear to reporters that he looked forward eagerly to his new assignment. Cary was and is an egghead liberal (he once worked for Stevenson), and an avowed idealist, but he also has a reputation for being tough and practical. The reputation will plainly be put to a severe test.

How many blackbirds?

Before getting too worked up about the alleged laxity of the SEC, and certainly before prying further into the tangled financial affairs of Bellanca, Penn-Texas, Swan-Finch, Louis Wolfson, *et al.*, it is well to put the job of the agency into perspective. In the first place it should go without saying, but unfortunately doesn't, that if it takes more than a single swallow to make a summer, it surely takes more than several blackbirds to prove that there is a national scandal in the broad field of security dealings. Every weekday of the year barring holidays, of which Wall Street is fond, millions of dollars worth of securities change hands—in 1961 over $60 billion worth—with scarcely a sign of dishonest trading. And the securities broker, who in one breath may imply that something is amiss with the SEC inspection system, will in the next be expatiating on the honesty and probity of the financial markets. The truth is that the overwhelming majority of the financial community observes such a high code of ethics that a large part of its daily business is transacted on the strength of the spoken word; and that the great exchanges of the country, as well as the National Association of Securities Dealers, are largely self-policing. Were this not so, no apparatus of SEC regulation and inspection could ever work any more than a police force, however big, could possibly enforce the mildest traffic laws in a great city without large-scale voluntary compliance.

But, second, the basic work of the Securities and Exchange Commission is precisely what the newspaper headlines never illuminate when they turn the spotlight on a Wolfson or a Birrell. That work, which occupies easily 60 per cent of the commission's effort, is to see to it that public issues of securities are properly registered, and that corporations continue to submit exact and reliable financial data as to their operations. Over the years this extraordinary service has worked out better than many of its most sanguine advocates would have believed possible. When the original securities legislation was passed in the wake of the 1929 collapse and Franklin Roosevelt's resounding talk about having driven "the money changers . . . from their high seats in the temple," great was the outcry of those affected. Yet in the past quarter-century brokers, dealers, and lawyers have learned to live with the basic laws of the land and indeed, in the case of a good many lawyers, to live off them. In a *Fortune* article at the time Arthur Dean, one of Wall Street's more prominent attorneys, drew attention to the severe and vague liability provisions of the 1933 Securities Act and stated that "the mind despairs" of how they would be interpreted. Many believed that the new laws would lead to an overwhelming and unwholesome volume of private stockholders' suits against companies registering with the SEC, thus binding the hands of management and cluttering the channels of legitimate enterprise. Such fears have proved unfounded. Indeed, it can be argued that it would be a good thing if private investors today *were* bringing lawsuits against corporations in cases of financial malfeasance. For this would indicate public awareness that in the last analysis it is up to the investor, both before and after he buys securities, to protect his own interests rather than think that his government can do the whole job for him.

This leads to a third and crucial point. Under state blue-sky laws, government agencies sometimes have the power to pick and choose among securities that private parties are offering on the market and to bar an issue that they consider unsound. This is not and never has been the purpose of national legislation in this field. That purpose is "full disclosure" of fact rather than active government responsibility for the kinds of securities issued in this country. "If men wish to form a company whose avowed objective is to pitch dollars off the Empire State Building," remarked a former employee of the SEC recently, "there is nothing or little in the law to stop them so long as they tell people what they propose to do." The SEC does not undertake to prevent investors, once they have been given the truth, from getting burnt as the result of bad judgment; nor is it a collection agency for those who think they have been swindled and who can always instigate private legal action. Finally, while the SEC was set up to administer certain highly complicated laws, it is itself the child of law. While it does itself possess certain sanctions, such as delisting a security or revoking a broker-dealer registration, it fundamentally has to rely on the civil and criminal courts for stronger punitive action against offenders. It is conceivable, of course, that the commission's current investigations will lead to legislation substantially broadening its powers.

Meanwhile, the job Congress has set the SEC is an extraordinarily difficult one. If the agency moves too slowly against the crooks it will be accused of lying down on its job. If on the other hand it flings its weight about arbitrarily it will be accused, and rightly accused, of burning down the country's financial house in order to get some very dubious roast pig. To hold the balance true requires a commission and a staff of outstanding character and ability, and here the agency faces a much tougher problem than it did in its early and formative years.

The faded glamour

During the first and second New Deals the SEC was a glamour outfit, which easily attracted the bright young graduates of the country's leading law schools. It was chairmanned by such near legendary figures as Joseph P. Kennedy, James Landis, former dean of Harvard Law School, and the late Jerome Frank, who intellectually was as much at home in the scholastic logic of Thomas Aquinas as in the niceties of administrative law. (On being gently reminded that one of his opinions was perhaps overlong and over-intricate for the occasion, Frank snapped back: "Make me a sum-mary but add it in as an appendix!") Those exciting days, when a job in the agency was a liberal education at government expense, would probably have come to an end anyway as the SEC came to be ac-cepted by the financial community. They were ended instead by World War II, when corporate issues slumped to as low as $1 billion a year, and when the SEC was unceremoniously packed off from Washington, D.C., to temporary lodgings in Philadelphia, where its staff busied themselves with studies of the Japanese railroad system and the condition of European harbors.

After the war the SEC returned to Washington but it never fully recovered its old prestige. Membership on the five-man commission, which is appointed by the President, came to be viewed as a stepping-stone to other office or as a duty, but scarcely as a privilege, and staff recruitment continued to languish. The demise of the Truman re-gime and the coming of the Eisenhower Administration did not greatly change matters. Under Eisenhower, the commission had three different chairmen: Ralph Demmler, who at the end of twenty-three months gave up the job to return to a lucrative Pittsburgh law prac-tice; J. Sinclair Armstrong, whose youthful enthusiasm did much to stir up the agency but who after a couple of years found more exciting duties as Assistant Secretary of the Navy; and Edward Gadsby, who spent no little time and effort in trying to soothe ruffled feelings left by his predecessor both inside and outside the agency.

An experienced administrator, Chairman Gadsby emphasized that by the very nature of its work the success or failure of the SEC de-pended basically on its permanent staff. Hence like Armstrong before him he bent every effort to try to repair the damage of the war years and was in part successful. Back in June, 1941, the SEC had some 1683 employees, an all-time record. Thereafter (partly as the result of attrition but more because the SEC had largely completed its work under the Public Utility Holding Company Act) employment dropped off rapidly, reaching an all-time low of 666 men and women in 1955. When Gadsby left office in January, 1961, the SEC had some 900 employees in Washington and its field offices, and its budget for the 1961 fiscal year ran to $7,100,000. It is interesting to note that, while egging on the commission to pursue larger objectives, in ap-propriating funds for special investigation Congress did nothing to beef up the commission's permanent staff. The investigation itself is being run by a former SEC officer, Milton Cohen, who was persuaded to take time off from his law practice in Chicago. One danger in the present situation is that Cohen's investigation will end by imposing new responsibilities on the SEC, but that Congress will continue to be laggard in providing the wherewithal for an expanded permanent staff.

What holds the agency together is, of course, a small inner group of trained lawyers, accountants, and administrators, and here it faces severe competition from higher paying jobs in industry. "Personnel," remarked Chairman Gadsby, "has been an acute problem for years. It's never been big enough . . . When we have to work within a given time limit we do it, but it's at the expense of something else." The problem has persisted under Cary's administration. The commission's growing workload, and resources for coping with it, can be traced in the box on page 199.

Penny stocks and all that

What burns up the SEC time, talent, and money, moreover, is paradoxically the least important and in some ways most trivial part of its work. Even when the volume of security offerings is large, it is not too much of a job nowadays to get major corporations to stick to the rules of registration and continuing disclosure of fact. Much more harassing and expensive is the task of policing the shoestring promoter and the fringe operator, who always put in their appearance when security markets are active. In the 1920s and into the 1930s, Wall Street produced the phenomenon of the "bucket shop"—the so-called broker who took an order to buy General Motors at a given price, "bucketed" the order, and went off with the money. Today the gadfly is the so-called boiler-room operator, who seeks to sell over the telephone securities that have little or no worth—oil stocks, uranium or other mining stocks, as the case may be.

To check this kind of monkey business, responsibility falls heavily on the SEC's New York office, which employs 184 people. Under aggressive Paul Windels, Jr., who ran the office in 1956–1961, it took action against some 200 suspect boiler-room operators, sometimes permanently and sometimes, unfortunately, only to find that the culprit changed his venue and started all over again. (Recently the administrator of the New York office has been Llewellyn P. Young, who has run things much more quietly than Windels; it is perhaps too early to evaluate his performance.) What troubled Windels was that his means of meting out punishment was limited—a point that applies, of course, to most SEC operations. Much can be accomplished by publicity and by letting it be known that SEC investigators are on the prowl. Again it is not too hard to get a restraining order or injunction in the civil courts against malefactors, but this carries no financial penalty unless the defendant breaks the order and is then found in contempt of court. What really hurts is a successful criminal proceeding, and for this the SEC merely prepares the case and then turns it over to the Department of Justice, recommending prosecution. But all too often the Justice Department has other and more important fish to fry—especially as SEC cases are highly technical, difficult to understand, and even more difficult to present to a judge or a jury.

The Canadian curtain

But this is not the only difficulty that lies in the way of preventing the sale of worthless or near worthless stocks. A more frustrating fact is that many "problem stocks" are of Canadian origin and the SEC lacks effective jurisdiction over dealers or companies that operate across what has been called the Canadian "Iron Curtain." How much money has been funneled out of the U.S. into questionable Canadian securities is impossible to estimate: it's been reckoned as high as $100 million or more per year. Efforts of the U.S. and Canadian governments to control this flow have not been overly successful though there is some cooperation between the SEC and Canadian provincial authorities. One of the weapons the agency devised back in 1951 for meeting this problem was the "blacklisting" of certain Canadian securities. Once a stock has been placed on the restricted list it becomes dangerous for a U.S. broker or dealer to execute a buy order (though he may take a sell order).

However, it is hard for the SEC to keep the list up to date, and by the time a stock has been blacklisted the chances are that investors have been sucked in and the money is gone. Frequently, moreover, it's a simple matter for the Canadian promoters to change the name of the security and begin their operations all over again. Thus, back in the Thirties, Canadians put together a company called Ascot Gold Mines. Later it became Hugh Malartic Gold Mines Ltd. and still later the New Hugh Malartic Mines. By 1957 the company had become Alba Explorations and made a new issue of stock.

In 1958, Alba stood second on the SEC's restricted list, and its high-pressure sales campaign in this country had just about fizzled out. That perhaps was just as well since at last reckoning its accounts receivable ran to $2400 against liabilities of $73,000.

Javelin jitters

Critics of the SEC feel that it should have moved on situations like Alba much faster, and the agency is far from claiming that its record in this respect is perfect. On the other hand, blacklisting a stock can be a two-edged sword: it may hamper the promoter but it may also harm the investor just as much. For instance, there is the case of Canadian Javelin, a mining company with some potentially valuable ore bodies in Labrador and Newfoundland, which has been traded in U.S. over-the-counter markets for several years. In July, 1958, U.S. brokers discovered that large blocks of Javelin were being inexplicably dumped in the U.S. and its price fell from $16 to $13 a share. The SEC then announced that it was putting Javelin on the restricted list on the grounds that some of its "control" stock was being sold in this country and should be registered. This move simply increased the selling pressure and the stock dropped to $7 per share in Canada, even though Javelin's management and key shareholders stated they wanted it to become an American company and would comply with the SEC's requirements. Javelin was later restored to good standing, but meanwhile investors who sold out with the idea that something was very wrong with the company had suffered, while those who sold short gained. Whatever the merits of this case, it illustrates the fact that when the SEC takes action against a security it is itself affecting the market though it is not actually "in" it. As in the case of the policeman "protecting" the corner store, the danger is always that the bystanders no less than the culprit will get hurt.

Playing the technicalities

This point should also be held in mind in approaching a series of famous U.S. cases—Penn-Texas, Bellanca, and the doings of Lowell Birrell—where the SEC has been under severe criticism. What seems appalling at first glance is that in some of these cases there has been very obvious manipulation of corporate finances going on right under the nose of the SEC without its being able, or feeling able, to protect the shareholder. Once again, however, it should be recalled that the security laws do not make the SEC arbiter as to whether corporations should or should not do certain things. Its mission is basically to see that they tell the public what they are doing. If, to take an extreme example, a corporation president raids the till of his company, he is certainly subject to prosecution by stockholders or state and federal legal authorities. But action by the SEC would normally have to be based on the contention that the company has not reported on what he is doing, or has issued new stock without so registering it. "We work," says an experienced SEC attorney, "always on the basis of what to the public are technicalities."

And the technicalities are by no means always present. Thus, in the famous case of Penn-Texas (now Fairbanks, Whitney), there is little doubt that Leopold D. Silberstein indulged in some very fancy dealings when he enlarged this company into a sprawling empire through acquisitions and mergers that included Industrial Brownhoist, Niles-Bement-Pond, and other enterprises. While he ran the company, he increased Penn-Texas stock from about 150,000 shares to 4,600,000, depleted its earning power, and saddled the company with large debts. Yet under an SEC ruling (Rule 133), stock issued in the course of a merger is not regarded as a "public offering," and hence does not usually have to be registered. Moreover, Silberstein was careful to report his acquisitions to the SEC and hence satisfied the technical requirements of the 1934 Securities Exchange Act as regards disclosure. Where Silberstein came to grief was in his failure to get control of Fairbanks, Morse after two proxy battles in 1956 and 1957. Here there was widespread suspicion that Silberstein was using Swiss agents to acquire shares of the company. But Swiss banks hold obdurately to the sound tradition of protecting the identity of their customers. And the SEC is scarcely in a position to break down this protection of individual property rights abroad, though it is trying to restrain Americans from abusing it. The net of the whole affair was that Silberstein was able to do much as he chose with Penn-Texas assets until finally ousted by its board of directors.

Bellanca and Swan-Finch

In some other scandals the SEC has had more to go on, but still has been slow on the uptake. In expanding the Bellanca Corp., for instance, Sydney Albert, a salvager of used machinery from Akron, Ohio, pulled off some deals that rivaled those of Silberstein (including

massive borrowing on his company's credit) but signally failed to report his doings either to his shareholders or to the SEC—as he was
bound to do, since Bellanca was registered on the American Exchange. Yet it was not until after Bellanca shares had risen from
4⅜ in 1954 to 30½ in July, 1955, and then had plunged to 3 in
the stock-market reversal of 1956, that the SEC got active; and it
was not until April, 1957, that it temporarily suspended trading in
the issue. With Bellanca shares now worthless, many an investor feels
that the SEC should have acted earlier when Bellanca was buoyantly
rising, and the SEC itself grants at least part of the criticism.

More baffling is the case of Lowell Birrell, who between 1954 and
1957 pulled off some extraordinary maneuvers in Swan-Finch, an oil
company, and eventually escaped the country with a reputed $10
million in his pocket. Birrell's career is chronicled in Chapter
Eight. The point about it that bears on the SEC is the ease with which
he was able to unload unregistered stock on the public—usually
by posting shares as collateral for loans, then defaulting on the
loans, so that the shares were thrown on the market by the loan
company. In April, 1957, the SEC finally obtained a temporary restraining order that brought Birrell's operations in Swan-Finch to a
halt, but by that time the harm had been done. Given Birrell's
reputation as a manipulator, the SEC might well have moved faster.
At the same time, it should be emphasized that the agency was able
to stop Birrell only on the technicality that his maneuvers constituted an underwriting. Once more there is a wide gap between
sensing that something is wrong in the security markets and getting
a legal redress that will stick.

Wolfson and Goldfine

Compared to the Penn-Texas, Bellanca, and Swan-Finch cases,
the highly publicized doings of Louis Wolfson and Bernard Goldfine
turn out to be pretty small potatoes. Among his manifold other activities, Wolfson had acquired some 400,000 shares in American
Motors, or 7 per cent of its outstanding stock. In June, 1958, the
New York *Times* carried a story quoting a "spokesman" for Mr.
Wolfson—who turned out to be one of his long-time associates, Alex
Rittmaster—to the effect that Wolfson was "about one-quarter of the
way home" in selling out his American Motors holdings—an odd
statement for anyone trying to unload a stock.

Investigation by the SEC quickly disclosed that Mr. Wolfson had in fact sold *all* of his American Motors stock some weeks before, and that furthermore 132,000 shares had been sold short in accounts held in the names of members of his family and in two accounts in which he held a part interest. The SEC then obtained a temporary injunction barring Wolfson and his associates from trading in American Motors. Wolfson at first protested the injunction, but before the case got to court he signed a consent judgment in which he agreed not to make "false and misleading statements" about the stock. At the same time, however, he said under oath that he had not violated the security laws, and had not intentionally misled the public. The SEC remains somewhat skeptical but is inclined to let the matter rest. Shareholders in American Motors were not too seriously hurt, and in fact Wolfson's accounts had to cover their short sales at higher prices and take a substantial loss. In getting Wolfson to sign the consent judgment, the SEC feels that it acted not only promptly but efficaciously. And as matters turned out, the big publicity given the case was in almost inverse proportion to its real importance.

This is likewise true of the Goldfine case, which leapt into prominence largely as the result of Bernard Goldfine's relations with Sherman Adams. In the course of its recent investigation into various administrative agencies, a congressional committee stumbled on the fact that Goldfine had called Adams to ask him to look into difficulties that his East Boston Co. was having with the SEC. As it turned out, these difficulties were of long standing, and as it furthermore turned out, Mr. Goldfine had failed to file proper reports with the SEC between 1948 and 1954. In 1955 the SEC finally took court action against him, and, on the strength of this action, a shareholder later revived a private suit demanding a full accounting of Goldfine's activities and charging that he misused company assets. The cases have since been settled, but the substance of the criticism of the SEC is simply that it took so long in making him disclose his operations despite frequent complaints by the Boston Stock Exchange. There is no evidence that this was due to political pressure. The explanation seems to be that the SEC had other business on hand. Moreover, it should be noted that at no time would anything much have been gained by delisting East Boston. Goldfine, like many another businessman, has himself complained of the expense and bother of keeping up with the requirements for listed securities. Nothing might have pleased him better than to be thrown off the Boston Exchange.

Throwing its weight

The extraordinary publicity given to these and other affairs could be salutary if it served to put the SEC on its toes. It also, however, involves an implicit danger—the agency, stung by congressional criticism, may now throw its weight around in all directions, and in the process disrupt normal and legitimate financial business. Indeed, many in Wall Street believe that this is just what happened in the 1958 Arvida melee. Here Arthur V. Davis, former chairman of Aluminum Corp. of America, and at ninety-four still an energetic multi-millionaire, decided to incorporate some real estate that he owns in Florida and to sell shares in the new corporation, called Arvida, to the public. To this end he enlisted the services of Dominick & Dominick, and Carl M. Loeb, Rhoades, both well-entrenched brokerage and investment-banking firms. At a press conference in mid-September spokesmen for both firms discussed many details of the proposed offering, including a possible price of about $10 per share. Under the 1933 Security Act, however, it is illegal for underwriters to make any kind of public offering before a registration statement has been filed with the commission. In the case of Arvida, registration proceedings had not even begun. Accordingly the SEC rushed into court and tried to get an injuction to prevent any further "sales effort." In addition the commission announced it would start proceedings to determine whether the broker-dealer registration of Dominick & Dominick and Carl M. Loeb, Rhoades should be revoked. These proceedings went to the commission itself for adjudication, and the case was later dropped.

While such punishment if administered may be minor (it might turn out to be a suspension for only a week or two, and other Wall Street houses, including Kidder, Peabody, have suffered as much), it of course impugns the ability if not the integrity of the issuing houses, and it is no wonder the Arvida case stirred up a hornets' nest. There is little question that the Arvida underwriters were imprudent in holding their press conference, and the SEC has every reason to be vigilant about what goes on before a security is registered, as well as after. For if underwriters can purvey any kind of information they choose before the agency has finally passed on the offering, they can obviously short-circuit the enforcement of the truth-in-security laws. On the other hand, the Ford issues of 1956 received huge advance publicity and the SEC never raised a finger. It should also be pointed out that the SEC moved against the underwriters without even warning them in advance of what it was doing. Finally, it is ironic that after a good many failures (as in the cases of Bellanca and Swan-Finch) to prevent large-scale financial manipulations that did harm the public, the SEC should make so much of a case where little if any public harm could have been done. The law is the law, but if its net effect is to police those who require little policing while being ineffective against those who require much, then there is reason for public concern.

Economics vs. the law

The problem is a real one, and, indeed, always has been since the first truth-in-security laws were passed. The solution, however, is certainly not to give the SEC more legal power than it has today, as is so often suggested by Congressmen, including Senator Fulbright. The fact is that the SEC already has under present law as much power as any administrative agency can possibly handle and maybe too much. The great need is for the SEC itself to keep its eye fixed on the obvious intent of all securities legislation—namely, to give the public the truth and to let a healthy capital market operate and expand.

And on this point surely economic as well as legal considerations come, or should come, to bear. If the U.S. is to expand, national savings must pass easily and constantly into new as well as established ventures without being hung up on too much legal barbed wire. It is noteworthy in this connection that while the security legislation of the Thirties did not result in all the disasters that some predicted, it did give rise to the phenomenon of "private placement," wherein corporations avoid the expense and delay of registration proceedings by selling their securities directly to a few large buyers—principally insurance companies. In recent years private placements have run to about a third of all corporate issues—some $4.2 billion in 1961 out of a total of $12.7 billion. While there is nothing technically wrong with the practice, it is by no means as healthy as the sale of securities in the open market where many purchasers have a chance to participate, which encourages the dispersion rather then the concentration of corporate ownership.

The capital market

More seriously, there has always been some question as to whether the security laws and their administration did not impede the flow of new capital, especially into smaller corporate enterprises. While the capital market is certainly active today, it should nevertheless be noted that some of this activity, about 7 per cent in 1961, is in refunding. But "refunding America," while no doubt necessary, is scarcely Wall Street's most important function. Moreover, whether in refunding or in new issues, the problem of the small corporation vis-à-vis the large remains. Corporate giants like A.T.&T. and U. S. Steel can always afford the legal talent to see them through the rigors of SEC surveillance. Wall Street abounds with competent lawyers to do the job and to do the job well. But smaller and newer companies resent both the expense and the delays involved.

For this reason Congress wisely exempted issues of under $300,000 from the registration mill. It is a hopeful sign that the SEC itself now favors lifting this limit to $500,000, and perhaps it should be raised to $1 million. This is only one possible reform but it points in the right direction. No doubt any easing of SEC requirements could pave the way for more "scandals in securities." But some chances will have to be taken, and it is past time for the public to realize that its real protection lies not in government enforcement of the doctrine of *caveat venditor*, but in common-sense understanding of the more ancient doctrine of *caveat emptor*.

In any case, it would be a national misfortune if the very real personal losses wrought by the appearance of a Birrell, or by the occasional and unintentional peccadilloes and mistakes of this or that Wall Street underwriter, or the understandable desire of the SEC to prove itself a good watchdog, should obscure larger objectives. The precondition of capitalism is the free flow of private capital. And if we are to come anywhere near the goal of $7 billion of new equity financing per year by 1965, the channels of capital formation need to be dredged and broadened rather than constricted.

THE SEC—A GROWTH SITUATION

EMPLOYMENT AND PRINCIPAL WORK-LOAD TRENDS
Fiscal Years 1950 to 1960

	1950	1951	1952	1953	1954	1955	1956	1957	1958	1959	1960
Registration filings	496	544	665	621	649	849	981	943	913	1,226	1,628
Regulation A filings	1,375	1,358	1,494	1,528	1,175	1,628	1,463	919	732	854	1,049
Preliminary proxy statements filed	1,711	1,805	1,850	1,821	1,858	1,934	2,016	1,991	1,994	2,024	2,133
Annual reports filed	2,872	2,937	2,994	3,056	3,086	3,145	3,241	3,394	3,645	3,692	3,854
Broker-dealer inspections	906	922	827	686	788	822	952	1,214	1,452	1,471	1,499
Investigations opened	550	725	511	462	343	392	362	512	447	523	519
Criminal cases referred	18	29	14	18	19	8	17	26	15	45	53
Administrative proceedings completed(1)	89	118	56	64	48	34	43	65	96	131	106
Injunction actions filed	34	21	27	22	19	31	35	71	65	60	86
Average employment	1,062	1,040	930	813	750	700	707	778	836	904	945
Per cent of employment in regional offices	31%	32%	34%	35%	35%	37%	37%	38%	39%	41%	41%

(1) Limited to cases in which order for hearing was issued by the commission.

THE SEC'S PLEA TO INVESTORS

The homily below is taken from an SEC brochure explaining the functions of the agency. It indicates how much the commission itself would like to retire the illusion that government regulation of securities guarantees their worth.

Investigate Before You Invest

Avoid unnecessary losses in the purchase of securities by following this ten-point guide to safer investments:

1. Before buying—*Think!*
2. Don't deal with strange securities firms. (*Consult your broker.*)
3. Beware of securities offered over the telephone by strangers.
4. Don't listen to high-pressure sales talk.
5. Beware of promises of spectacular profits.
6. Be sure you understand the risks of loss.
7. Don't buy on tips and rumors—*Get all the facts!*
8. *Tell the salesman to:* Put all the information and advice in writing and mail it to you—*Save it!*
9. If you don't understand all the written information—*Consult a person who does!*
10. Give at least as much consideration to buying securities as you would to . . . any valuable property.

Appendix

Should Financial Reporting Be "Flexible"?

The rules of the auditing profession, though often the subject of argument, are seldom argued in public. But at the September, 1960, meeting of the American Institute of Certified Public Accountants, in Philadelphia, two distinguished auditors made speeches setting forth quite different ideas about the principles—and practices— of their profession. The speeches were actually billed as a "debate"; it would probably be more realistic to view them simply as two different views of an old and sticky problem.

The problem, in essence, is this: Auditors feel that they must retain an element of judgment in their handling of financial reports, because corporate finance is so complicated, and the words used to describe some transactions are so ambiguous, that there is no way to systematize the reporting once and for all. But if auditors exercise much judgment, then they will surely disagree, and the public will be uncertain what to believe about the published reports. Where should the limits of judgment be set—or can a line be drawn at all? Is there a "right" way to prepare a financial report? Or is it all just a matter of definition?

The first speaker was Leonard Spacek of Arthur Andersen & Co.; the second was Maurice Peloubet of Pogson, Peloubet. Mr. Spacek argued in general that the profession's principles had already been stretched too far, and that auditors were drifting away from "fairness." Mr. Peloubet argued the case for maximum flexibility, and derided the notion that there is one right way to report a transaction. Their talks are reprinted here in full. In addition, Mr. Spacek has written a letter to *Fortune* commenting on some of Mr. Peloubet's statements, and Mr. Peloubet has written commenting on both Mr. Spacek's statements and his letter. These "rebuttals" are also printed below, with minor deletions.

Are Accounting Principles Generally Accepted or Generally Ignored?

LEONARD SPACEK

A discussion of the question as to whether accounting principles are generally accepted or generally ignored would be incomplete without a program for solution of the problems that now confront us. Then, too, in my public discussions of these problems, I have been asked many times to make my comments as specific as possible. Accordingly, after considering the question as to the acceptance of accounting principles, I am going to briefly discuss ways of eliminating those practices which I consider objectionable.

If generally accepted accounting principles are those now being followed by the profession, and if acceptance means (as the dictionary says) "an act of accepting; favorable reception; approval," then, as a profession, we are accepting what we call accounting principles. Many business enterprises are likewise accepting the same accounting principles as our profession.

However, when it comes to the public and to the stockholders, it is my opinion that our accounting principles are more nearly tolerated than accepted. Tolerate means "to bear up under; or to endure." We have no evidence that the wide variety of alternative accounting principles and practices that we now offer are being other than endured on a suffer-it-to-be-so-now basis, insofar as the public is concerned. Accordingly, we are either ignorant of the inadequacies of the practices we are now accepting, or we are not responsive to the task we have led the public to think we are performing as certified public accountants. Either way, the situation calls for action on the part of the profession.

One of the first questions that comes to mind in thinking about this problem is "who should do the accepting—that is, by whom should our accounting principles be accepted?" The fact that the public has used the financial statements prepared on the basis of what we choose to label generally accepted accounting principles, does not confirm public acceptance of these so-called principles any more than did the existence of the rigged TV quiz programs prove their public acceptance before the public learned the basis on which they were presented.

Illustrations of this nonacceptability to the public can be found whenever accounting principles become factors in lawsuits or in claims before our courts. But aside from court cases, which usually involve technical features of controversy, there are numerous illustrations of the nonacceptance of many of our accounting practices in the everyday press reports, such as the following comments in the August 1, 1960, issue of *Forbes Magazine:*

"There is also another symptom of the company's new order of efficiency, but it is perhaps more suggestive than conclusive. In every year since 1955, whether or not its sales volume was temporarily trending up or down, the company has been able to increase its earnings. There are so many ways of accomplishing this by mere bookkeeping tricks that financial specialists are wont these days to view any such performance skeptically. So many costs can at option legitimately be anticipated or deferred, expensed or capitalized, that no corporate earnings figure is now regarded by sophisticates as absolute and objective. Windfalls such as those deriving from favorable market prices for a commodity can have a pleasant but misleading effect on stated earnings; so can variations in the rate of remitted dividends received from foreign subsidiaries."

As a profession, we have ignored the basic necessity of developing and stating the reasoning as to why the accounting principles we follow should be accepted by the public, just as the networks failed to tell the public the basis of their quiz programs. When this reasoning is stated, the public will then say whether it is valid. If it is not valid, disapproval will come quickly.

Until we as a profession tell the public why the principles of accounting that we have accepted and applied should also be accepted by the public, the public cannot be expected to know or understand the meaning of the certified financial statements. Neither can the public be expected to accept them as being reliable, nor what is still more important, to require the reporting companies to observe them. In nearly all cases where accounting principles come

under scrutiny, it is under circumstances where something has
turned up wrong.

Therefore, until we have demonstrated the fairness of the accounting produced by the principles accepted and used, we are not
in a position to ask the public to accept the application of these
principles in our regular certified reports. But even more important
to everyone, until the profession properly develops and publicly
supports, on an authoritative basis, the reasoning necessary to establish acceptance of the principles used, we are in no position to tell
the public why our accounting principles should not be held responsible when something goes wrong in the financial reporting of
our business entities. It is this job of firming up the principles of
accounting by clearly stating the reasons for their existence, that
has been ignored. Until this is accomplished, it cannot be assumed
that what we as a profession are doing will be accepted by the
public when the public does not and cannot know the reasons for the
existence of the present practices.

The fairness of the accounting that results from the use of our
accounting principles must be demonstrated; otherwise, when the
unfairness of many of our principles is determined or discovered,
the result may be to destroy the whole of our services, as the taint
of unfairness destroyed the good as well as the unfair quiz programs.

I first undertook public discussion of the inadequate basis of accounting principles about three years ago. The request I then made
of the profession was that the reasoning underlying principles currently followed by the profession be developed to demonstrate that
their application produces fair financial accounting and reporting.
In illustrating the need for such a demonstration of fairness, the lack
of uniformity of accounting principles applied to comparable sets
of facts, was pointed out.

In reviewing the comments with respect to accounting principles
that have come forth in the last three years, I note that they have
largely been defensive. Among them was the argument that uniformity was a strait jacket, a bar to progress. But so far as I know, not
one single treatise has been presented to show the fairness of the
various financial statements that would result from the application
of alternative accepted accounting principles to a given set of
facts. No one has defended a single set of specific alternative accounting principles by contending that both were fair, and by
advancing sound reasoning in demonstration of that fairness.

If uniformity in generally accepted accounting principles is basically bad, is it unreasonable to ask why not one of our professional leaders who holds this view has come forth (1) with a specific case where uniformity would result in damage to the reported financial condition of a business entity and to the economic rights of the various segments of the business community interested therein, or (2) with a case where the alternative principles now followed would produce rightful advantages for all of the various segments involved? If we are to continue such alternatives, our need is for the reasoning and proof as to how we in the profession can justify accepting such alternative accounting principles, other than by merely showing that any such alternative practices are followed in other instances.

The objection has also been voiced that uniformity would eliminate flexibility in accounting principles. But to my knowledge, not one person has attempted to show where flexibility in the choice of alternative principles of accounting would result in financial statements that were fair to all segments of the business community. The arguments were only that flexibility was good, per se, and that the elimination of flexibility was bad, per se. Yet with respect to no single set of facts to be accounted for was the theory of flexibility applied and reasoning advanced to show why the "flexible" results were proper or fair.

Assuming for the moment that flexibility of principles is needed for a transition period to permit improvement in accepted accounting principles, would not the proof of this contention demonstrate its merit by eventual elimination of the less desirable practices? If flexibility would produce such improvement, could it not be illustrated? Yet examination of the record shows that the alternative methods of accounting for intangible drilling costs (either by expensing them currently or by capitalizing and amortizing them) are each as old as the other. The alternative treatment of deferred income taxes is as old as the laws that permitted deferral of the taxes. The alternative treatment of pension costs is as old as the requirement that pensions be paid. Flexibility, as such, has not brought improvement; in fact, the less desirable practices have tended to drive out, or at least to retard acceptance of, the good.

It is easy to prove the fallacy of the contention that flexibility is a good influence on accounting. Flexibility has been used as an excuse to prevent improvement, not to advance it. Improvement in accounting principles comes from demonstrating the unfairness of the effect on the financial statements of the accounting for transactions

under existing principles, and then establishing new ones (or eliminating alternatives) which do not produce such unfairness.

Still other accountants have argued that elimination of alternative
accounting principles in endeavoring to accomplish uniformity
would prevent experimentation. But no one has produced or illustrated a single experiment in the choice and application of accounting principles that would have been prevented by the elimination of alternative accounting principles.

In my opinion, the present array of accepted accounting principles applicable to a similar set of facts retards the adoption of
improvements in accounting. Any accounting principle can and
should be changed when analysis of the reasoning underlying it shows
that it falls short of its purpose of producing a fair presentation of
the facts of any given financial transaction.

The use of alternative principles of accounting as a basis for
experimentation is the very antithesis of what would ordinarily be assumed as a fact from the presence of the word "accepted" in the
phrase "generally accepted accounting principles." No one would
guess that the word "accepted" embraced "experimentation"; even
to suggest such a possibility would indicate lack of integrity. Such
an idea would be equivalent to a doctor planning a medical experiment on a regular patient while he is on the operating table. The
very thought is a chilling shock to a professional man's integrity.
Ordinarily the reader of financial statements would assume from the
phrase "accepted principles" that no experimentation was involved,
but that definite rules were applicable to each transaction and that
the accounting treatment for the transactions was in accordance
with those specific rules. If the phrase were to be truthfully and
clearly stated, it would read something like this, "in accordance with
one or another of the generally accepted alternative accounting
principles." Even this clarification would prevent any experimentation outside the bounds of the accepted alternatives now existing.
A concept that alternative accounting principles permit the adoption of additional alternatives that have not already come under the
umbrella of generally accepted principles, would worsen an already
intolerable practice from the viewpoint of the welfare of the public.

So far as I have been able to see, no one has demonstrated any
merit in nonuniformity, flexibility and experimentation in accounting
principles. Of course, this does not prove that merit cannot be demonstrated. I do not believe it can; but then maybe others can do it.
The only support advanced thus far for the acceptance of alter-

native accounting principles as being right, is the contention that accounting principles cannot be defined because they must be flexible, they must not be rigid; and they must permit experimentation, they must not inhibit new ideas. Standing alone, these are all generalized contentions that are without merit or proof of their truthfulness.

The opportunity of examining our accounting principles and supporting them with adequate reasoning, is still within our hands, if we choose to take advantage of it before we are forced to do so. The initiative is still ours. We have taken the first organizational step through the establishment of the Accounting Principles Board.

But until this Board acts, we should ask ourselves, "What are the consequences of the lack of authoritative support for the accounting practices being followed by our profession, which we cannot support as fair?" In reasoning out the answer to this question, we will find that the consequences are misrepresentations. We should then ask, "When do such misrepresentations by the members of our profession become problems for us?" It is easy to find the answer to this question, too. It is when these misrepresentations get our members into trouble; when the spotlight shines on a particular practice that was unjustified in the first instance; when we could not bring forth reasoning acceptable to the public, that would justify our practices.

This "hard-way" process of finding our trouble spots is no different in the accounting profession than in any other activity. TV quiz shows were accepted practice until the limelight disclosed them to the public. They were like misrepresentations made through accepted accounting principles. They were known by the individuals involved. The participants knew that shows were misrepresented, but the practice was justified in their minds because other similar shows were doing the same thing. Prearrangement was, therefore, rationalized as being accepted practice. The authority was not what was *proper* practice, but what was *accepted* practice. There was no law that said quiz shows could not be prearranged.

This same kind of reasoning was used by the Institute committee on professional ethics in attempting to justify the noncompliance of the usual type of auditors' certificate on railroad financial statements with the Institute's professional-conduct rule 5(e). This rule, as you know, requires the auditor to direct attention to any material departure from generally accepted accounting principles. Also, reporting standard Number 1 approved by the Institute membership requires that the auditors' report "shall state whether the financial statements presented are in accordance with generally accepted principles of accounting." But the usual type of audit certificate on railroad statements makes no reference at all to *generally accepted* accounting principles or the effect of departures therefrom; it refers only to conformity with accounting principles prescribed or authorized by the Interstate Commerce Commission. The ethics committee made no specific finding that the accounting practices followed by railroads under ICC requirements were right or were in accordance with generally accepted accounting principles. The committee's decision that the usual railroad audit certificate is not a violation of Rule 5(e) was not made on the basis of the reasoning that should be employed to show that the certified statements were fair and proper; it was made rather on the basis of presumption and custom—i.e., what most accountants and the railroads were doing, not what they ought to be doing.

In the recent case of the irregularities in the Sister Kenny Foundation, that I am sure you have all read about, the auditors allowed the management a high degree of nonuniformity, flexibility and experimentation in reporting fund-raising costs for a nine-year period. For some of the years, the amount of funds raised by the campaign was shown net, without disclosing the costs, which were very high in relation to the funds received; for other years, the funds received were reported gross, and an expense item was shown for the fund-raising costs, but it included only a part of such costs; the rest was effectively buried in other amounts. At no time during this period was there a clear statement of the funds received from the campaign and the cost of obtaining them.

As a result, the public was not adequately informed and contributed millions of dollars for charitable purposes that were siphoned off for noncharitable uses. Even with all of the criticism that might now be leveled at the accounting followed, it is doubtful that such unsupportable practices would have come to light if there had not been a simultaneous allegation of waste and unlawful diversion of funds. How much of this was the result of bad management and how much was misappropriation of funds, is yet to be determined.

This case is a clear example of the consequences of not having authoritative standards of accounting that were required to be imposed; it is an illustration of the absence of discipline in the application of accounting standards. Insofar as the accounting and reporting practices followed were concerned, they did not meet standards of accountability that were acceptable to the public.

They did not meet the disciplinary test of fair reporting demanded by the various segments of the public. Had sound principles for financial accounting been established by the profession on the objective standard of fairness to all segments of the public, it is doubtful that such consequences as occurred in this case would have been allowed to develop, at least to the same extent.

The profession cannot avoid some share of the responsibility for such cases as the Sister Kenny Foundation reporting, under the standards it has allowed to exist. It is unfortunate that, in this case, a local accounting firm must bear the brunt of the inadequacies of our professional practices.

The profession itself has not set up the means by which to question or judge whether the accounting being followed in a given case is proper. It is hoped that thought now being given to the problem of substandard practices will provide a way for bringing such matters before appropriate Institute or state committees, and that the members who performed the accounting that is under scrutiny can be required to bring full information before such committees for consideration. This would enable the profession to hold the information in confidence, and at the same time permit the performing members to be admonished and instructed as to where the accounting followed did not conform to proper standards. But the professional committees must have the intestinal fortitude to require adherence to established principles of accounting that are supported by sound reasoning; they must not use their committee positions to justify unprofessional work, as was done in the railroad certificate case. Authoritative statements of sound accounting principles and practices will, of course, have to be developed as a basis for judging whether or not the accounting under consideration was substandard.

No decision of material consequence in accounting is final until it is decided rightly; and this applies to the decisions of the Accounting Principles Board and all of the American Institute committees which issue authoritative pronouncements on accounting principles and practices. Those who would swing such pronouncements in the direction of support for their own viewpoints and practices, irrespective of the rightness or soundness thereof, are only seeking to delay the day of reckoning. Make no mistake—that day will come. Let us hope we do not wait until Congress gets around to specifying what day it is.

When mention is made of the accounting-principle problems that face the profession, almost everyone wants to know what the problem areas are considered to be, and what the various points of view with respect to them are. This is particularly true of those individuals who have not made a study of these problem areas. It is difficult, if not impossible, in an address of this kind to cover such problems even in a general way that will convey any reasonable comprehension of them.

For the purpose of providing information and correlating discussion within our own firm, we have prepared a booklet on the accounting problem areas which we believe are of most immediate concern. Perhaps the best way I can here deal with specific instances of accounting and reporting problems of the profession is to say that copies of this booklet are available to anyone in the profession who would like to have them. And we, in turn, would welcome similar discussion material from others in our profession who wish to state their views on these or additional problems.

Even our discussion booklet, which consists of 125 pages of printed material on 20 different problem areas, includes only brief comments on each. To indicate the approach, I might say that our comments on each problem are divided into the following six sections:

The problem.

Existing practices.

Our firm's viewpoint.

The profession's position, as expressed by the Institute.

S.E.C. requirements.

Analyses and discussion of the problem.

We would like very much to have the views and reasoning of those who differ with us, so we can study them in the same way that others will study our views and our reasons therefor. In fact, we believe that those who hold other opinions have a professional responsibility to state them, along with the reasoning in support of their positions. Merely to recite the differences in practices or points of view without giving the thinking that underlies the positions taken contributes little or nothing to the solution of the problems.

Now how should the profession go about doing what must be done to establish sound accounting principles on a solid foundation of objective standards?

The new Accounting Principles Board has been established and provided with a research staff. The plan for the Board was conceived by the Special Committe on Research Program, in a spirit of earnest desire to meet this pressing need. The plan proposes a process for meeting the major deficiencies in the accounting principles that we are now observing.

The Board was conceived also with the idea that its members would be open-minded and unprejudiced in their thinking; that they would establish sound accounting principles on the basis of the fairness of the financial accounting that would result; and that objective reasoning as to fairness of financial accounting to all segments of the business community would be the criterion of the Board's decisions.

The plan calls first for the determination and establishment of the basic postulates (or objective standards, as I prefer to call them) as the foundation on which the accounting principles are to be formulated. The postulates are to be supported by reasoning derived from the economic and political environment and from the modes of thought and customs of all segments of the business community. Then, a fairly broad set of coordinated accounting principles is to be formulated on the basis of the postulate foundation.

The program contemplates that in connection with the Board's research studies, the professional practitioners and other interested parties will submit memorandums (or briefs) giving their views and reasoning on the research projects announced. This will require every public accountant—either individual or firm—having convictions on any principle or project under consideration to file a memorandum advocating and supporting the views held, so that others may examine them and may present their own views and reasons, whatever they may be. The Board will fail in its task if the basis for its pronouncements on accounting postulates and principles is generated solely within itself, without vigorous outside advocacy. This approach would merely provide the means for insulating the viewpoints of the Board members from professional analysis. It would be the cowardly approach—it would prove the lack of independence of those who do not file briefs stating and arguing their own views, but who at the same time, refuse to accept the views of those who do file with the Board. On that basis the Board's efforts would be of little import.

It is the conclusion of the study made by our firm that the objective standard or basic accounting postulate underlying all accounting principles is simple—it is that of "fairness"—fairness demonstrated as to all segments of the business community. The results of our study in arriving at this conclusion are set forth in our first brief entitled "The Postulate of Accounting—What it is, how it is determined, and how it should be used," recently filed with the Accounting Principles Board. Since all material filed with the Board is of public record, we shall be glad to make copies of our brief available to anyone wishing to have it. I am sure that all of us in the profession will welcome similar statements filed by others who have convictions and viewpoints on this first problem before the Board.

If the manner in which this objective standard of fairness to each segment of the business community is specifically reasoned out for each accounting principle adopted by the Board, that principle will be acceptable to, and will be accepted by, the entire public. Then and only then will the ostensible needs for nonuniformity, flexibility, nonrigidity and experimentation in accounting principles be viewed in their true light, as diversionary generalizations without meaning or purpose. Improvements are the result of action taken to meet the needs of the public; they do not result from defense of the status quo.

We accountants like to talk in generalities, and yet all of our work involves specific applications. Therefore, we must supply the reasoning underlying specific applications of accounting principles. We should be able to take any balance sheet or income statement and explain for every accounting principle applied why it produces fairness in those financial statements. This can be done if the entire profession will open-mindedly follow the course laid out in the Special Committee report that recommended the creation of the Accounting Principles Board.

Is Further Uniformity Desirable or Possible?

MAURICE E. PELOUBET

By the beginning of 1961 we will have a new national administration. There is little doubt that inflation will continue. The only question is the rate. It may be 2 per cent a year or less as has been the case for the last eight years or it may be at a more rapid rate. The question seems to be the degree, rather than the fact of the progressive deterioration of the value of the dollar.

Where this will end no one knows but we have at least one certainty and one probability: the certainty is that we will, for some time to come, live in an atmosphere of change and disturbance in practically all fields and all countries; the probability is that our present creeping inflation will continue at a greater or lesser rate for at least four or five years or until a war of substantial size breaks out.

This is a general and, I hope, objective view of the present situation. I have tried to eliminate prejudice and to present a practical view of the world we must live in and work with. All this is not so far from accounting principles as may at first appear. Accounting is a method of description and we must understand what we are describing before we can make intelligible statements about it.

As I see it, the relation between basic generally accepted accounting principles and accounting procedures or techniques is something like the relation between the Ten Commandments and the great body of statute law, court decisions, and administrative regulations. The Ten Commandments neither change nor vary and they embody the basic principles of human conduct, but they must be implemented by specific laws and rules. Accounting procedures, methods and techniques are many and varied and are constantly changing and developing. On the other hand, with one exception accounting principles have not changed since accounting took on the characteristics of a profession.

The basic principles apply to all situations where the methods and techniques are used and determine whether or not these methods and techniques are permissible and appropriate.

The first principle is adequate disclosure, sufficient, as the SEC. phrases it, to make the statements not misleading. Adequate disclosure does not require the search for or the attainment of some sort of *absolute truth,* invariable as the speed of light. This *exists nowhere else and will not be found in the practice of accounting.*

It does require that the conventions and assumptions on which the accounts are prepared should be clearly stated. Under some circumstances the effect of alternative conventions or assumptions should be shown, particularly if changes in basis have been made.

The requirement that no opinion on a statement should be given when the auditor has not been able to satisfy himself on vital and material points flows from the principle of adequate disclosure. In the same way, when procedures have been adopted which might, in the opinion of the auditor, make the statements misleading, but are not such as to make it impossible to give an opinion on the statements, he must take an exception or qualify his report.

The second principle may be stated as the principle of conservatism. It is sometimes summed up as "Cut the losses and let the profits run." In general this means that the accounts should show a situation no better than the existing one, and where any possible error is on the unfavorable side. Inventories reduced to market, bad debt reserves, obsolete plant written off before its physical life has expired and reserves for known but undetermined contingencies are examples of the application of this principle.

A third principle is materiality, analogous to the legal maxim "de minimis non curat lex." If an item is treated incorrectly or inconsistently and is relatively so small that however it is treated it will not make the statements misleading, the auditor or accountant is not required to withhold an opinion or to qualify his report.

The application of this principle calls for the exercise of mature and careful judgment. The size of the item, the size of the company, and the significance of the item in relation to others should all be weighed before a decision as to materiality is made.

A fourth principle, an extension, perhaps of the first, is that accounting is, essentially, a description of business and financial and frequently other facts, by agreed conventional symbols and under agreed conventional assumptions. Some of these are: the continuity of a going concern, the validity of the inventory methods used, the preparation of the accounts from the point of view of the original investors, the disregard of any changes in value of the company's property—although this is now being challenged widely—and the disregard of any change in the fixed or long-term liabilities regardless of changes in purchasing power.

These and other conventions have been almost universally accepted. They may, however, change in the near future but this does not mean that accounts will cease to be presented on a conventional basis. Income is, therefore, the result of the application of agreed and understood conventions.

A fifth principle, which might be described as insuring the validity of the income account and its corollary, the treatment of the balance sheet as a collection of residual items arrived at on conventional bases is probably the only real change or development in basic accounting principles in this century. This has been necessary because of the increased importance of the ascertainment of periodical earnings and the recognition of the growing difficulties of establishing income by a comparison of net worth at the beginning and end of an accounting period.

This principle was illustrated and explained in the *six rules* adopted by the membership of the Institute in *1934,* the first five of which had been recommended in 1933 to the New York Stock Exchange by the Institute's Committee on Cooperation with Stock Exchanges. These are reprinted in full in Chapter I of Accounting Research Bulletin ⚜43, issued by the Committee on Accounting Procedure in 1953. The basic purpose of these rules is to insure that all items affecting income are, in fact, included in the income account, and they prohibit the use of accounts such as capital surplus or certain reserve accounts as devices to permit the exclusion of items properly affecting income from the income account.

There are two answers to the question posed in the title of this paper. So far as these basic and generally accepted accounting principles are concerned, the greatest possible uniformity is desirable, and apart from their acceptance by the profession and the business community they are now being enforced by state and national professional societies, by the Federal Government, through the Securities and Exchange Commission and other agencies, and by the increasing number of states whose accountancy laws include a code of ethics written into the statute. I repeat that the most complete uniformity of practice and enforcement of these generally accepted principles is not only desirable but essential.

They are the simple and fundamental commandments, but they cannot be enforced and implemented without a great deal of specific consideration of methods, procedures and techniques. We do not legislate the Ten Commandments and we do not legislate the basic accounting principles. However, the application and working out of these principles requires a continuous development of procedures, methods and techniques which in many respects is analogous to statutory law, court decisions and the regulations and rulings of government departments.

The inauguration of the new research program of the American Institute of Certified Public Accountants and the organization of the Accounting Principles Board must necessarily, and properly, have the effect of legislating for the profession.

In itself this is neither good nor bad. Large groups, political, religious or professional, must have rules of conduct and codes under which to operate. What is important is how these rules and codes are formulated, what they are to do and how they can be changed, improved or repealed, in whole or in part.

Accounting, as a modern financial, economic and technical development, has condensed into seventy or eighty years a change and growth equal and parallel to the development of civil and criminal law over many centuries.

Accounting in this country in the late eighteen nineties and early nineteen hundreds was in the stage when custom and habit were almost the only criteria. Individuals of incisive mind and strong character exercised a powerful, but entirely unofficial and extra-legal influence on the thought and conduct of their fellow accountants.

This was the formative period described in the introduction to Sir Henry Maine's inquiry into the origins of law:

"The jurists had in their analysis of legal sovereignty postulated the commands of a supreme lawgiver by simply ignoring the fact that, in point of time, custom precedes legislation and that early law is . . . a habit and not a conscious exercise of the volition of a lawgiver or a legislature."[1]

[1] *Ancient Law,* Sir Henry Maine, E. P. Dutton & Co., N.Y., p. vii.

Some years later these practices and ideas began to be condensed and formulated into textbooks which had as much authority as the eminence of their authors warranted. In many cases this was very considerable and as new generations of accountants studied these books their influence was greatly extended.

This may be likened to the period in Roman law when the jurisconsults, the compilers and commentators, were the basic source of law.

To a certain extent accountancy is still in that period and it may be that the Accounting Principles Board will be the body which will start the movement from a mass of textbook literature, quasi-official statements by accounting organizations, and piecemeal recognition of some accounting principles and procedures by the courts and executive agencies to a systematic codification of accounting methods and principles. This might take the form of an encyclopaedic compendium of accounting principles and methods something like the "Corpus Juris" first compiled in the days of the Roman Empire and carried through to our own day.

So long as such a compilation is not intended to be rigid and unalterable it is a desirable objective. Obviously the present is not the time in which to promulgate any work of this kind as a final and unchangeable authority, but it would be of great value if means were provided whereby it could be altered or amplified to suit changing times and conditions.

There are some statements in the leaflet "The New Accounting Research Program" which, at first sight, appear alarming but which, on analysis, are seen to be little more than the results of misplaced emphasis and an effort to condense and simplify the report to Council of the Special Committee on Research Program (*Journal of Accountancy,* December 1958 p. 62).

However, as this has been circulated to the membership some explanation seems to be in order.

The statement in the leaflet that "These pronouncements will be the authoritative determination of the applicable accepted accounting principles" does not, read in the context of the December, 1958 report, have the somewhat arbitrary meaning which could be given to the statement standing alone.

The December, 1958 report makes it clear that the pronouncements will, in effect, stand or fall on their merits in the same way as the statements issued by the former Committee on Accounting Procedure.

The leaflet says "the areas of difference in accounting must be narrowed." This is a desirable end, provided that all we are proposing is that differences in accounting methods be narrowed. There is always, however, a tendency to describe different things or conditions in the same terms merely to be uniform.

A case in point is the financial statements of natural resource enterprises. Some deduct an allowance for depletion of mineral deposits, some do not, and some of the larger enterprises deduct depletion on some mines and deposits and not on others.

It would be hard to imagine greater disparity but the reason for this is not to be found in the wishes or desires of the management or the accountants. It is not the result of a fortuitous or capricious choice of several equally acceptable methods. The method employed is dictated by the facts. Where the limits or the content of a deposit are accurately known it is generally possible to arrive at a depletion allowance roughly equal to the progressive exhaustion of capital.

An exception to this rule is where the deposit is so large as to be, from a financial point of view, inexhaustible. A mine with an ore supply sufficient for 150 years operation would not ordinarily calculate depletion on a unit of mineral available 50 or 75 years from now as this has a present value of practically nothing. As each year's operations exhaust part of the valued ore another year's supply comes into the valued zone.

A mine where it is impracticable to develop ore more than, say, a year ahead, does not and should not ordinarily attempt to calculate a precise and specific depletion allowance as this would be so inaccurate or uncertain as to be misleading. Instead adequate statistics on production and ore reserves give all the information available. A statement disclaiming any relation between book and current values should also be made. An attempt to arrive at a precise depletion allowance, under these circumstances, could hardly fail to be misleading.

These differences, while expressed in accounting terms, are not differences in accounting. They are differences in facts and situations, expressed in differing accounting terms.

It is possible the next Congress may pass legislation to reform the depreciation allowance by recognizing, in some way, the impact of changing price levels.

A difference of opinion will immediately arise on how and whether the effect of inflation should be shown in the accounts. The difference will be a difference in the recognition of facts, not a difference in accounting methods.

The treatment of foreign currencies and foreign currency assets in consolidated accounts is another example. Currencies may be hard, soft, blocked, free or dedicated to specific purposes. One method of accounting would hardly fit more than one condition.

Another approach to consolidated accounts for integrated enterprises is that taken by N. V. Philips' Gloeilampenfabrieken, described in Prof. A. Goudeket's article in the July 1960 *Journal of Accountancy*. Here the method is, basically, to reduce all currencies and other assets to a purchasing power standard.

This is a far cry from the old-style consolidated statement for an international enterprise, where foreign currencies and assets were reduced to a gold-standard head-office currency. There may still be situations where this treatment is acceptable, even though the head-office currency may be a managed one.

In any event narrowing of differences in accounting methods, procedures and techniques, seems to me to be overemphasized. Generally speaking it is desirable to describe the same things in the same way but it is far more important to allow for change and improvement than to endeavor to enforce a Byzantine rigidity merely for the sake of uniformity.

Not quite a year ago Leonard Spacek, speaking to the financial accounting class at the Harvard Graduate School of Business Administration, made a clear and simple statement of the position of those who seem to want uniformity of methods and procedures at any price.

His position is not unlike that of many financial analysts who would like to take the accounts of all the members of a particular industry, spread them out in columns with uniform captions at the sides and determine by a simple formula their relative value and desirability as investments.

There is so much truth included in what Mr. Spacek says and so much justification for the desires of the analyst that it makes the task of exposing the fallacies or, more properly, the limitations of the thesis that complete uniformity is always possible and desirable, both difficult and ungrateful.

At the outset let me say that I am closer to loving uniformity for uniformity's sake than I am to any devotion to diversity as such.

Every accounting firm which numbers among its clients a manufacturing enterprise with plants spread all over the country putting out similar products, a chain of supermarkets or variety stores or a chain of restaurants knows the value of uniformity in accounting statements and statistics.

Uniformity is essential for control. Furthermore, uniformity and consistency are much more important than theoretical correctness. Fixed expenses may be omitted or estimated, inventories may, and often are, taken at sales price and depreciation may be omitted or calculated on some method other than that used in the financial accounts.

Conventional methods consistently employed give better control results than sporadic attempts at "truth" or "real values."

In some industries, notably retail trade, conditions are similar enough for reliable and useful total statistics to be compiled which form valuable yardsticks against which the results of an individual enterprise can be judged.

It might also be possible to arrive at some method of uniform reporting for industries where the units are small and conditions do not vary greatly: printers or tool and die shops, for instance.

But when we get into the area with which we are most concerned, the larger corporate enterprise, we find that no amount of uniform accounting will produce truly comparable results because the enterprises and the conditions under which they operate are not comparable.

In Mr. Spacek's paper[2] he sets up, not a straw man but a pair of straw twins. He assumes two companies with exactly the same physical operations, sales and costs and assumes that a choice of permissible accounting methods can increase conservatively calculated profits of $480,000 to $1,076,000, income taxes increasing at the same time $484,000.

Mr. Spacek assumes that Company B's management has decided to do everything possible to bolster the reported earnings per share. A primary result of this is assumed to be an increase in the market quotations for Company B's stock as compared with that of Company A.

In the example given, most of the differences in income between Company A and Company B are not the results of the application of accounting principles, methods or techniques at all, but are the results of policy decisions taken by the Company. The use of stock options as a management incentive, the way a pension fund shall be

[2] This refers to the imaginary profit-and-loss statement reproduced on page 37.

treated, and whether or not research costs should be deferred are certainly management decisions and not the result of the application of any accounting principles, methods, or techniques. It is true that management decisions on these questions will affect the accounts and will affect the earnings in the same way as any other management decisions, for example, the decision to build a new plant, or to make a new product, but the only function of accounting in relation to these decisions is to reflect their results in the accounts.

If any of these decisions represented a change in policy in the period, it would probably be necessary to make some statement in the year of change of the effect on income.

I gather that Mr. Spacek thinks that there is something wrong or at least doubtful in these management decisions. Is he proposing to tell management that they should not compensate executives by stock options, but should give them cash bonuses? I do not think that is the function of the accountant or auditor.

In the year in which a change was made from compensating executives by bonus, and doing the same thing by stock options, the stock option plan would be described in appropriate detail and the effect on the accounts would be indicated. All of this has nothing whatever to do with uniformity of accounting methods or techniques.

The choice of an inventory method is also a management decision. Here again, in the year of change the effect should be shown. It might be possible for management to choose an inventory method so completely inappropriate to the business as to require an exception in the accountant's report, for example, valuation at sales price, which would require an exception by the auditor.

Depreciation is another question for management decision. It has been widely stated, and it is my own personal opinion, in which I am happy to agree with Mr. Spacek, that depreciation provisions and reserves are generally inadequate. They are, however, calculated on a basis of agreed and accepted conventions. In any statements to third parties, the valuation of depreciable property, depreciation reserves, and depreciation provisions are subject to disclaimers, explicit or implicit, of any responsibility for current or actual values of property and, consequently, the adequacy of depreciation reserves. Both Mr. Spacek and I would like to see this condition changed. Our only point of disagreement is that I believe the change must be initiated by management with, of course, the assistance of their accounting advisers, and Mr. Spacek seems to believe that there is some way that the initiative can be taken by the accountants.

The impossibility of presenting the accounts of different companies in the same industry on a completely comparable basis arises from the fact that physical and financial conditions and management policies are different, and this must be reflected differently in the accounts. The accountant, public or private, cannot influence management decisions in any other way or to any greater extent than is warranted by his role as adviser.

In most industries, particularly manufacturing and those having to do with natural resources the various units are quite dissimilar. An integrated steel or nonferrous metal enterprise will commonly, but not invariably, include railroads, steamships, power plants, coal mines, lumbering operations and saw mills, as well as metal mines and metal producing plants which may have as an end product pig iron, steel for further fabrication, or refined copper, zinc and lead.

Other integrated enterprises may carry fabrication to the point of semi-finished material for other manufacturers or to goods for direct consumption.

These enterprises commonly issue consolidated statements which show the stockholder the net result of all the various types of business undertaken by the enterprise. Consolidated accounts cannot show much more and no amount of uniformity in accounting would make the accounts of a medium sized steel company producing special purpose and high-speed alloys comparable with those of a large, fully integrated steel company.

General Motors and Chrysler are both important units in the electrical appliance business, as are Westinghouse and General Electric. Each has interests and products not common to the others. No amount of uniformity would make their accounts comparable.

These are what we might call rationally integrated enterprises where all the activities have some relationship to each other. When we come to the increasingly large number of aggregations of quite dissimilar activities the impossibility of comparablity is even more evident. It is even doubtful whether a consolidated account is the proper form of statement for, say, a mixture of electronics, pharmaceuticals, metalworking and transportation, none related to the other in an operating way.

The fragmentation of these accounts by corporate entities would not necessarily result in statements which were comparable because in many cases quite diverse activities are carried on as mere divisions rather than separate companies.

There is little doubt that greater comparability and uniformity in accounting statements is necessary but the way to arrive at this is not through an attempt to make financial accounts, particularly consolidated accounts, do something they were never intended to do.

In the large consolidated enterprise, if statements are needed for special purposes they should be prepared so as to agree with the consolidated accounts, any differences being noted. Such statements generally can and should be prepared so as to be comparable with those of other companies prepared for the same purpose. They may be the statements of a subsidiary or a division.

The statements for investors, labor unions and the various government agencies would be quite different from each other. The investor is interested in total results. A labor union is interested, usually, in the subsidiaries or divisions in which its members work. The government has a variety of interests; taxation, statistics, welfare and many others.

These are the areas in which uniformity in methods and techniques is possible and desirable because, if we isolate similar conditions we can and should describe them uniformly.

However, the generally accepted accounting principles: adequate disclosure, conservatism, materiality, the use of agreed conventional methods of presentation and the preservation of the integrity of the income account, should be uniformly applied and should have behind them the full weight of any authority the Accounting Principles Board may have.

These policing functions are most important but they should be sharply distinguished from the research and development function which should have for its purpose the improvement of methods and the solution of problems rather than the satisfaction of an overmastering desire for uniformity.

We have a full quota of such problems now. A few others in addition to the five described in the leaflet to the membership are:

1. Direct costing, with its tax and management implications;

2. Insufficient depreciation from inflationary and technological causes, with the consequent doubt cast on the validity of the financial statements;

3. Inventory and income account problems revolving around the LIFO principle.[3]

[3] Six projects have already been started: "(1) Basic accounting postulates; (2) Broad accounting principles; (3) Accounting for income taxes; (4) Business combinations; (5) Long-term leases; (6) Accounting for nonprofit organizations."

While it would be presumptuous to try to tell the Accounting Principles Board how to do its work it is the right and, perhaps, duty of every member to say what he thinks ought to be done. Exercising that right, I would say the Board has two general spheres of action, the moral or ethical and the technical. There may be some overlapping but, in general, these spheres are reasonably well defined.

In the field of technical development no permanently positive or authoritative statements are possible or desirable. Here the problem is one of experimentation and testing. When the experimental period is over the new method will be accepted on its merits and will be uniformly applied where it is appropriate.

The oath of Hippocrates is still a valid basis for medical ethics, but no one would think of deciding on the value of a new drug or treatment by a majority vote of a committee.

Direct costing is a case in point. It is used by some companies and not by others. It is applied differently in different organizations and is used for different purposes. In, perhaps, three to five years this may be developed into an acceptable method which will be generally used.

In the meantime nothing should be done to discourage experimentation or development by a premature statement on a developing method.

The deliberations of this panel should be of great help to the Accounting Principles Board in determining its general purposes and objectives and to the membership in clarifying and explaining them.

As I understand it, the function of the Accounting Principles Board will be similar to that of the former Accounting Procedure Committee except that its research facilities will be expanded and its scope broadened. Instead of doing little more than cover current problems as they arise it will also formulate the basic principles and philosophy of accounting, a work of immense value but often neglected for more immediate and urgent but often less important problems.

Every accountant interested in the progress and development of his profession should take a keen interest in the operation of the Board, particularly as the problems are being worked over and before the Board has arrived at any conclusions. Suggestions at that time will be more effective than protests after a statement is issued.

There can be no question of the importance and value of a body such as the Accounting Principles Board and its staff. Even if a private firm or organization could do the work it would not have the authority and standing of the Board.

We should all, I think, wish the Board well and help as much as possible by advice and constructive criticism, which we are assured will be welcome.

Rejoinder by Mr. Spacek

To answer Mr. Peloubet's paper adequately would take a long treatise analyzing and commenting on each point. On an over-all basis I gather Mr. Peloubet thinks companies are comparable only when they are in the same business, and that principles of accounting are dependent on what policy decisions management wants to make in that business. This is an error. I do not feel that the operations of a steel company are ever directly or indirectly comparable with those of a merchandising company, but profit results of their operations, if accounted for on the same accounting principles, would show the net accomplishment of each operation and thus would determine a return on investment in comparable terms.

Mr. Peloubet seems to think that accounting first requires operating conditions and activities that are strictly comparable. For instance, he states:

"The statements for investors, labor unions and the various government agencies would be quite different from each other. The investor is interested in total results. A labor union is interested, usually, in the subsidiaries or divisions in which its members work. The government has a variety of interests; taxation, statistics, welfare and many others.

"These are the areas in which uniformity in methods and techniques is possible and desirable because, if we isolate similar conditions we can and should describe them uniformly."

He does not see that if all divisions or subsidiaries observe comparable sound principles of accounting, the combination of their results in the company as a whole will produce reports that are in accordance with comparable sound accounting principles. The whole is the sum of all its parts. If the accounting principles are all sound for each division, the results on a combined basis will also be sound, and they will be equally applicable to labor, investor or any other user.

As to reporting for tax purposes—Federal taxes are controlled by statute arbitrarily enacted by Congress to raise funds; equity is not the objective.

Mr. Peloubet says my position is not unlike the financial analysts "who would like to take the accounts of all the members of a particular industry, spread them out in columns with uniform captions at the sides and determine by a simple formula their relative value and desirability as investments."

This is exactly what the analyst does, whether he is an adviser, a company president or a working man who is doing his best to manage his own money. He compares the net accomplishment of all companies with each other to make his decisions. He may use whatever method he wishes to value the various investments with which he is concerned, but the financial accounting reports to which he applies his valuation method should be based on consistently applied sound accounting principles. The investors and other users depend upon the accountant to furnish such financial reports. If the accountant does not do it, his work is worthless. Mr. Peloubet illustrates this further in the following statement:

"General Motors and Chrysler are both important units in the electrical appliance business, as are Westinghouse and General Electric. Each has interests and products not common to the others. No amount of uniformity would make their accounts comparable."

Here he is dead wrong, if he is talking about uniformity in accounting principles. The business operation activities, of course, are not comparable, but accounting principles consistently applied to each company would make their financial position and operating results comparable as to what was accomplished. The public already assumes that they are comparable. These are the financial results on which investors base their investment choices.

On accounting principles Mr. Peloubet presumes that companies' policy decisions on such matters as (a) the adequacy of depreciation provisions and depreciation reserves, (b) the validity of the inventory methods used, (c) the omission of depletion provisions (since, he claims, it is better to make no depletion provision than to use estimated depletion, although estimates are always the basis of depletion and depreciation), must be accepted by the accountant; he also presumes that the accountant may not consider these decisions, as to their soundness and propriety in determining the fair financial accomplishments in making his examination and expressing his opinion on the statements. This is completely in error, if measured by what stockholders and management think we as outside accountants are doing. He also states that the accounting practices for stock options, pensions, research costs are purely management decisions, and that the requirements of proper and sound accounting stand in the way of entering into such arrangements or activities. This is absolutely wrong unless management wants to enter into such arrangements without disclosing the actual "price" paid for them on behalf of the stockholders. In such a case, it is not the accounting that stops the transaction but the disclosure of the price paid. If the transaction justifies the price, what objection can there be to an accounting that properly records the price?

Mr. Peloubet says "the choice of inventory method is also a management decision." True; but that does not remove it from the review as to its soundness of the accounting, by the public accountant who is asked to express his opinion on the fairness of the financial statements.

Mr. Peloubet seems to infer that whatever management does must be accepted by the public accountant, unless it cannot be justified by any precedent or reason whatsoever. If this is correct, he must have a very different kind of client from those that we serve. Our clients expect us to review and apply disciplinary accounting principles to what has been recorded, so that we not only can say they have followed sound accounting but that we can stand behind them in defending it.

We would not be in position to do this if we merely took the view that the company could have followed directly opposite accounting practices and that we would also have approved them, thus completely destroying the value of our examination and opinion on behalf of the stockholders and others who may rely on the statements. In those cases where generally accepted accounting principles have embraced widely varying or extremely flexible practices, we have had to accept them under the rules of the Securities and Exchange Commission and the profession, but we have criticized these practices and have urged the profession to join us in their correction. We not only have a responsibility to require a correct accounting but also state *why* it is correct.

Mr. Peloubet views accountancy as being at a stage comparable to that of the "period in Roman law when the jurisconsults, the compilers and commentators, were the basic source of law." This view would have to prevail if his ideas as to the ineffectiveness of public accounting reports was to be supported. However, while I believe the profession as a whole is behind in the proper standards of practice, a large share of the profession has advanced beyond the stage Mr. Peloubet refers to. The accounting practices among professional public accounting firms differ greatly, as he points out. But at least the public and most companies think they are receiving a much more disciplinary check of corporate reports than Mr. Peloubet would lead them to believe. And a large segment of the public accounting profession, including small practitioners, is responding to that expectation.

Mr. Peloubet excuses the present unsatisfactory stage of the public accounting profession by pointing to the rapid growth of its modern version. However, that does not excuse the constant opposition within the profession to updating its practices in order to serve the very important needs which the public expects it to fulfill.

Mr. Peloubet also seems to look to the agencies of the Federal government to assist in enforcing uniformity of generally accepted accounting principles. The fallacy of this view is clearly evident in the actions of the Interstate Commerce Commission in prescribing a system of accounts for railroads that now not only is obsolete and outdated, but is valueless from a management viewpoint and produces outright misrepresentation of the financial position and operating results of the railroads. It was not enough for the ICC to impose this accounting on railroads for ineffective and unnecessary regulatory use; ICC now proposes a rule that no railroad shall issue an annual report inconsistent with this prescribed accounting—even though it is obsolete and produces misleading results—thus denying the public its right to the truth in any fashion. This is central government dictation of erroneous reporting and the enactment of concurrent laws and regulations to prevent the reporting of the actual facts.

Such is the dictatorial course of accounting by the government fiat. The truth of the railroads' financial plight cannot be told until the properties themselves collapse. The profession, true to Mr. Peloubet's description, found that since the practices followed by the railroads had been in effect for such a long period, they had become generally accepted. Thus, the very fact they were obsolete, was the basis for accepting them. Neither the profession nor the Interstate Commerce Commission made any pretense of proving or explaining that such financial statements were sound and truthful.

The test of an acceptable accounting principle, according to

Mr. Peloubet and some members of the profession, seems to be only that there be some basis of rationalization. This is an easy way to justify present accounting practices that do not provide the public with financial accounting reports that it can rely upon for the financial facts it needs. Fortunately, the whole profession does not share this philosophy of "justify what we're doing at all costs."

—October 20, 1960

Rejoinder by Mr. Peloubet

The real difficulty in any discussion like that between Mr. Spacek and me is that the terms are seldom clear and definite. I think Mr. Spacek's letter of October 20 goes much further than before in defining his terms and thus makes it much easier for me to indicate the large areas of agreement between us and the smaller but no less important areas of differences.

As I said in Philadelphia, there are certain generally accepted accounting principles—adequate disclosure, conservatism, materiality, use of agreed conventional methods of presentation and the preservation of the integrity of the income account. There is no question here of alternatives or of choice on anybody's part about the application of these principles. They are required by sound business practice, by the ethics of the accounting profession and by a number of provisions in both state and federal laws and regulations.

Obviously, what these principles do is to govern the application of accounting methods and procedures. Here, judgment is required and the final responsibility is with the management of the company, not with its professional advisers. It is equally obvious that the company's professional advisers must form their own opinions as to whether the application of any specific accounting method is such as to make the statements misleading. Generally, this is not a difficult determination to make. If the statements indicate clearly what methods are being used, the reader of the accounts should be in no doubt about the nature and significance of results.

For example, two important points on which I believe Mr. Spacek and I agree completely are, that the use of the LIFO inventory method is generally desirable and that there is, in general, some overstatement of earnings of companies which include among their assets large amounts of long-term depreciable property. We both believe that the use of the LIFO inventory method usually produces a more realistic income account. It is also true that the use of this method at the same time produces inventory values on the balance sheet which are much below any market or realizable value, an example of assets carried on a conventional basis. If we state, under the principle of adequate disclosure, that inventories are valued on the LIFO method together with any appropriate details, it is perfectly clear to the reader of the accounts that the income account is realistic and the balance sheet valuation of inventory is not. On the other hand, if it is stated that inventories are carried at first-in, first-out, or FIFO, it is equally clear that, if there has been an increase in commodity prices or labor rates in the accounting period, there is an unrealized inventory profit in the income account and the inventory in the balance sheet approximates current costs or market. The accounting method differs, but the accounting principle, that of adequate disclosure under which the method and facts are described, is the same in each case. Which inventory method to use is a management decision and neither the accounting profession nor regulatory bodies such as the SEC can require that one or the other method be used. However, both the profession and the SEC insist on adequate disclosure.

One method of accounting for fixed assets and depreciable property is to carry them and to depreciate them on the basis of original cost. This method is almost universally used and under the same principle of adequate disclosure the basis of valuation and depreciation is generally stated with a disclaimer which, in turn, states that the values of fixed property do not represent current values which can only be determined by a current appraisal.

There are other examples of alternative accounting methods which can apply to a particular situation, for example, the treatment of various types of deferred expense. Here again the choice of an acceptable method is with management, but the auditor must apply the accounting principles calling for adequate disclosure, conservatism and the use of agreed conventional methods of presentation. Principles of accounting are not dependent on management choice or decision but the use of particular methods of accounting is.

Another aspect of the principle of adequate disclosure is the requirement of consistency. Here, management has no choice. It must be consistent or it must show and explain fully the results of any inconsistency.

Mr. Spacek in his letter makes it clearer, at least to me, what he means by comparability. This, apparently, in his view, applies only to the end result, the net income or earnings per share. This type of limited comparability is, of course, useful and valuable and is not too difficult to achieve. I agree completely with the statement that if all divisions or subsidiaries of an integrated enterprise prepare their accounts properly, the aggregate income will also be stated on sound principles and as a total result may well be compared with the total result of another integrated enterprise. The type of comparability which I had in mind was a little more specialized and specific than that envisioned by Mr. Spacek. I was thinking of statements where all the items were comparable, where the sales-cost ratio, the inventory turnover figure, the proportion or ratio of selling and general expense to sales or other similar ratios could be determined. This is the type of comparison which I think it is generally impossible to make between companies of any size because the conditions under which they are organized and operate are so different. Comparability here is difficult, but to the extent it can be achieved is of great value.

As I pointed out in the Philadelphia paper, retail trade organizations have been able to prepare useful statistics along this line and I believe some trade associations have done good work in this way for their members. On the other hand, anyone who has ever tried to work with Treasury statistics of income knows how little comparability there is between members of the industry groups. Mr. Spacek makes this clear in the last full paragraph on the second page of his letter.

Mr. Spacek says that I seem to infer that whatever management does must be accepted by the public accountant if it can be justified by any precedent or reason whatsoever. I have, of course, taken no such position. If my view and that of my friends on what accounting principles really are is correct, these are definitely "disciplinary" and they certainly are applied to the client's statements. I have tried previously to explain the difference between accounting methods and principles.

Mr. Spacek's allusion to generally accepted accounting principles as widely varying or extremely flexible practices is another example of his confusion between principles and practices or methods. While I would be the last one to say that the Securities and Exchange Commission has not had a beneficial effect on accounting and auditing principles and practices, I think it is quite incorrect to say that the SEC has done anything towards enforcing uniformity of practices. It has, of course, required uniform adherence to accounting principles. As a matter of fact the accounting profession, through the pronouncements of the Accounting Procedure Committee and the Auditing Procedure Committee of the AICPA, has really assisted the government by formulating accepted principles and practices in its pronouncements later adopted or ratified by the SEC.

I think we may sum up the differences between Mr. Spacek and myself by saying that whether my statement of accounting principles includes all the principles or whether I have included something that should have been left out, I have at least tried to make a distinction between principles which are unvarying and generally applicable, and methods and practices which are subject to change and improvement and which are applicable in some situations and not in others. Mr. Spacek has these hopelessly confused. He says very little about principles as such and constantly refers to various practices and methods as principles. I do not think the profession has to apologize for the fact that its methods and practices are continually changing and, I hope, improving. If we have this condition of change and improvement, we obviously must have some who use one method and some who use another. This has nothing to do with the application of accounting principles which can take care of any given situation.

As a footnote, I might add that the increasing support for the use of cash flow statements may sharpen up the disclosure of the differences between the different methods of accounting. This would be particularly true in the treatment of deferred charges and differences in inventory methods.

It seemed to me that it would be more useful to indicate the areas of difference and agreement between Mr. Spacek and me, rather than to attempt a point by point answer to his letter.

—October 31, 1960

Index